PORTUGAL

Hippocrene Companion Guide to

PORTUGAL

T. J. Kubiak

HIPPOCRENE BOOKS
New York

For information, address: Hippocrene Books, Inc.
171 Madison Avenue, New York, NY 10016

Library of Congress Cataloging-in-Publication Data

Kubiak, T. J.
    Hippocrene companion guide to Portugal / T. Kubiak.
    Includes index.
    ISBN 0-87052-739-8
    1. Portugal—Description and travel—1981-   —Guide-books.
I. Title.
DP516.K83   1989
914.69'0444—dc19   89-30270
                                                CIP

*Dedicated to
our Portuguese Friends*

Acknowledgments

I gratefully acknowledge the assistance and encouragement of the following individuals: first, my wife, Lavinia, for her insight, directional assistance, itinerary planning, notes, comments and expert observations concerning historic events and architectural details, and her research into the history of Portugal and certain Portuguese decorative arts; Mrs. Mary Kay Kasitz, whose typing, grammatical criticism, and technical advice kept my thoughts and pages in order; my Portuguese friend and correspondent Dra. Ana Firmino, lecturer in geography at the New University of Lisbon, who kept me informed of the latest developments in Portugal; Professor Manuel Santo, Jr., of Faro, Portugal, who corresponded faithfully and advised me on current events and all things political in nature; my daughter Sarah and son Alex, who first ventured to Portugal with me many years ago and found places there that I would not have known otherwise; my colleagues at Eastern Kentucky University for their encouragement in this project, particularly Mr. William G. Adams, professor of geography, for his expert aid in producing the map of Portugal and Professor Kathleen Hill, who helped me to learn the Portuguese language and its peculiarities; finally, the U.S. Council for the International Exchange of Scholars for the Fulbright-Hays Grant, which allowed me to study and lecture in Portugal as a Senior Fulbright Scholar.

Contents

Introduction

And you my Tejo's nymphs since you did raise
My wit t'a more than ordinary flame;
If I in low, yet tuneful verse, the praise
Of your sweet River always did proclaim:
Inspire me now with high and thundering ways:
Give me them clear and flowing like this stream:
That to your waters Pheobus may ordain
They do not envy those of Hippocrene.
From *Os Lusiadas* (The Lusiads), Canto One,
verse 4, written in 1572 by Luis de Camões (1524–80).

Camões may not, in fact, have envied the Muses; he saw Portugal for what it was. Today the visitor sees Portugal for what it is. Portugal in general, and Lisbon in particular, are different than their European counterparts. Lisbon feels, tastes, smells, sounds, and looks different than any other European capital. It is small enough to be enjoyed on foot, a walking city more intimate than larger European capitals. The country of Portugal is also small and can easily be traversed in a few days. Despite its diminutive size,

Portugal is packed with sights of interest to the tourist. Because of these qualities it is easy to write a guide to the sights of the country. But this book is not merely a sight-seeing guide to Lisbon and Portugal. It is also a story of spaces, places, tastes, frustrations, surprises, people, and the land. It is organized to address the concerns of visitors to Portugal, focusing on accommodations, food, and sights. Interspersed are perceptions, insights, and tidbits of history and language. This book is for visitors who wish to learn about the country as they travel, not merely to buy souvenirs.

I have tried to avoid the use of superlatives where none are due. Many travel and guide books create something that does not exist. In this treatment of Portugal I attempt to be truly objective. Not every sight in this Iberian land is beautiful or breathtaking. Any foreign city has sights that are interesting but not necessarily spectacular. In Lisbon there are several superlative vistas and innumerable interesting places to go and things to see. Even some shabby and run-down areas can be of interest to the traveler. All is discussed objectively and candidly.

I have also tried to avoid another pitfall of the foreign resident writer. Some travel writers fall in love with the people of a country and tend to describe them as if they were of a single national character. Realistically, not all people of a country are alike and certainly not all Portuguese have identical characteristics, although there are some qualities that they do have in common. For the sake of truth in travel, I do not look at Portugal and the Portuguese through rose-colored glasses. There are many charming characteristics of the country and people, and we came to love the country as a second home. But day-to-day encounters with Portuguese life also left us with many frustrations.

Travel *is* experience, and experienced travelers know that travel isn't always easy. It can be demanding, frustrating, and sometimes uncomfortable, but it is usually worth the experience. Portugal is not simply a destination; it is a unique cultural experience. When traveling in this authentic country, North American visitors must make certain cultural adjustments. They must realize that Portugal is not a fast-food society. Therefore, a major goal of this book is to inform the reader what to expect and what not to expect in this special country.

CHAPTER 1

Sense Appeal

*E*very country and even some cities have distinctive sights, sounds, and aromas associated with them. Visual impressions may be pleasing or offensive. This is also true of aromas.

The dominant visual impression of Portugal, Lisbon in particular, is the colorful variety of structural surfaces: ceramic tile walls and floors, orange tile roofs, intricate mosaic sidewalks, and pastel stucco buildings.

Lisbon's aroma is also distinct. Like individual homes, cities and countries tend to be dominated by particular olfactory ambiances that only incoming visitors can detect. What, for example, is the dominant aroma visitors associate with the United States? Once the visitor leaves the exhaust fumes of the airport and the freeway, what is the prevailing smell? Many visitors to the United States agree that its cities are generally engulfed in the aroma of fried foods. The smell of frying hamburgers and french fries is the foreigner's most common olfactory perception of America.

T. S. Eliot once wrote that Rudyard Kipling's gift was to make people realize that the first condition of understanding a foreign country is to *smell* it. There is much truth in this concept. One's memory of a place is often based upon odorous impressions. The memory of a good place may be destroyed by a bad smell; a bad place may be remembered by a pleasing scent.

Portugal has a distinctive aroma. As one leaves the airport, the

11

pervasive smell is of seafood. It is a fact that the myriad restaurants throughout the city of Libson serve rich varieties and large amounts of seafood. Their kitchen activities fill the air at all hours with the sometimes pungent smell of the sea. Near the waterfront the sensation is intensified by the many fish markets and the activities of the fishermen.

Under this blanket of the scents of the sea waft other aromas, depending upon the time of year. In winter the street vendors' charcoal braziers and roasting chestnuts add their aromatic accent to the urban milieu. In spring food stores and street vendors stock mounds of strawberries. Their sweet fragrance blends with the standard aromas of the pungent cheeses, sausages, and cabbages. In summer, as elsewhere, auto exhaust seems to peak. Lisbon and other Portuguese cities have huge fleets of taxis. Many are old, and these inefficient fuel and oil burners can mask the impact of even the ripest codfish. In autumn, as the air cools and the breezes increase, the air clears and is refreshed again by the smells of the street vendors' produce. Through the seasons, however, the dominant olfactory sensation remains seafood.

Other aromas are localized. For example, nearly every city block has its *pasteleria*. This shop is an important social institution and will be discussed in detail later in this volume. As the name implies, it specializes in baking and selling tasty pastries. Here the Portuguese linger over a welcome coffee break; so intermingled with the luscious fragrance of fresh pastries is the glorious smell of the aromatic Portuguese coffee. Nearby will surely be a *padaria*, or bakery, where all of one's senses can cooperate.

Sounds. Sounds, too, are associated with places. They are not as strongly embedded in the psyche as aromas, but one does imprint certain auditory associations. In Lisbon one can hear the rattle, the metallic bumps, and the squeals of the trams and trolleys, punctuated by the conductor's bell ringing. These streetcars are a delight to ride and a joy to see and photograph.

One sound unique to every country is its language. Grammatically and visually close to Spanish, the Portuguese language sounds totally different. The sound is more eastern European than Iberian. The language contains many nasal dipthongs, hard consonants, and silent vowels. Later in this volume certain key phrases of the language will be reviewed so that the reader can acquire a feeling for pronunciation. At any rate, the sound of the language gives a unique overtone to the bellows and cries of street vendors and hawkers.

In the densely populated neighborhoods of Lisbon and in the small towns and villages throughout the country, the early morning sound heard above the crowing of the roosters is the greeting *"Bom dia."* This sing-song greeting is extended to one and all as the greeters pass on their individual traverse. At times it seems as if whole neighborhoods are speaking the lilting phrase. Once the early morning song subsides, the predominant sound is the chirp of the ubiquitous canaries, whose gilded cages hang near the doorway of nearly every home. Mixed in are the sloshing and swishing of women scrubbing steps and entryways, the dripping of wet laundry on the cobblestones, and occasional singing of a mournful *Fado* song. The *Fado* is a Portuguese product that will be elaborated upon later in this volume.

As in other cities, not all sounds are of songs and canaries. Lisbon has traffic and lots of it. Rush hour is chaotic and aggravated by the city's narrow streets. In a city, however, the clatter and roar of motor vehicles is not unique and is accepted as part of urban life. But one sound that visitors may find particularly distressing is that of motorcycles. Their cacophony is not unique to Portugal but seems to be pervasive in southern Europe. Many tourists have spent sleepless nights in Greece, Italy, and Spain because of the din of underpowered and unmuffled motorbikes. These noisy vehicles have rudely disturbed many otherwise pleasant moments of southern European charm. There are a number of reasons for the ear-splitting diaphonics of these motorcycles. For the sake of fuel economy, their engines are small. This may seem to be an advantage for noise control, but it is not. The result is that the unmuffled exhaust emits a high-pitched, ear-splitting whine that reverberates off the walls of the narrow streets. Compounded with machismo and youthful exuberance, the noise level can be very unpleasant. Some riders believe that removing the muffler increases power and engine efficiency, but this is not true.

There are at least two types of motorbikes. The first includes the very old, smoke-belching bikes used by delivery men or as primary transport by low-income families. These are always underpowered and require heavy use of the throttle. The second category is the newer bikes driven at full throttle by their relatively well-off youthful owners.

There are laws pertaining to such annoyances. People complain, to be sure, but there is wholesale disregard for the laws, as well as total lack of enforcement by the authorities. Although the law requires all motorcycles to be equipped with mufflers, virtually none are. The British seem to be particularly sensitive to this issue. Since the British constitute a sizable proportion of tourists to Portugal, the problem should be solved soon. Amongst the authorities, the general mood is one of indifference toward the din. A typical reaction is a shrug of the shoulders and a shake of the head, as if to say, "What can be done?"

Spaces and Scale. Americans who travel abroad are often struck by the smaller size of everyday items such as napkins, chairs, and even toilet tissue. Portugal—because of its size, population growth, and the high cost of energy and land—seems to be even more down-sized than other European countries. The American sense of necessary space is unknown here. Proprietors of the tiniest restaurants will crowd diminutive tables and chairs into already bursting spaces. Claustrophobic souls will find the two-person elevator cars intimidating. Persons requiring elbow room should avoid small restaurants at the beginning of lunch hour, and those demanding breathing space should avoid buses and subways during rush hours. The space requirement for the average Portuguese is not nearly what the average American finds essential.

This diminution of space influences many things: houses, streets, parks, and belvederes. Lisbon is laced with parks, squares, overlooks, and botanical gardens, each is built on a small, human scale.

Portuguese attitudes toward personal space differ from the American view. A group of six Americans would probably space themselves around a small room, while six Portuguese would likely crowd together in one section of the room. This phenomenon of small personal space requirements is evident when people are waiting for service at a post office window. The clerks seem to move in slow motion while the stoic patrons inch their way nearer and nearer to the window. The result is a very close crowd, trying its best to encourage progress by shuffling, sighing, and nudging while peering over the shoulder of the lucky person at the window.

The interior spaces of Lisbon also reflect this attitude toward space and scale. Soaring open spaces are unknown in public buildings. Not even in the expensive new hotels at the top of Avenida da Liberdade is there a sense of spaciousness. The Portuguese can easily identify a public building constructed during the Salazar years. To the average American such a building has a normal size entry and interior. To the Portuguese it is a monumental structure of outlandishly egotistical proportions, indicating the waste and self-indulgence of the dictator.

Taste. The sense of taste is probably treated more lavishly in Portugal than any other sense. The dominant flavors in Portugal are garlic, olive oil, white wine, coffee, and seafood. Nearly every Portuguese dish is flavored with garlic, and many are prepared with olive oil. Meals are usually served with the fine light wine known as *vinho verde*. Most days begin and end with the incredibly rich Portuguese blend of coffee served espresso style, *bica*. Many Portuguese dishes use a rich selection of seafood and provide a great variety of taste sensations. The cheeses, breads, soups, and wines keep visitors' taste buds sharp.

Color. The predominant colors of Portugal include the deep blue of the sky, the brilliant white of the whitewashed houses, the orange of the tiled roofs, and the green of the gardens. In both city scapes and rural views the montages of color seem to be composed by a master designer. Subtle shades of blue, green, and red combine to give feeling to the classic decorative tiles, *azulejos*. The pastels of stuccoed buildings blend to create a Portuguese patina, a unique blend of wall-wort, mildew, and weathering that is pleasant and pictuesque.

Finally, Portugal possesses an intangible quality that the visitor senses almost immediately. It is the fact that Portugal has yet to enter totally into the modern era. There are few structures that would be considered modern in an architectural sense. But most visitors find that inchoate feeling desirable. There is a feeling of stepping back in time that mellows the mood and enlivens the spirit. Of another age, Portugal is genuine. There are no artificial attractions, no amusement arcades or theme parks of any description. Every sight and situation is genuine. There is a feeling of authenticity.

CHAPTER 2

People and Personalities: O Povo

*I*t is difficult to generalize about a group of individuals that number ten million, even in a country as small and as culturally and socially homogeneous as Portugal. Portugal, for its small size, is remarkably diverse in landscape features and topography. Its area is 35,383 square miles (92,000 square kilometers), roughly the size of the state of Maine or the country of Austria. (Spain is 5.5 times its size.) Yet within that relatively small space lives an incredible diversity of people and personalities.

Portugal is often thought of as an island. Historically, Portugal has turned its back to Europe. With few historic ties to continental Europe, Portugal has always looked to the sea and to the past. For that world view, Portugal has paid dearly. It is an island of underdevelopment in the affluence of Europe. It is an island of unique attitudes, attitudes that are characterized by a longing for the unattainable past and its glories.

There is great difficulty in validating the idea of a national character, with the consequent generalizations about an entire population group. But if there is one overriding characteristic that nearly all Portuguese share, it is that longing for the great and glorious past, the romantic past, the rich past. This attitude is described best in the Portuguese word *saudade*. It is more than mere nostalgia or fond remembrance. *Saudade* is a yearning for the past that never can happen again. This feeling pervades the life of the Portuguese. It refers not only to the great national glories of the past eight hundred years but also to individuals. A perfect example is the mystique of the *Fado*. All classic *Fado* songs have the *saudade* theme. Speak to individuals about the state of the economy and you hear comments such as "It was much better last year" or "We were much better off before the revolution." Comment about the wet winter weather and you will get "Last year it was perfect." Refer to the state of education, the arts, or politics and the response is always the same. There was always a better time in the past when the situation was nearly ideal, but, of course, this will never be realized again. It seems that the Portuguese are happiest when they are slightly sad.

Closely related to *saudade* is the need to apologize for the present. If the past was so great, then how can the present compare? They must, therefore, apologize for it to the visitor. "We can't compare our wines to the French; I'm sorry." "I'm sorry, but our language is so difficult to pronounce." "Portugal has no great literature." "You must realize we are not as rich as America, so our roads are in bad shape." "Yes, the beach is pretty, but not as pretty as. . . ." On and on the apologies extend.

Rarely will one hear a negative comparison with Spain. The Portuguese prefer, if not to ignore the Spanish, at least not to recognize the differences. Indeed, there are differences. Americans tend to think of Spain and Portugal as one and the same. But they are as different as Austria and Hungary, as different as Switzerland and Italy.

In Portugal there is none of the Spanish bravado typified by the *"Viva yo!"* machismo: "Hurray for me!" Some people suggest that the *"Viva yo!"* attitude begs a following ". . . and to hell with you!" In Portugal there is no corresponding behavior.

The Portuguese tend to be exceptionally helpful and polite. Sometimes that helpfulness can be embarrassing and sometimes more than is needed or wanted. A person trying to speak the complex language with its difficult pronunciation is accorded infinite patience. The usual response to language errors is a polite correction, a smile of understanding, or a lapse into English. Never will one see the impatience of the Spanish, French, or Italians. That innate helpfulness can destroy one's motivation to practice Portuguese. In an effort to ease a visitor's language anxiety, the Portuguese try to speak in English. That can hardly be classified as a fault.

In Portuguese there is no directly translatable word for the English word "anxiety." The vast majority of people in Portugal seem to possess infinite quantities of patience. Dealing with simple everyday activities, in fact, requires tremendous patience. The post office, laundry, grocery store, travel agent, and bank, all can be sources of stress. Latin countries seem to be enamored with red tape, bureaucracy, and meaningless paper shuffling. Portugal is no exception. You cannot hurry through a banking transaction. You cannot buy even the smallest item in the smallest store without great ceremony. Everything is wrapped with precise and intricate care, tied with string, and handed, finally, to the customer with a smile. I believe this purchasing and then the wrapping ceremony to be symbolic red tape. Who cares if other customers are lined up? No one is in a hurry! There is no anxiety. There is curiosity, however. Everyone in that line (more accurately, crowd) needs to know what you bought, the quantity, and at what price. At the post office the persons behind you have a need to know your business. At a bank the notion of a private transaction does not exist. People will actually stand beside you at the teller's window, waiting their turn patiently but also finding out what you are doing.

The concept of a waiting line or queue is nebulous in most Latin countries. In Spain, where you can find American fast-food establishments, the counter scene is chaos. No one lines up in the American or northern European fashion. Instead, everyone pushes toward the counter in hopes of placing an order. In Portugal no such American institutions have arrived. There is one imitation called Max Burger, and the counter scene there is unfathomable to the American mind. Enter a *pastelaria* at lunch time. Try to find an orderly queue at the take-out counter. There is none! The strange thing is that the system, or lack of one, doesn't seem to create anxiety for the Portuguese. Your anxiety will leave once you relax and realize that *there is no system!*. There is nothing to understand. It *is* as you find it.

Kindness and gentleness seem to pervade a society that has little violence. Violent crimes of murder, rape, armed robbery are almost nonexistent. Although acts of political violence are increasing in Portugal, the incidents are fewer in number and much less violent than elsewhere. It is as if the "terrorists" are concerned with the safety of their victims.

In Portugal violent American television programs, films, and videos are never shown. One never sees a fight among teenagers or a violent argument among patrons in crowded drinking establishments. One never sees a dog mistreated. One never sees children being spanked.

Portugal was the first country in Europe to do away with capital punishment. That is indicative of the people's attitude toward life, crime, and punishment. A policeman stands at every bank. His duties are obvious, but his job is unbelievably boring. Banks are the only places where one sees police in Portugal.

The attitude toward animals is also remarkable. The Portuguese form of bullfighting is much less brutal than the Spanish form; the bulls are never killed in the ring. One never sees dogs being mistreated by people. They are scolded, to be sure, but never hurt. The result is that most dogs in Portugal seem friendly and appear to be as polite as their masters. Even stray dogs seem to apologize for being strays and then seek your forgiveness with their eyes.

We were meandering through the lovely little town of Évora one Saturday morning. Two small dogs decided to tag along. A kind word to them assured them we were to be trusted and maybe even a source of some much needed food. To this day, I feel that those dogs led us to the Saturday market. Walking slightly ahead, they kept glancing back to make sure we were following. Since we had no plans anyway, we simply tagged along with them. In appreciation for showing us the market, I bought them each a bone from the meat vendor. We didn't see them again until the next morning. Both were waiting patiently and politely near our *pousada*. I'm sure that if they could have spoken, they would have asked in polite broken English as best they could, "Where to today, folks?"

Even the sheep in Portugal are treated with special care. One evening we were driving with a Portuguese friend north of Lisbon and noticed a particularly bucolic scene that I wished to photograph. Almost sunset, the golden sun was illuminating a shepherd and his flock in a back-lighted glow. As we stopped the car, the shepherd was excitedly calling and beckoning us to come and see. We arrived just in time to witness the birth of a lamb. The shepherd was as proud as a new father and shared his pride with us. As we watched the lamb take its first steps, he described the individual characteristics of his animals. I noticed that each ram wore a leather apronlike device strapped around its belly. The shepherd confirmed that this was a birth-control apparatus to prevent the coupling of ram and ewe. If lambs were born of conceptions at this time, the pastures would not support them at a critical time after birth. The Portuguese have chosen not to produce lambs for slaughter, only to replenish the herd for wool. Portuguese people simply do not eat lamb as other Europeans do.

The custom of kissing cheeks as a greeting between friends is often associated with the French. In Portugal rarely would two friends, male and female or two females, meet without the cheek-kissing ceremony. Never would one meet someone without shaking hands. Good friends also include the kissing routine. Both men and women offer their hands for a polite and short greeting. Handshakes are not of the vigorous American style but rather short, light squeezes along with a verbal greeting and smile. Mere acquaintances, men and women, would never kiss but would always shake hands.

Salutations and honorary titles, both written and spoken, are always used. In the written form, everyone is addressed in personal and business letters as *"Exmo.,"* an abbreviated form of "your excellency." This is always in addition to *"Senhor," "Senhora,"* or other appropriate title.

Everyone must be greeted with a title. In polite company one never calls another by the first name. It always must be proceeded by the person's title. Other than *Sr.* and *Sra.*, all lawyers and other college (or equivalent) graduates are titled *(Doutor) (Doutora)* "Doctor." Engineers and architects and other professionals are so designated in a greeting. Professors are never called merely *"Senhor."* The list is endless. If you really want to show great respect for someone, your salutation might be, for example, *"Exmo. Senhor Professor."*

An important trait of the Portuguese is that they are not obnoxious. When American teenagers visit the beach in Estoril during summer, they are amazed by several things. First, they are amazed by the nonchalance of the topless sunbathers. Second, they can't believe how quiet the beach is. There are no "boom boxes" blaring noise. There are no obnoxious groups of beer-drinking troublemakers. There are no loud Frisbee or volleyball games. Many

American teenagers would have trouble relating to the Portuguese beach scene and might even deem the beach boring.

Generally, the people are much quieter than Americans. Most Portuguese would find it improper to speak in a normal volume on the train, on buses, or on the street. Most people speak quietly, as if they are shy about what they are saying. This general attitude of subdued silence is diametrically opposed, however, to the pervasive noise pollution of the ever-present motorbike.

Although the Portuguese tend to speak softly, their bars and homes are filled with loud music and they seem to revel in it. When they are asked how they can endure the incredible din in a small café, the answer is always the same: the Portuguese *enjoy* noise. Even the most distinguished-looking and conservative government officials, physicians, professors, or bureaucrats seem not to be bothered by high noise levels. A group of Lisbon professionals taking a weekend journey to Spain in a chartered motor coach will "enjoy" the bus radio at much higher levels than most American and British adults can tolerate. No Portuguese will complain. Why would one object to such fun sounds? Yet, paradoxically, in conversation the speakers always speak softly.

Americans and northern Europeans also tend to think of Latins as religiously conservative while politically volatile. In Portugal it is true that the political environment is marked by government turnovers at frequent intervals. It is also true that the history of Portugal is, in many respects, a history of church-state relations. The church helped Portugal achieve its independence and world status. But that relationship has not always been a rosy one. Strong anticlerical sentiment has been voiced at various times since the 1700s. During the twentieth century the church has had much influence, and religious traditions pervade all of Portuguese life. According to church statistics, nearly everyone (95%) is baptized into the Roman Catholic Church. Other surveys and unofficial observations indicate that only a small percentage of the population regularly attends Sunday Mass. Church attendance is, however, only one indication of fidelity to religious beliefs.

Regardless of people's growing indifference toward the church as Portugal modernizes, the importance of religion in the rural population still manifests itself very deeply. The religion of rural Portugal is personal and familiar. People often form intense prayerful relationships with the saints, by-passing the clergy in personal religious practice. The number of priests is declining and, as a result, many of the rural village churches are empty on Sunday, but in-home worship continues with intense fervor. Historically priests in Portugal have not been as highly regarded as religious leaders in other Latin countries. It seems as if the people would rather communicate through the saints than use a priest as a mediator with God. On the other hand, the authority of priests is not questioned in matters of church governance or law. Today the role of the clergy seems more secular than spiritual. It appears quite likely that religion could survive very well in Portugal even without the clergy.

Although generalizations about a country and its people are difficult and should be avoided, some generalities seem appropriate to Portugal. The country is truly homogeneous in a cultural and social sense. Most Portuguese are polite, quiet, conservative, religious, kind, helpful, patient, and sad. Each individual, though, has different combinations of these traits. Some people recognize the futility of *saudade* and look happily toward the future. Some people cannot bear to stand in crowded lines and have less than an infinite quantity of patience. Some Portuguese even hate loud music. All individuals vary within the framework of the Portuguese national character. But politeness is one trait that seems to be in every individual. Rarely will one encounter rudeness as it is defined in Portugal. It is not considered rude to join an already close crowd; it is not rude to push through a crowded bus. But it is considered rude to stretch one's limbs in public; to yawn and stretch one's arms or torso is blatantly improper behavior. It is considered impolite not to extend one's hand or use proper titles in greeting. It is impolite to point or call a waiter with a snap of the fingers. It is impolite to speak loudly. Above all, it is considered a major social blunder to treat a visitor to Portugal as if he or she were not an honored guest.

CHAPTER 3

Accommodations, Money, Shopping, and Other Things to Know

On some journeys, getting there is the whole point. But arriving in Portugal means that the adventure is just beginning. Upon arrival, the traveler's primary concern is lodging. The package-tour participant has nothing to arrange and will be assured of excellent accommodations at no less than a three-star hotel. The hotels in Portugal are officially graded into categories based primarily on price and the level of service the operators provide. The top of the line, the five-star hotels, are represented by such deluxe institutions as the Hotel Altes in Lisbon, the Hotel Albatroz in Cascais, the Enfante de Sagres in Porto, and the Palacio in Estoril. Four-star hotels are impeccable and a good buy, but three-star hotels are the best buy and are always clean and comfortable. For example, the

Hotel Miraparque is in the district of the fine hotels (at the upper end of Av. da Liberdade), but is quiet, low-keyed, friendly, and much less expensive.

No matter the hotel choice, prices remain reasonable throughout the country. Portugal still is the least expensive, overall, of any European destination. Even with some inflation and devaluation, the relative strength of the dollar, yen, or pound against the Portuguese *escudo* adds up to a bargain when coupled with the genuinely low prices.

The staff at most Lisbon hotels is virtually permanent. There appears to be little turnover. On a return visit to a hotel after a few years, you will quite likely be greeted by the same doorman, desk personnel, bartenders, and waiters. The reason is that these people are professionals in lodging service, not temporary workers. They have chosen their position, and view it as a lifework, regarding themselves as career waiters or bartenders. Many times, in the smaller hotels, the jobs are shared or rotated. This attitude toward service should be respected.

The *Pousadas* of Portugal, operated by the government through its *Pousada* organization, are a class of tourist lodging all visitors should consider. Do not let the term "government operated" turn you against the idea. These are all five-star hotels operated on government subsidy to encourage tourism. But the best part is that many of the *Pousadas* of Portugal are historic buildings, castles, palaces, and monastaries. These are splendidly restored structures. A few, however, have been recently built. All reflect the culture of the region in which they stand. Each possesses a unique character and charm and may be furnished in local style using locally produced fabrics. Where appropriate, the furnishings are period antiques.

The word *pousada* means "inn" or "resting place" and the *Pousadas* of Portugal are this, indeed. Comfort is the rule. The food is excellent; each restaurant offers not only specialty regional cuisine but international dishes as well.

They are strategically located to form a logical network so one can visit all parts of the country while staying only in *Pousadas*. Of the thirty, some examples include the Pousada do Castelo in Óbidos. This one is housed in one of the loveliest medieval castles in Portugal and in a town of unbelievable charm. The *Pousada dos Loios* in *Évora* is a fifteenth-century convent amid Roman ruins, fountains, and great vistas of the plains of Alentejo. Another choice is the newly built *Pousada* occupying a site overlooking the beaches of Sagres Point and Cape St. Vincent. It is the *Pousada do Infante* in *Sagres*. This place is spectacular by anyone's measure. All *Pousadas*, however, offer something special in distinctive settings.

Prices are kept reasonable by government subsidies, otherwise the average tourist could not afford such luxury. This makes the system one of the great travel bargains in the world. Advance reservations are highly recommended. *Pousadas* can be booked through a travel agent or direct with: Pousada Organization, EN-ATUR, Av. Santa Joana Princesa, 10A, 1700 Lisboa, Portugal.

The *estalagem* is the counterpart to an American motel. These are all four-star establishments that cater to the motoring tourist. The restaurants associated with the inns are always exceptional. Some *estalagems* are modern structures, and some are converted mansions or specially designed roadhouses. An example is the *estalagem* in *Batalha*. Called the *Estalagem do Mestre Alfonso Domingues*, it has only twenty-two rooms. All of the very comfortable rooms have a view of the Gothic-style cathedral of the Batalha Monastery with its colossal equestrian statue. The restaurant is considered a four-star establishment and compares favorably with its counterparts in Lisbon. This is a marvelous place to spend the night after a day of bumpy Portuguese road travel.

In Portugal the owners of many beautiful old houses have opened them to the traveling public. The variety is great. They include old manor houses, elegant country homes, *quintas* (farm houses), and even some traditional cottages tucked away in out-of-the-way villages. Staying in homes is a perfect way to learn the Portuguese way of life. For information or reservations contact: Associocão das Casas do Tourismo de Habitacão, Largo do Princepe Real, 32, 1000 Lisboa, Portugal.

In the area of budget accommodations, the choices are innumerable. They are the *pensãos*. These also carry a Portuguese government rating, but it is best to have a look at the rooms before booking in. Most are clean and very inexpensive. Usually the bath is down the hall. For location, a *pensão* is ideal. There are so many that travelers can easily find one close to everything and anything. They seem to be everywhere. For a few dollars, a couple can be guaranteed a clean place to sleep. In fact, *pensãos* are the accommodations of choice for the traveling Portuguese. It is the *pensão* where the traveling salesman will stay. Portuguese families on holiday, youths, and some budget-minded tourists tend to fill the *pensãos* quickly.

In addition, the Portuguese government provides a system of youth hostels throughout the country to accommodate a huge demand for very inexpensive sleeping. The hostels are clean and well run, and there is no apparent age limit, even though mostly young people stay in them. Some people indicate displeasure with the early closing hours. For example, midnight is closing time and lights-out for the hostel located in the historic Prince Henry's school in Sagres. This is much too early for youths on vacation.

Camping is also a popular and frugal way in which to tour the country, and there are some good campgrounds in nearly every region of Portugal. For the urban camper, the camper who wisely chooses to be near Libson, the best campground is located in the huge *Monsanto Parque* just a few minutes to the west of town. Additionally there are many camping or caravan sites along the entire coastal zone.

It should be noted that all hotel, *estalagem*, and *Pousada* room tariffs include the continental breakfast. Experienced tourists generally agree that the continental breakfast in Portugal is unparalled in other southern European countries. This is due primarily to the quality of the bread, rolls, and coffee.

The room bill also includes a small service charge that covers all service except the extraordinary. Any gratuities beyond the standard service charges are purely discretionary. Most tourists leave a few extra *escudos* for good service. Most hotel staff persons will have earned it and appreciate the kindness.

In Lisbon and Porto all hotels are convenient to the major tourist sights by the nature of the cities' compactness and because inexpensive public transport or taxi service is available. Hotel location, therefore, is never a problem. *Estalagems* tend to be located in more suburban or peripheral sites. Each *Pousada* location is unique.

Money

The *escudo* is the currency unit in Portugal. All prices for goods and services and menu items are shown with the *escudo* amount first, followed by the "$" sign. Subdivisions of the *escudo*, *centavos*, are then indicated. For example, two hundred eighty *escudos* and fifty *centavos* would appear as: 280$50. The "$" acts as a decimal point. There are 100 *centavos* to the *escudo*. Paper money is issued by the Bank of Portugal in 50$, 100$, 500$, 1000$, 5000$, and 10,000$ denominations. The Bank of Portugal also mints coins in denominations of 1, 2$50, 5, 10, 20, 50, and 100$ *(escudos)*. The casual tourist normally will not deal with the 10,000$ note as its use is limited to major transactions. The most commonly used notes will be the 100$ and 1000$ bills. One thousand *escudos* are called the *conto*. This slang word originated in years past when one thousand *escudos* was an incredible amount of money. The word *conto* translates literally into English as "tall tale" or "yarn." If one spoke of possessing or using a 1000$ note, one was telling an outrageous tale.

A word of caution about the 1000$ note. There is a tendency for the visitor, as she or he exchanges dollars or pounds for *escudos*, to ask for the 1000$ note simply as a matter of space economy in one's pocket. With a favorable exchange rate, one receives many more *escudos* than dollars or pounds. For example, at an exchange rate of 150 *escudos* per dollar, one would receive 15,000 *escudos* for 100 dollars. Small notes accounting for 15,000 *escudos* would be too large a wad of money to manage neatly. Unfortunately, there are still many circumstances in which the presentation of the 1000$ note for payment is frowned upon: in early morning hours before cash can be accumulated, in small shops or restaurants that do not keep a large amount of cash on hand, and with street vendors, tram conductors, or bus and taxi drivers. If the tab is small, many individuals will refuse to take the 1000$. The wise tourist carries several smaller bills or coins for such encounters. The 1000$ note seems to be a trivial amount to the tourist, but in Portugal it's still a *conto*.

There is no limit to the amount of cash or traveler's checks one may bring into the country. But there is a minimum: each visitor is required to have sufficient funds to cover expenses for the planned visit. The minimum is equivalent to 5000$ per person. When leaving Portugal, however, one is not permitted to take more than 50,000$ or the equivalent of 100,000$ in foreign currency. The complex reasons for this seemingly unnecessary rule rest upon the nature of the Portuguese economy relative to its European neighbors. The rule was not made to affect the casual tourist but to discourage the Portuguese themselves from leaving the country for extended periods and spending locally generated currency on foreign goods and services. The rule has been effective. One cannot venture very far with only 50,000$ (about $350).

A bank is the best place to exchange currency to *escudos*. Hotels will change money, but one receives the poorest rates of exchange, always in the hotel's favor. Bank rates change with the money market since the *escudo* is a hard currency traded in the international money markets. Most banks have a special window indicating the exchange function. The sign *"Câmbio"* indicates where to change cash or checks. Traveler's checks are readily accepted, but one must show one's passport at the bank.

Morning banking hours are 8:30 to 11:45 A.M. Banks reopen at 1:00 P.M. and close again at 3:30 P.M. (1300–1530h) on weekdays. The bank branches at the Lisbon Airport are open twenty-four hours a day.

During banking transactions in Portugal, tourists should be prepared to step back in time. The banking system is not yet totally computerized. The result is much time-consuming paperwork and shuffling of documents. The somewhat cumbersome system often requires, for example, the presentation of documents and currency at one window, while payment in *escudos* occurs at a cashier's window elsewhere in the bank. In the larger Lisbon banks, you are given a number and wait for the number to appear or be called before approaching the cashier. Do not expect orderly lines at the bank counter or cashier's window. Banking in Latin countries is akin to the purchase of cheeseburgers in the United States. No transaction is private, and visitors must be patient.

The visitor planning an extended stay in Portugal should open a checking account. Branch offices of the same bank do not do business interchangeably; so an account in a bank with several branches does not offer the convenience expected. One cannot, for example, make deposits and cash checks or international money orders at sister banks in the same system. One should open an account in the most convenient location to one's needs.

Credit cards are commonly accepted at most hotels, shops, and larger restaurants in Lisbon and resort areas. In smaller towns and cities and small Lisbon restaurants, one should expect cash transactions only.

Mail

It is easy to buy postage stamps, *selos*, for postcards or letters in the *correio*, or post office. Merely join the crowd in what appears to be a line at a post office counter. Portugal, like other Latin countries, is mired in bureaucracy. Many other official transactions take place at the post office in addition to posting mail: tax collection, fee payment, license applications, and many other mysterious activities requiring reams of paper and many signatures. Some *correios* have express windows selling only stamps. To purchase stamps you need only the simple phrase *"Selos, por favor."* Show the items to be posted to the clerk, who will issue the proper stamps.

Telephones

Telephoning in Portugal is sometimes not as easy as elsewhere in Europe. The switching system has not been completely modernized and wrong numbers are a constant nuisance. Business phones are generally difficult to reach. Pay telephones, the mainstay of the populace, are of several varieties, each of which requires a different procedure for operation. It is easier and better to place calls through the hotel operator. For long distance and international calls, inquire about the hotel's surcharge. The surcharge can vary between 50 and 200 percent of the actual call tariff.

Rental Cars

For car rentals, most hotels and all travel agents can make arrangements. During the winter months—the low season—there are substantial discounts. During the main tourist months of the spring and summer, prices are much higher. Portugal remains, however, one of the least expensive countries in Europe for renting autos.

To be strictly legal when renting a vehicle outside of your own country, you need an international driver's license. Such a document is acquired before leaving your country of origin. In practice, however, the rental companies never ask for a license. Residents of European Economic Community countries carry pink EEC driving permits that are recognized by all member countries. Any detailed questions concerning international driving regulations can be directed toward your automobile club. For information concerning driving in Portugal, direct questions to the Auto Club of Portugal in Lisbon (Automvel Clube de Portugal).

Gasoline is very expensive in Portugal. It is second only in price to that of Italy and is nearly three times the U.S. price. Price is the principal reason why tourists should rent the smallest car that meets the needs of their travel group comfortably. There is no need for large gas-guzzling vehicles.

Driving in Portugal can be a pleasurable experience if you follow a few rules. The novice to Portuguese motoring should try to avoid Lisbon and the heavily traveled four-lane highways near Lisbon. After gaining experience and confidence, you can attempt driving in city traffic. Follow signs carefully. Finding your way around this small country is easy. Forget the idea of route numbers. The highways are numbered, but the numbering system is indicated only by small, nearly invisible concrete markers along the roadside. The best advice is to drive from town to town, moving in the indicated direction to the next destination, following the arrow signs. Europeans, including the Portuguese, travel cross-country mainly by using landmarks, towns, and cities as indicators of direction and progress. Route numbers are unimportant.

Portuguese roads are in critical condition and tend to wear out the vehicle, driver, and passengers. Most roads were originally constructed from individually laid stone blocks or brick. Over the years these uneven surfaces have been covered and patched with asphalt in an effort to make the roads more modern and efficient, but the net result has been disastrous: bumpy, noisy, and sometimes intolerable roads. Money for road improvement is a low priority item in a struggling economy. Cross-country travelers should not expect a smooth ride, but for the intrepid tourist, the rewards of driving through the lovely countryside are many times worth the bumps. It seems as if the Ministry of Tourism deliberately created the views, the vistas, and the impression of a timeless Iberian landscape to reward the tourist in spite of the Ministry of Highways' shortcomings.

Local drivers, as anywhere else in the world, can be impatient with gawking tourists. One must be extremely careful! Unfortunately, Portugal has the highest highway accident rate in Europe. The reasons for this appalling situation relate to the perception of what is and what is not safe driving. There is a strong tendency to pass on curves, on hills, and in dense fog. For the average Portuguese driver the ideal passing situation would be a combination of all three. A typical Portuguese response to criticism of such irresponsible driving would be a joking remark to the effect, "In Portugal the roads are like cartoons. They always stretch wider for one more car. There is always room." But the statistics show that this is not always true.

If you are careful, take the time to observe, watch the signs, are cognizant of other traffic, drive defensively, and ignore the terrible road surfaces, you will have a great time.

Laundry

All hotels will make arrangements for the guests' laundry to be handled efficiently. But if you are staying longer than two or three weeks, you will need a less expensive alternative.

Condominiums or apartments in resort areas will probably be equipped with washers and dryers. A word of caution is necessary: the dryers tend to operate at very high temperatures. You need to be careful of permanent press or delicate fabrics. If the rental unit has no washer and dryer, you will need to find a convenient laundry. There are many, but they are surprisingly expensive. Inquire about a laundromat or a self-serve laundry. A laundromat will be a surprise. The self-serve system requires that you load the clothes into the washer, add detergent, and then leave for about one and a half hours. When you return, the clothes are dry, folded, and bagged. This is all for about one-tenth the price of a regular laundry where clothes are washed, dried, and ironed. The self-serve laundry personnel merely fold the clothes. Again, the dryers tend to be very hot, so caution should be given to permanent press fabrics. Do not expect rapid service. Do expect very clean clothes and courteous service. It is customary, as in all service sectors, to tip the laundry personnel a small amount as you pay the bill. (Note: the best brand of laundry detergent is "Polo.")

Grocery Shopping

"When in Rome," as the saying goes, do as the locals do. Naturally, then, the best way to buy groceries is in the open-air markets. Unfortunately, in modern Portugal most markets are only weekly affairs. In outdoor markets, things seemed to be fresher if not less expensive, and the atmosphere is always exuberant and fun.

Between market days there are other alternatives for stocking the pantry. For example, there are hundreds of very small (15 ft. by 25 ft.) market spaces crammed full of many necessary items. These little shops are everywhere in Lisbon and elsewhere in Portugal. Usually the produce is overflowing onto the sidewalk. Hams, cheeses, and sausages are hung from the rafters. The entire space is crowded with food. Portugal also has its version of the supermarket, known simply as the *super-mercado*. The Portuguese-style supermarket is generally smaller than those in the United States, but the principle is the same: self-serve from well-stocked shelves. Meats and produce are still individually weighed and wrapped, however.

The ultimate Portuguese *super-mercado* is the Lisbon area chain store known as *Pão d'Açucar Jumbo Super-Mercado*. This is more like an American supermarket than any other. An American will appreciate the familiar arrangement of a logically laid-out format to entice the consumer. But the *Pão d'Açucar* also has shoes, photographic processing, lawn furniture, flowers, snack bars, and garden and plumbing equipment. Additionally, there are several differences that distinguish Portuguese *super-mercados* from American supermarkets. These differences include the many aspects of quality and selection. When it comes to the quality and selection of bread, the Portuguese market excels. *Pão d'Açucar* has a bakery that is open to view, where the fresh loaves of at least a dozen varieties of bread are placed in bins for selection. The aroma fills the building and livens the spirit as no other aroma can.

Grocery stores usually have a wide selection of quality wines and liquors. Imported liquors, scotch and gin in particular, are very expensive due to high import duties and other taxes. There is also a wide selection of cheeses in the supermarket. Quality is always high. The supermarket is the best place to stock up for a picnic of bread, cheese, and wine.

Junk-food addicts will not be satisfied with Portuguese grocery stores. There is no such thing as a giant bag of potato chips, corn chips, pretzels, or the myriad variety of snacks that occupy an entire supermarket aisle in the United States. This disappointment can lead to new taste frontiers. Many tourists try locally produced olives, sardines, and other goodies like figs, almonds, and raisins to satisfy their craving for snack food.

Do not expect a big selection of frozen foods. Energy is very costly in Portugal, and frozen food items are superfluous to the Portuguese family lifestyle. Only recently have frozen entrees been offered on the market. Occasionally there are frozen pizza and other expensive and exotic items in the frozen food case. Frozen foods do not take up much space, even in a *super-mercado*.

Fresh produce, however, occupies a sizable portion of the *super-mercado*'s space. Most visitors from the United States and Britain expect to purchase blemish-free fruit and perfect vegetables offered in lovely displays. Apparently, looks are not as important as taste to the Portuguese consumer. Generally, apples, oranges, and other fruits are bruised and spotted. Yet their taste seems unaffected. Often there is noticeable insect damage in leafy vegetables. This indicates the sparing use of insecticides.

Always expect abundances and special prices on certain seasonal items, such as strawberries, oranges, turnips. Do not expect to see produce such as cauliflower, broccoli, head lettuce, celery, brussel sprouts, or peas. Do expect to see an abundance of cabbage, leaf lettuce, potatoes, tomatoes, leeks, olives, bananas, apples, and oranges. The olives are worth mentioning again. Many claim that Portuguese olives are the best of southern Europe. Certainly, they are the least expensive.

In the seafood department, expect freshness. Seasonal varieties of the bounty of the sea are usually available in large quantities and at special prices. At times sardines are very inexpensive. At other times, the clams are "on special." Snails are overly abundant in the spring and early summer, so prices are correspondingly low.

Regular fare includes tuna, hake, octopus, eels, skate, sole, grouper, and sea bass. Rarely are sharks sold in any of the markets or fish auctions. The Portuguese have never eaten shark meat to any serious degree. A recent plan issued by the Ministry of the Sea, however, foresees government promotion of shark fishing from the port of Sesimbra. Sharks are caught with nets and lines, but those few sharks now taken are not used as food. The liver is removed and the fish is discarded. The new plan is to encourage the use of the meat as well.

The meat department at the *super-mercado* is also startling to the average American or Briton. By American standards, the meat department is paltry. Beef in Portugal is expensive, tough, and not worth buying. The cuts in the stores are unidentifiable and the quality is obviously poor. There are no good steaks or roasts. The better cuts of beef are marketed to tourist hotels; so little is available to the Portuguese consumer.

Pork is leaner than one might expect, but the cuts are not standard. The color of pork is almost beef red. The meat is from farm-raised, free-ranging hogs and is not the mass-produced pork common in the United States and northern Europe.

Poultry is very lean but a good buy. Grown by individual farmers, the chickens are free-ranging and, therefore, accumulate less fat. If you buy only seafood and poultry (chicken), you can eat well and cheaply.

The deli or prepared foods department is a treat. Available are fried fish fillets, rice, salads, cod cakes, roasted chicken, vegetables, and a wide variety of seasonal dishes at reasonable prices, despite the obvious cost of preparation. Labor, particularly unskilled labor, is cheap.

Expect to find a good selection of yogurt. Fresh milk, however, is a rarity in the city. Usually available is super-pasteurized, unchilled milk marketed in one-liter cartons. The shelf life of this type of milk is apparently unlimited.

Do not expect to find ketchup, peanut butter, mayonnaise, pickles, instant stuffing, or other convenience foods. There is little processed food produced in Portugal, and such items are not imported. There is no market for such items because of their high cost.

Canned foods include a wide variety of beans, a few vegetables, tuna, and sardines. Little else is offered. Necessarily then, the diet will be more healthful with more vegetable fiber, less red meat, more fish and poultry, and more vegetable protein.

At a Portuguese *super-mercado* the consumer must supply shopping bags or be prepared to pay a few *escudos* for the plastic bags supplied by the store. The consumer must also be prepared to bag groceries. This service is not provided. Such a situation is particularly puzzling, given both the availability and low cost of labor.

Transportation

Getting around in Lisbon can be fun. The myriad modes of transportation available make traversing the city an adventure. There are taxis, buses, subways, funiculars, trolleys, trams, and a street elevator.

Upon arrival at the Lisbon airport you will need a taxi. Beware of the hawker in the official-looking uniform waiting in the area just beyond the customs zone. He is looking for the obviously sleepy tourist in a hurry to get to a hotel. Once spotted, the tourist is directed to the hawker's taxi. This is not the metered variety but an expensive, unmetered Mercedes. For such "services" the un-suspecting tourist is charged twice the regular fare into the city. This practice is illegal but nevertheless allowed to exist. Instead of being misled into wastefulness, follow the signs to the taxi stand where you can hire a cab to the hotel for a surprisingly small amount compared to other European taxis. Those staying along the Estoril coast should expect to pay nearly twenty-five dollars for the forty-five-minute drive.

All official taxis are painted black and green. They are ubiq-uitous—except in the very early morning. One very interesting aspect of taxi service in Portugal is its relative organization. That is, there are very orderly queues of both taxis and potential clients at various busy transportation locations. This is a surprise since or-derly lines are not an essential part of the Portuguese way of life. Taxi drivers will not allow entry to their vehicles if the queue is ignored.

Compared to taxis elsewhere in the world, Lisbon's are inexpen-sive. Coupling relatively low fares with the second highest fuel costs in Europe, even the casual observer must wonder how a cabbie can make a profit after a day's cruising. Profit or not, like all big city taxi drivers, Lisbon's also try to scare the wits out of the passenger in the first tenth of a mile. If they somehow do not succeed, their manhood has been abridged and the scare tactics continue. Drivers seem to revel in the narrow streets of Bairro Alto, drive with glee and abandon over the hills of Alfama, and hurl their vehicles at breakneck speeds down the avenues and boule-vards. Most trips are hair-raising and heart stopping. This, how-ever, is regular stuff for the Lisbon taxi driver.

During the regular day-to-day Lisbon traffic, taxis are constantly in motion, either consigning some hapless passenger to a breathless adventure ride or cruising slowly and calmly seeking passengers or stalking pedestrians. The Lisbon taxi driver seems to assume that everyone will clear a path for his mighty little black and green marauder. Since auto horns are not permitted in Lisbon (what a blessing that is!), the only way the driver can warn others in his path is by blinking his headlights. But because of trying to save the lights, this is only rarely used as a warning signal. Usually, it is up to the pedestrian to be wary.

Walking in Lisbon can be a pleasant experience. Lisbon is a small capital city and, therefore, a walking city. From the hotels at the upper end of Av. da Liberdade to the shopping district of Baixa (low district), it is a relatively easy thirty- to forty-five-minute stroll. The pedestrian seems to be the taxi driver's target, so crossing streets in Lisbon is tricky business.

As a strolling pedestrian one should begin to see the city at its heart, the *Rossio*. This is the main square, the gathering place, the center. But it is not a pedestrian setting. For example, in the middle of the square are flower sellers with their brightly colored bouquets, long pampa grasses, and dried flowers. Visiting their stalls, however, is a challenge. Instead of a people place, the Rossio of today is a transport hub. In busy Lisbon the Rossio has become the transfer point for subway, buses, trams, and taxis, as well as a well-traveled roundabout for general auto traffic. The result is that crossing on foot to the interior to buy or browse for flowers can be very risky. The pedestrian is better served by striking out in any direction away from Rossio.

The next best way to see Lisbon is by tram or trolley (locally known as *eléctricos*). Many of the little streetcars were built in the last century but, by a miracle of maintenance, are still operating happily. You can buy a transport map of Lisbon at the transportation kiosks at both Cais de Sodré and the street elevator. Notice how the tram lines lead to all parts of old Lisbon. Look for the overhead hanging sign *"Paragem."* That sign indicates a tram stop and does not coincide with a bus stop. First-time visitors are often confused and frustrated by a lack of knowledge of the system. Pick a route and hop on the first tram that passes.

There is a certain etiquette in tram riding. To board a tram properly, always enter from the rear door and exit through the front past the driver. Each car will have a conductor/ticket taker. The conductor's function is to collect the fare and to signal the driver (with the classic trolley bell) that all passengers are aboard. The conductor will ask each passenger where he or she is going and charge the fare accordingly. A tourist who rides for sightseeing only, merely says, *"Volta"*—meaning roughly "returning" or "round trip." The conductor should understand. This is a cheerful transport mode. The people are friendlier and more relaxed than those on the buses; the pace is slower and of a different era. Consequently, the conductor can be very helpful. Tourists often have a special stop at particular tourist attractions. The conductor, if asked, will let you know it is coming up.

Many first-time riders try to board the tram at the front. Tourists are kindly told by the conductor that this is not done. The key word is "kindly." A proper exit is through the front door past the tram operator. Confronted with a different culture or unknown system, tourists often feel stupid, embarrassed, and awkward. In Portugal, unlike elsewhere in Europe, such mistakes evoke a smile or a joke, never anger.

According to local custom and concensus of many visitors, the best place to ride a tram is on the rear platform, where the rider can see the passing scene unobstructed and get a feeling for and a whiff of Lisbon. From that vantage point, one can see it all, smell it all, and even watch the young boys trying to hitch a free ride while keeping out of the conductor's view. Although a tram ride is bumpy, squeaky, and full of jolts and rattles, it is the best way to see Lisbon.

Ride several lines. The tourists' favorites include tram #15 from the Cais de Sodré to Belém. This is a cut-rate and scenic way to ride to the many historic sights in Belém. Other good rides include #25 or #26 from near the Cais de Sodré on Rua de São Pablo through Bairro Alto to the Basilica Estrela. Number 28 from the area of the Camões square also runs to the Basilica. Another good one is #29 or #30 through Bairro Alto from the Cais de Sodré. Take #10 or 11 from Baixa (Rua de Conçencão) to the Graça area. This is an interesting ride through the fringes of old Alfama and very close to the entrance to the Castelo S. Jorge.

Buses are less interesting than trams, but the myriad routes and frequent service make the bus system easy to use and efficient. Be advised that buses are crowded during the morning and late afternoon rush hours. The Portuguese concept of space applies very well in a bus: the less space one has the better. According to many, the best bus ride is #37 from Rossio to the castle entrance. The bus that plies this route is an ancient, coughing beast that is narrow enough to negotiate the fringes of Alfama. The streets are steep but so narrow that brake failure is not a worry. The vehicle could not roll very far in the twisting maze of old Lisbon even if it had no brakes and was totally out of control.

The subway or metro system is frankly not very interesting. The system is clean and efficient but doesn't offer much service to the tourist. The limited coverage does not shuttle the tourist to any of the principal sights. The design accommodates mostly the people of Lisbon as they go about their daily commuting. The trains seem to be crowded at most times of the day. For subway aficionados, it is worth a ride.

For the trams, buses, and subway, tourist passes are available at a modest cost. The passes can be purchased at all Transportation Public Information locations. The pass is valid for seven days and can be used at any hour of the day. Books of single transport tickets can also be purchased. Both forms offer genuine savings. Using the tickets saves about 50 percent of an already modest fare. The tourist who plans not to use the transport pass system must pay a fare on each boarding. This necessitates some communication with the driver or conductor as to destination and charges. To become informed as to the fare to any destination, study the route and ticket information at each bus stop. The map will show the location of the stop. It is easy then to calculate the fare or number of tickets needed to reach your destination by simply following the lines indicating the route and required *modulos*. A *modulo* is a fare or zone indicator. On trams, the conductor takes your fare or validates your ticket. On buses and the subway you must validate the *modulo* tickets at the small orange-colored, box-like device near the driver. It is best to watch other passengers and do as they do. Do not discard any ticket until after disembarking. The system is basically an honor system, but from time to time an inspector boards to check passes or ticket validations.

Two unusual forms of public transportation in Lisbon include the *funicular* and the *street elevator*. The street elevator is easily found in the Baixa area. The elevator lifts one from the Baixa (low area) to the street level of Bairro Alto (high neighborhood). At the upper end of the elevator platform there is a great view of Lisbon. For that reason alone it is worth the ride. The structure itself is intriguing. Designed by Eiffel and built in the nineteenth century, it is pleasing to look at and definitely a structure worth studying from all angles.

There are three funiculars in operation in Lisbon. Known as the *"elevadores,"* they too are an alluring link to the nineteenth century and offer an inexpensive way to arrive at interesting places. One funicular is on Av. da Liberdade in the Restauradores area just to the north of Rossio. This one should not be missed because the ride transports you to the summit of one of Lisbon's hills to Bairro Alto and a beautiful park and overlook of Lisbon. Another, also convenient to Av. da Liberdade but one block to the west at Rua da Boavista, transports you up another Lisbon hill on the east side of the city. A similar but opposite view of the city awaits the rider there.

Tourists preferring a water-level view of the city, a view the great explorers and seafarers of centuries past enjoyed, must take the ferry at the slip near Praça do Commerçio. For a few *escudos* they can ride the smooth ferry across the wide river to Caçilhas. There are some great seafood specialty restaurants near the slip on the opposite side. These restaurants serve the best fried baby eels in town. A lunch or dinner break is appropriate. The return trip offers expansive vistas of the city and its hills. A twilight return is best to catch the setting sun as it brightens the tile roofs and glistens off the pastel cityscape.

There are also ferries from Cais de Sodré to Caçilhas and from Belém to Trafaria and Porto Brandão. But none of these offers a great view of the city.

To travel to the south of the country by rail, the first leg of the journey begins at the CP ferry slip just west of the Praça do Commerçio. Included in the price of the rail ticket is the half-hour ferry ride across the estuary to the station at Barreiro. The ferry crossing offers interesting views of the ship building and repair facilities (the world's largest), the industrial zones, and a far view of the hills of Lisbon.

Portugal's trains serve all of the major cities and towns within the country and connect easily with the rail system of Europe. Portugal is part of the Eurorailpass system. There is daily service from London's Victoria Station by way of Paris. Passengers bound for Porto change trains at Pampilhosa. The London-Lisbon journey is approximately twenty-five hours. The Sud Express between Paris and Lisbon has first and second class cars, a dining car, and sleeping cars in both classes.

The train station at Sta. Apolonia in Lisbon is for train journeys to the north of Portugal and east to Spain. Incidentally, Saint Apolonia is the patron saint of those suffering from toothaches, which, of course, has not one bit of relevance to the train station of the same name. The station is accessible by tram, taxi, or bus. For a tourist with luggage, it is not within reasonable walking distance of the major hotels. The station itself is unremarkable and even a bit shabby in a run-down waterfront area. It is not worth a special visit.

Within the country Portuguese Railways (CP) provide a good

network of service. Fares are some of the lowest in Europe and various discounts are available. The tourist can purchase tourist passes, family tickets, and senior citizen discount tickets. The senior discounts amount to 50 percent of already low fares. One must present proof of age (sixty-five and over). Portuguese rail systems also honor the Inter-Rail ticket for those under twenty-six years of age. Children under four travel free of charge. Children between four and twelve years of age travel for half fare. There is also a convenient Porto/Lisbon/Faro motorail service during the summer months.

The electric train, known as the Estoril Line, runs from Cais de Sodré in Lisbon to Cascais along the Estoril Coast. This is one of the least expensive and most efficiently operated commuter trains in Europe. It is always on time—to the second. Locals often set their watches by these trains. The smooth half-hour journey takes travelers to the beaches at Estoril and the quaint town of Cascais at the end of the line. The route follows the Tagus River to its mouth at the Atlantic. The scenery is urban on the right and maritime on the left as the train passes Belém, Jeronemos Monastery, and beyond. The stations along the line represent Lisbon's western suburbs. Be advised that this is a commuter line and the trains are packed at rush hours. Try to avoid the early morning (7:00 A.M. to 9:00 A.M.) and later afternoon (5:00 P.M. to 7:00 P.M.) trains. The cars vary widely in comfort depending on their age. Look for the newer models for the best ride and comfortable upholstered seats. The Portuguese take pride in the fact that the train is spotlessly clean. Litter, graffiti, and cigarette butts are never seen on the train. Smoking and snacking are forbidden. The ticket takers are pleasant but do not tolerate any rowdiness and loud behavior. The short trip along the Estoril coast is one of the more pleasant Portuguese transportation experiences. There is a similar line that leaves the station near Rossio for the fast twenty or thirty miles to Sintra. The Sintra train is a bit more crowded and tends to remain so throughout the day.

Tourismo

The government of the Republic of Portugal, in its effort to encourage tourism and to aid tourists in their enjoyment of the country, has established a *Tourismo* office in each city or town in the country. Tourists who need advice, information or accommodations, transportation, *pousada* reservations, or help of any sort, should look to the *Tourismo*. It simply appears as a large white "T" on a dark blue background.

The staff speak excellent English and are always helpful and courteous. The tourist can rely on *Tourismo* for many helpful hints. The staff are more than happy to accommodate American and British idiosyncracies and sometimes trivial requests. The value of this service to the tourist is beyond question. Do not hesitate to avail yourself of the service. Many experienced visitors first stop at *Tourismo* for maps and other information as they enter a city or town. In Lisbon there are three locations. One is on Av. da Liberdade at the lower end. Another is at the upper end, near the hotels. In Estoril, the *Tourismo* is in the arcade building near the casino, convenient to hotels and the beaches.

Travel Agents

For other travel arrangements such as hotel bookings, rail tickets, air travel, and other routine trips and excursion details, enjoy the use of the many travel agencies throughout the city. The best, according to experienced travelers are the Wagon-Lits/Thomas Cook agencies in Lisbon and Estoril. Use them to buy your rail tickets. It is particularly gratifying to avoid the lines at the station. Unfortunately, Portuguese travel agents charge a fee for telephone and telex if they make international reservations. This is explained away by the fact that agents receive low commissions. At any rate, be prepared to pay the added small fee for "T and T."

Medical Care

In preparing to visit Portugal, tourists are not required to have any specific vaccinations. However, it is recommended that long-term visitors have tetanus, polio, and diptheria boosters as a precaution. Some physicians may recommend a gamma globulin shot also. Generally, travelers need not be concerned about health and disease issues. The water is safe to drink in the larger cities and there are no specific food problems. The sensitive individual, however, may prefer to order bottled water and avoid raw foods in rural areas.

If you should become ill while in Lisbon or elsewhere in Portugal, you have several options for medical care. In a hotel, call the desk for the house physician. A less expensive alternative is to go to the *British Hospital* in Lisbon on Rua S. de Carvalho, 49. You can also call any *Turismo* office for a list of English-speaking physicians. The same list is, of course, provided by the Consular Office at the U.S. Embassy. Doctors' and surgeons' fees are comparable to those in the United States. There are several hospitals in Lisbon: *The Hospital Particular,* the *CUF, Santa Maria,* and the *Red Cross Hospital.* These are among the better hospitals for emergency care. In the Algarve area the tourist is best served by the *Hospital Distrital* in Faro.

The Portuguese emergency telephone number is "115."

Farmaçias or drugstores are open during normal business hours. At other times, one drugstore in each neighborhood is available for emergency needs on a 24-hour basis. Such information is listed on each drugstore's door.

Hours

Mealtimes in Portugal are fairly standard. Hotels offer continental breakfast between 7:00 A.M. and 10:00 A.M. Lunch is between midday and 2:30 P.M. and dinner no earlier than 7:30 P.M. Traditionally a snack is served at about 5:00 P.M. This teatime snack is simply called *lanche.*

Banks, as mentioned, are open to the public from 8:30 A.M. to 11:45 A.M. and reopen from 1:00 P.M. to 3:30 P.M.

Shops usually open at 9:00 A.M. and close for lunch at 1:00 P.M. They reopen at 3:00 P.M. and remain open until 7:00 P.M. This custom of closing for the long lunch is rigidly observed. Since little business can be conducted during this period, visitors should enjoy the leisure along with the Portuguese. About the only thing one can accomplish during these hours is to have a long leisurely meal.

Most museums are also closed during this lunch period. Museum open hours are usually 10:00 A.M. to 5:00 P.M., but many museums may be closed from 12:30 P.M. to 2:00 P.M. Schedules should be checked before a museum visit. For many tourists the practice of lunch closing is very frustrating and illogical. The obvious solution to this annoying practice would be to stagger lunch breaks for the staff while maintaining regular visitor hours.

Shopping

When tourists shop, clothing sizes often present problems of conversion. The following table is provided to aid in the selection of the proper clothing sizes.

SIZE CONVERSION TABLE

Men's Suits and Overcoats							
British	36	38	40	42	44	46	48
American	36	38	40	42	44	46	48
Continental	46	48	50	52	54	56	58
Men's Shirts							
British	14	15	16	17			
American	14	15	16	17			
Continental	36	38	41	43			
Men's Shoes							
British	7	8	9	10	11	12	13
American	7	8	9	10	11	12	13
Continental	41	42	43	44	45	46	47
Men's Socks							
British	10	11	12	13			
American	10	11	12	13			
Continental	39	40	41	42			
Women's Shoes							
British	4	5	6	7	8	9	
American	4	5	6	7	8	9	
Continental	34	35	36	37	38	39	
Women's Suits and Dresses							
British	10	12	14	16	18	20	22
American	8	10	12	14	16	18	20
Continental	34	40	42	44	46	48	50
Stockings							
British	8	9	10	11			
American	—	9	10	11			
Continental	0	2	4	6			

Electricity

The electric current in Portugal is AC 220/380 volts with a frequency of 50Hz. Americans need both a voltage converter and plug adapter. British tourists will require only the plug adapter since the Portuguese wall outlets are of the continental two-pin variety.

Customs

Tourists are seldom asked to produce anything for customs officials but their passports. Rarely is the baggage of foreign nationals
searched. Customs regulations specify that clothing and items for
personal use can be temporarily imported. Visitors over seventeen
years of age may take the following into Portugal duty free: two
bottles of table wine, one liter of spirits, 200 cigarettes or 250g. of
tobacco, one-fourth liter of toilet water, 50g. of perfume. It is not
permitted to import fresh meat into Portugal.

The initial entry stamp allows the visitor a sixty-day stay before
the entry stamp must be renewed. Tourists staying more than sixty
days must apply for an extension at any police station. It is necessary to do so a few days before the original sixty days is about to
expire to avoid delays and hassles. This should not be a serious
problem, but the bureaucracy seems to enjoy paperwork. If you are
near the Spanish border, take a short side trip and get a new sixty-
day entry visa upon reentry. Long-term American visitors (more
than thirty days) are asked to register with the Consular Office of
the U.S. Embassy. The U.S. Embassy is located on the Av. Forcas
Armadas, Lisbon (tel. 783003 or 787131).

Miscellaneous Items

There are many surprises in any country in which one travels. In
fact, that is the very source of some of travel's great pleasures. The
longer the visit, the more surprises, pleasures, and, indeed, frustrations one encounters. The previous pages have provided the
usual pertinent travel information, but the following items are
usually not mentioned in guidebooks. For example, if you rent a
car and are brave enough to drive in Lisbon, you may have a good
deal of difficulty finding a place to park. Many of Lisbon's grand
old boulevards and stately avenues are now choked with parked
cars. It is difficult to find a formerly green space that is not clogged
with autos. So desperate are some drivers that they actually leave
their cars parked on the narrow sidewalks. There are few public or
private parking lots or garages because land is too costly and
precious to devote to such extravagant space users. The auto
owners and renters are on their own. The once beautiful Praça do
Comércio on the banks of the river in Baixa has been converted into

a huge parking lot. The cars now destroy the ambiance the square certainly had in the past. The grand seaward entry into the once mighty colonial empire is now an ugly car park.

Mosaic sidewalks are, indeed, a delightful aspect of Lisbon and tend to enliven street scenes throughout the country. Designs of small stones are meticulously laid out in elaborate patterns. From the top of a double-decker bus you can get a splendid view of some important and unusual sidewalk art. This is a national art form and is seldom given the credit it deserves. There are problems associated with these lovely and special sidewalks, however. Because the stones (roughly three-inch cubes) are individually placed in a sandy medium, they quickly take on irregular surface features. Often the stones become loose and dislodged, causing holes to develop. For the uninitiated woman walking the sidewalks in high heels, the experience can be, to say the least, hazardous. Tourists will marvel at the dexterity and ease with which the smartly-dressed Portuguese women negotiate these pitted and undulating walkways with never a falter. For the tourist who finds these surfaces to be obstacles to high-heeled progress, the going is less than smooth.

Visitors may also find that many of the walkways are too narrow for two people to walk side by side. Lisbon is an old city, built not for cars but for horses and buggies. As the streets were widened over the years, sidewalk space was sacrificed. In old Lisbon the narrow streets had little need for sidewalks because they were laid out in a nonmotorized era. In new Lisbon the sidewalk space has been sacrificed for vehicle space.

As in any big city the residents of Lisbon have pets. Dogs in particular must be walked for their relief and exercise. Even though the city officials are concerned and have launched an all-out assault on offenders, the sidewalks still offer many unwanted piles of dog droppings. Couple this problem with the irregular surface of the sidewalks and a newcomer spends much of his time watching the walkway for both pitfalls and pet-falls.

Lisbon also seems to be, like any other big town, in a constant state of repair. Minor construction and repair jobs are evident everywhere. This, of course, is a positive manifestation of a dynamic urban environment. The negative aspect is that the visitor is confronted, it seems, with construction remnants in the most conspicuous places. To the consternation of many tourists, construction materials (stone, concrete, sand) are piled in small amounts at nearly every major monument. It is difficult to determine if these materials are left over or about to be used. One of the peculiarities of this country is that construction and repairs never seem to end.

Because of the nature of the economy (to be discussed later), beggers are an unfortunate aspect of the street scene in Lisbon. Some, of course, are legitimate and there is no reason not to donate a few *escudos* to their cause. There are some, however, in the resort areas that appear to be professionals. At times, entire families of professional beggars descend on the resort hotels and practice their profession aggressively. These should not be encouraged. Young boys will often spot an American and hold out a hand for a coin or two. Usually the booty is spent on ice cream. No harm in that. Tourists must realize that the mere fact that they are able to visit other countries indicates to most local people that they are, by local standards, very wealthy. The tourist, in fact, may not be wealthy by American or British standards. Visiting a foreign land is beyond the wildest dreams of most of the world's population, however. No wonder tourists are expected to be frivolous with their money. Tourists are expected to be wealthy even if they are not. Near Rossio in Lisbon there are many beggars. A few coins for these desperate people are always appreciated. Unfortunately, the Portuguese welfare system is overwhelmed as the result of recent economic problems. The only alternative for a few is begging. The tourist should be patient and sympathetic to this need and make it a point to drop a few coins into the tin of an old couple crouched near the Café Suiça.

Movie theaters and the manner of their operation are an interesting new experience for most Americans. The first pleasant surprise is how inexpensive they are. The second surprise is how clean and neat the theaters are. Another aspect most Americans do not expect is the system of reserved seating for every showing. You can acutally buy tickets well in advance and request specific seats. Being cognizant of that system prevents mishaps. Usually Americans happily enter the theater and choose seats in the typical American way—wherever they want to sit, they sit! In Portugal patrons must check their ticket stubs and allow ushers to direct them to their reserved seats. The system of reserved seats is strictly adhered to and enforced, although it does seem rather odd and silly at times. For example, when the patrons are few, they still tend to be bunched together in one section of the theater. The Portuguese do not break the formation. Yet another surprise is that, unlike in most other European countries, American movies are shown in the English version with Portuguese subtitles. This makes easy viewing for visitors who speak English. So, remember to allow an usher to direct you to your seat, a service for which a small tip is expected.

Another surprising movie theater custom that is unknown in the United States is the short intermission immediately after the previews of coming attractions. The theatergoers expect this short break and quickly retreat to the lobby for a smoke, coffee, beer, glass of wine, or pastry before the main feature begins. There is never any smoking, eating, or drinking in the auditorium. This makes for a cordial environment free of noise and litter. The final surprise is the midmovie intermission. No matter the film, the need for a smoke brings the feature to a sudden halt, and the patrons again rush to the lobby for coffee and a cigarette.

There are many other surprises in Portugal. One very interesting surprise is the high quality of workmanship in many sectors. It is most apparent in the construction industry. The building quality is impeccable. The detail in construction and finish is painstakingly fine. This same pride in workmanship and thoroughness is also evident in the manufacture of handmade items like woolens, jewelry, and Portugal's famous wines. In fact, Portuguese workmen are prized elsewhere in Europe. They have created a good reputation as migrant laborers. The construction industry throughout Europe eagerly seeks the Portuguese workman based upon a long tradition of quality craftsmanship and diligent work habits.

Tourists are also struck by the clarity and blueness of the sky. They will seldom see a deeper blue to contrast with the lush green of the countryside, the multicolored flowers everywhere, and the whitewashed houses with orange-tiled roofs. It is as if Portugal were put together by painters bent on perfect composition and color choices. Always a pleasant surprise is the realization that all of this is genuine, authentic, real. There is nothing artificial in Portugal. The longer one lingers in Portugal, the more one appreciates these lovely vignettes of color and form.

CHAPTER 4

Food and Drink:
A National Pastime

Manifold are the pleasures of dining in Portugal. Allusions are made to food and drink throughout the entire volume. This chapter, however, is devoted entirely to the Portuguese national pastime—eating. There are few more engaging activities for a tourist than to discover and enjoy local cuisine. In Portugal this is easy to accomplish. Every restaurant favors Portuguese cuisine. Even the fanciest and most expensive continental-style restaurants in Lisbon always have a few typical Portuguese items on the menu.

It has been said that eating is the national pastime. Well, eating is not regarded with the same fervent emotion reserved for soccer matches, but it is close. The two-hour lunch break is as sacred in Portugal as the coffee break is in the United States. A Portuguese cannot function without the two-hour lunch. Everything closes and comes to a halt during midday. The only thing to do is find yourself a table at one of the hundreds of restaurants and enjoy the two-hours. During crucial soccer (*futebol*) matches, everyone is glued to the radio, but life goes on. During lunch, nothing happens but culinary work and the fun of a good meal.

There is good reason to take time at lunch. Usually the portions are enormous, the wine is plentiful, and no one else is in a hurry.

51

But, most of all, the food is luscious. Portuguese cuisine is not haughty or embellished with rich sauces. It is not gourmet, trendy, nor chic. It is simple provincial food prepared from recipes hundreds of years old, refined through years of experience to suit the simple tastes of a small country. One won't find food disguised or unrecognizable morsels hidden in sauces of cream and eggs. One won't find mysterious mixtures of ingredients *en casserole* or even stir-fried veggies. But one will be pleased with the low-cost, nutritious, and savory cuisine.

Portuguese cooking relies heavily on the ancient and classic combination of olive oil and garlic. Portuguese dishes are seldom overpowered by garlic, but garlic is nearly always present. The most widely used herbs are parsley, onions, and the pungent coriander (*cilantro*). The coriander imparts a unique flavor that is typical of certain dishes. Seasonings are basic: salt and pepper and sometimes the African red pepper known as *piri-piri*. Piri-piri is hotter than cayenne and can melt your socks if overdone. Restaurant-prepared foods tend to be a bit heavy with the salt, but you can ask for low-salt preparations. Bay leaf, rosemary, and a little oregano are used in some dishes, but nearly all food groups are aromatic and highly seasoned. There are exceptions that you will note as you read on.

Portion control is unheard of in Portugal. Standardization of menus is, likewise, an impossible concept for the Portuguese to understand. Chain-restaurant-type preprinted menus are unknown. Many menus are actually hand written on a daily or weekly basis. The result is that you will be amazed at the amounts of food served and thrilled with the variety of the menu. A typical first Portuguese dinner will probably be served in a small, impeccable, but rather plain dining room. Being unaccustomed, at first, to the serving portions, you will be startled as you watch the waiter serve *frango na pucara*, chicken cooked in a clay pot with a light stew sauce. By the time the waiter finishes serving, your dinner plate will be stacked with chicken pieces, potatoes, and carrots. This scene will take place only after enormous servings of fish, soup, and appetizers. You will face dessert problematically, but such servings are typical.

With a Portuguese friend in a small town in Algarve, I was served what I thought to be adequate portions of the rich *cataplana* of mussels, clams, and vegetables. My friend, however, was not at all pleased. He felt that the waiter had deliberately slighted the portions because we looked like tourists. As we were leaving the establishment, my friend cornered the waiter, and asked in no uncertain terms why we didn't get Portuguese-size portions. The waiter explained that they had mostly a tourist trade and that the British, Germans, and Americans often left more food on their plates than they ate. What waste! The management opted for smaller portions. It made sense, but a lesson was learned: stay away from restaurants that cater primarily to tourists. There are so many eating places in every town that to dine only in the tourist hotels or nearby cafés would be a waste of time and taste. You should also note that many of the dishes are toned down to the taste preferences of the tourist. The larger tourist hotels serving Portuguese food will go lightly on the garlic or olive oil or piri-piri in deference to what they feel the British or German tourists want. Americans seem to be more adventurous when it comes to food and can deal with spices or unusual tastes much better than the British. Americans tend to order local dishes and enjoy them. The English are much more conservative. Oil and garlic do not suit the English. You often see, in Algarve particularly, many English pubs or teahouses serving specifically British food. The Portuguese restaurants in the area serving typical dishes will often prepare the dishes with much less gusto and more blandness. But this happens everywhere in the world. Most tourists cannot relish true Indian curry, real Mexican food, or authentic Thai cuisine unless it is made more palatable to their tender tongues.

Soups

The soups of Portugal are few in number but all are hearty. It seems that every lunch and dinner begins with a bowl of soup. Some are so rich and thick that Americans and British would consider a bowl to be the meal. There is no such thing, incidentally, as a cup of soup. Soup is always served in a soup bowl of uncompromising dimensions.

Those varieties that are the most popular and most often found on restaurant menus include *caldo verde* and *sopa de legumes*. These are the classic Portuguese soups. The *caldo verde* (green soup) is a rich, thick cabbage and potato soup. What is known as cabbage in Portugal, we would call kale, but regular cabbage can be used too. The potatoes and greens are boiled with onions, garlic, olive oil, salt, and pepper until well done. The soup is then blended until almost smooth. Some potato chunks and bits of leaves give it texture. It is a simple soup but good, and if there is a standard menu item, this is it. *Caldo verde* is on nearly every menu.

Sopa de legumes is also a pureed soup and, as the name implies, has more vegetables than the *caldo verde*. Usually there are carrots, potatoes, kale, a bit of lettuce, and turnips, along with garlic and onions. The lot is cooked in beef stock and when blended has a bit more color than the *caldo*.

Another classic is the *sopa de alentejana*. This is a savory garlic soup served over stale bread with a poached egg. The soup calls for lots of olive oil for body, lots of garlic to give it its dominant taste, and fresh coriander to give it its uniqueness. Be advised that this soup is heavy with garlic flavor and aroma. Expect to sit alone on buses. Expect your traveling companion to avoid you. In fact, agree beforehand to both order the concoction.

Açorda is closely related to the *alentejana*. This is a characteristic peasant dish that is served everywhere in the country. It is more of a bread porridge and is the soup young children of all backgrounds are weaned upon. Very nourishing as well as tasty, it apparently soothes the beast in the child. You may see this on a menu. It is very much like the previous soup but lacks the poached eggs and has much less coriander, if any at all. It may even be served with well-beaten eggs in the broth for more richness.

When a restaurant offers fish stew (*caldeirada*) on its menu, it is likely it will also have fish soup (*sopa de peixe*). The reason is that the soup is merely the broth of the caldeirada. Unfortunately, the soup tends to be very salty since all of the seasoning collects in the broth. *Caldeirada* itself tends to be a high sodium dish so the broth is likewise highly saline. Be careful of this tasty treat.

In both fancy and simple restaurants you will find the specialties such as shrimp soup or cream of almond soup. In the more rural areas of the north, you are likely to find a heavy bean soup with sausage and pork stock. In general, south of Lisbon, the soups are lighter and more fragrant. North of Lisbon, the soups tend to be heavier, more brusque, and with a bit of a no-nonsense attitude about them.

Portugal even has a variety of gazpacho, popular in Spain. The Portuguese variety is much simpler, has fewer types of vegetables, and has the added treat of *chouriço* sausage.

You will also generally see several varities of chicken soup. Rarely are noodles used. More likely the chicken broth will be packed with meat, vegetables, and egg. In fact, nearly all the light broth varieties of soup are served with poached eggs.

Breads

Breads are, for many people, Portugal's major contribution to the culinary world. The rest of the world's breadmakers cannot hold a candle to those who produce the quality and variety of Portuguese breads. Bread is served with every meal. Breakfast, continental style, consists merely of coffee and a hard roll. If the rolls are fresh, they are unbelievable. There is little or no choice in the variety of bread that restaurants serve, but you will surely be served a large basket of bread (*pão*) and butter (*manteiga*), never margarine. Also, be aware that if you eat the bread and butter, there will be a small extra charge. The extra cost is minuscule, hardly noticeable. For a few pennies you will be served several varieties. Perhaps you will want to try some hard-crusted oval-shaped rolls or a thick-sliced, hard-crusted whole-wheat variety with big air pockets called *mistura*. There is also a uniform whole-wheat bread that is very dense and naturally sweet. In fact, there are at least a dozen varieties that you are likely to run across completely at random. All have a different shape, texture, and degree of hardness. All are wonderfully full of taste. Since the Portuguese rarely served or ate sandwiches until very recently, uniform loaves or sliced bread are never seen.

For fresh bread, of course, it is best to visit a bakery shop (*padaria*) to study the wide variety available. The *Pão d'Açucar* is a great place to visit if one wants to compare breads side by side and watch the loaves being prepared and baked. The *Pão* is a supermarket in Cascais near the Hotel Estoril Sol. The aroma of the market's *padaria* is mouth watering.

In Portugal breads are *haute cuisine*. Look forward to sitting at the table with a basket of fresh bread served immediately by the waiter. You could, if you wished, make a meal of the bread alone, but alas, people cannot live by bread alone, so order a bowl of *caldo verde* or *sopa de legumes*. That makes a terrific and nutritious lunch.

Dairy Products

Dairy products, including cheeses, butter, and ice cream, deserve uneven attention. Ice creams (*gelados*), for example, are not particularly outstanding compared to the Italian or American varieties. Portuguese ice cream is good but not outstanding in taste or variety. You won't ever find a store featuring thirty-one flavors—twelve, maybe, but never many more. Prepackaged ice-cream bars are sold everywhere by street vendors or small shops. The major brand is *Olá*. Again, there is not much to extol.

The butter is of high quality, but there is little to say about it. The cheeses of Portugal, on the other hand, are worth many descriptive phrases. The meager Portuguese output does not compare with the incredible variety produced by the French, but generally Portuguese quality is high.

Cheeses can be classified by the source of the raw material. *Leite de vaca*, cow's milk, is used to produce some very pleasant cheeses. Favorites are *Queijo Flamenga* and *Flamenquito*. Both are very mild cheeses with a nip that tastes great with chilled white wine or beer. They are very much like the Dutch Gouda or Edam cheeses and are similarily packaged in a wax coating wrapped in red plastic. The Portuguese also produce a nice Gruyere style cheese and a creamy Gervais. A hard cheese known as *Queijo de Ilha* is hard enough to grate. Produced in the Azores, this cheese is used often for cooking.

A second classification of cheese comes from the *leite de ovelha*, or ewe's milk. A Portuguese favorite is the very popular *Queijo de Serra*. The variety is produced from the milk of sheep of the Serra da Estrala (Mountains of the Stars). It is a soft cheese with enough firmness so that it can be sliced. For some people's taste, it is a bit strong. The *Queijo de Alentejo* is a trifle less pungent but still has the delicate creamy texture. The cheese produced near Lisbon in the Serra da Arrabida is milder yet and can be compared to a French Brie. This is worth a try and is often served as an appetizer in Lisbon restaurants. Look for *Queijo de Azeitão*. The *Queijo de Serpa*, though drier, has the same flavor as the former. In the vicinity of Évora, the cheese is *Queijo de Évora*. There are two other varieties of ewe's milk cheese that are flavorful. Buy *Queijo de Saloio* fresh in the winter and spring when it is best. During the remainder of the year it is served as a hard, dry variety. Likewise, the *Castello Branco* cheese, from the vicinity of the town by the same name, is best eaten fresh in the spring.

Goat's milk, *leite de cabra*, is the raw material for a very piquant, sharp, and strong cheese called *A Cabreiro Picante*. The name says it all. This is a cheese served in the *taberna* (tavern) and *cervejaria* (beer hall or pub) to liven the palate and increase consumption of spirits. *Rabacal* is another less pungent variety of goat's milk cheese.

Finally, the Portuguese have produced a combination goat and ewe's milk cheese called *Requeijão*. Many of the finer restaurants serve this unpasteurized cheese between courses or as an appetizer. Try it. It has a light, creamy texture and is usually served in small circular tin molds to hold its shape. It is reminiscent of strong but dry cottage cheese curds and must be eaten fresh, the fresher the better. The city of Tomar functions as the principal area of production for this cheese.

It is difficult to be indifferent about cheese. It is easy not to care one way or another about the stuff called "cheese products" or "processed cheese." They are nothing more than bland mixtures of vegetable oil, milk, chemicals, and coloring. But a real mountain cheese made from the milk of a sheep or goat is hard to ignore. You either like it or you don't. If a sharp goat cheese is in the vicinity, your nose will notice.

Eggs and Meats

Eggs are a very important part of the Portuguese meal. As noted earlier, many of the lighter soups are enhanced and enriched with eggs. But eggs, in addition to the soup course, play an integral role in the two-hour lunch. As part of the fancier meals, the egg dish will usually be a *tortilla*. In the Portuguese and Spanish meal, a *tortilla* is simply a flat omelette enhanced with chunks of ham or sausage. In less affluent families, the *tortilla* is often substituted for the meat course. Smaller restaurants, cafes, and pastelerias will always have an omelette on the menu. Generally the omelette is served plain, with ham, or sometimes with mushrooms. Fried eggs or scrambled eggs are available in nearly every restaurant. Look for the heading *"Ovos."* Fried eggs will be *ovos estrelados* (literally translated as "starry eggs"). Scrambled eggs are *ovos mexidos*, a boiled egg is *ovo cozida*, and the ever-present poached egg is *ovo escaliado*.

Beef, with the unappetizing designation *carne de vaca* (meat of the cattle) is not very good in Portugal. Beef cattle production is not emphasized in Portugal because land in a small country is precious and a sizable amount of land is needed to graze cattle. The marginal lands where cattle could be grazed are low in quality pasture and are systematically being reforested. The few purely beef dishes will be rather expensive. In the markets there is no grading of beef, there is little of it, and what is there is unusually cut. The truly good beef steaks (*bife*) are consumed in the large hotel restaurants, which charge high prices. On a binge, you may find good Chateaubriand at an expensive place like the Hotel Altes in Lisbon, but excellent beef of that sort is rare indeed. Generally, avoid beef at the market and in restaurants. There are, nevertheless, two popular lunch time dishes that are passable. One, called *bife a Portuguesa*, is simply a thin beefsteak grilled in a wine sauce and topped with fried eggs. Usually served with French fried potatoes on the side, the eggs and potatoes disguise the low quality meat. A second beef item that you can order if you are in a rush is called a *prego*, which translates into English as "nail." No one could explain how a hot steak sandwich ever came to be called a "nail" in Portuguese slang, but it is. The beef is not usually as hard as nails, but close.

A better choice than beef would be veal. Look for *vitela* on the menu. There are many pleasing and tasty veal dishes. A favorite is veal roast (*vitela assada*) with port wine sauce. Veal is more tender than beef and is generally cooked with aromatic herbs, onion, tomatoes, and garlic. Nearly every veal recipe calls for the use of wine, either in a marinade, basting liquid, or sauce. Port and Madeira wines seem to have been made for Portuguese veal.

In a hurry? Pop into a favorite Lisbon *pasteleria*, where you can get a fast and delicious lunch. This place, called *Tim-Tim* (Av. 5th Outobra, 113), serves wonderful fish fillets. Daily specials are posted on the door. Perhaps you decide to order the *vitela* special. When your plate is served, it looks much different than you expected. It is a plate of scrambled eggs, French fries, and a tomato slice. Scrambled with the eggs are whitish cubes that look like tofu. Thinking your waiter has misunderstood the order, you choose not to question but to accept the lunch as is. When you leave the little place, you look again at the menu posted in the window. Taking out your trusty pocket dictionary, you look up the word *cerebro*, which appears along with the known words *vitela* and *ovos*. To your surprise, you have enjoyed a plateful of scrambled eggs and veal brains!

The many ways veal can be prepared offers a wide range for the meat eater. The best is the *assada* (roast) with a wine sauce (*molho* or *atrevimento*) of port or Madeira.

According to most considered opinion, ground meat should be avoided. By law, Portuguese ground meat can contain many meat by-products other than beef. There are allowable amounts of mutton, goat, and horse, as well as beef. The Portuguese are relatively new at the hamburger business, and the strict quality control of the American fast-food industry has yet to reach Portugal. There are so many good things to eat, there is no reason to fall back on the hamburger. Teenagers who try a burger at a fast-food place in Lisbon often remark that the product is terrible. Considering that most American or British teenagers will eat anything called a burger, that judgment should be information enough.

The pork served in Portugal tastes better and tends to be leaner than American domestic pork. You will also notice that the meat itself has a richer and darker hue than North American pork. The reasons are not clear, but it really doesn't matter. Pork is served very imaginatively. The hearty grilled pork steaks of the north are mouth watering, especially those soaked in a wine marinade. The aroma of grilling pork steaks whets even the most blasé appetite. Everyone craves familiar food after being away from it for a time, and sometimes you feel you would sell your soul for something like a Big Mac. Whenever you have this problem, be sure to walk past a restaurant noted for its grilled pork steaks. The aroma will turn melancholy into savory passion.

In the south in the province of Alentejo, pork with clams has become the favorite pork dish. Many Lisbon restaurants have this on the menu. The pork should be tender after cooking for a longer than usual time in olive oil, garlic, onions, and a bit of tomato sauce, added to make the stew slightly reddish. The clams, added last, are allowed to stew with the meat for a while to blend those contrasting flavors.

Pork chops and pork roasts are not very popular in Portugal. The reason is that much of the pig is minced to make the great Portuguese sausages. Peasant societies elsewhere in the world have developed sausage as a way to preserve meat. Without refrigeration, pork could not be kept for very long periods of time. Pork does not dry well, and other preservatives such as salt and spices were historically very expensive. During the days of Europe's colonial era, spices were the medium of trade, and spice traders acquired great wealth. But what spices did to revolutionize meat preservation and, hence, sausage making, left a culinary legacy. The highly spiced or smoked sausages so common in rural areas of Europe are not excluded in Portugal. In fact, some fairly unusual forms evolved there. The most important Portuguese sausage is the *chouriço*. It is highly spiced, peppery, and smoky in flavor. The sausage has become a Portuguese staple—added to many stew dishes, sliced for appetizers or sandwiches, or tossed into omelettes. A decidedly Portuguese way of consuming large amounts of sausage is to order a plate of sausages at a traditional *Fado* house. The sausage is then grilled over a tiny brazier at your table. This peasant fare is both delicious and rich.

Linguiça is another favorite sausage. This smoked pork-tongue sausage originated in the northern mountain areas. Every food store has a stock of these dark sausages. Look for them hanging next to the reddish colored *chouriço* and the darkened hams.

Hams come in two varieties. The smoked variety from the areas of Chaves and Lamego are called *presunto*. These hams are luscious, very rich and very salty. When one orders an omelette with ham, this is the type of ham that will be served. It is often added to stews and other dishes as a savory flavoring to bolster otherwise bland combinations. The second type of ham is simply the generic *friambre*, as in a ham and cheese sandwich (*friambre y queijo*). This is a milder, less lean, cheaper type of ham.

Poultry is widely served. Chicken dishes predominate, but occasionally you will encounter a turkey dish worth ordering. On the menu look for *peru* if you want turkey and *frango* if you prefer chicken. The chicken is not the plump mass-produced kind Americans and Britons are accustomed to seeing in the grocery stores. Portuguese chickens are strange birds. They are skinny, bony, and have a look of poverty compared to our meaty, plump birds. But the taste is not the bland flavor we are used to. The chickens, though less meaty, are much tastier. These chickens were raised the way chickens used to be raised—on the farm, where their diet is varied. A standard Portuguese chicken recipe known as *frango na pucara*, calls for a chicken stewed in a clay pot with garlic, onions, tomatoes, and parsley.

Churrasco happens to be another very popular chicken preparation. This chicken is grilled or barbequed. The hot spot for this dish is in Cascais and is called *Frango Real*. To find it, just follow your nose. The aroma literally dominates the air for blocks around.

The Portuguese are fond of rabbits, not as pets, but as dinner. Some restaurants specialize in rabbit dishes. Most rabbit dishes originated in the rural north of the country. Look for the rabbit items under *coelho* on the menu.

Other game dishes are featured on menus from time to time but only rarely. Portugal is not endowed with great herds or flocks of wild game. Although venison is rarely served, *carne de veado* can be extremely tasty served with onions and potatoes in a stewlike concoction.

Mutton is fairly common in the mountain areas of the north but is rarely found on the menu in Lisbon restaurants. In rural areas watch for the menu item *carne de carneiro*. Lamb (*cordeiro*) is rarely served except in the mountain regions.

If you prefer goat meat (*carne de cabra*), there are many restaurants serving various goat dishes. More popular is *cabrito*, or kid goat. Even *cabrito* in restaurants tends to be very tough meat. It makes you wonder what the age limit is on "kids"!

Seafood

Portugal has always been a country that looked to the sea. The sea was the storehouse of food, the highway to discovery, and the track to the colonies. It was inevitable that Portuguese cuisine would reflect that marine heritage. The result is that Portugal is a seafood lover's paradise. The "catch of the day" and many other menu items in the seafood restaurants are probably caught only hours before they are served. Tons and tons of fresh fish are consumed daily in the country, yet the catch is many times greater than the local demand. As a result, Portugal does a sizable export business in fresh seafood. Its principal market is maintained in the remainder of Europe. Most of the seafood is shipped by truck and can easily be delivered to much of Europe within a day's time.

Bacalhau, or salt cod, remains one of the paradoxes of the Portuguese way of life. The people, without doubt, are devoted to dried salt cod. It is puzzling to think that salt cod, now very expensive, is the most popular seafood item of the people, given the plethora of fresh seafoods. Why? The answer to that defies explanation. The strong smelling, dried fish can be purchased in every grocery. The cost of fishing the now depleted banks off North America keeps the price high. Additionally, much salt cod is even shipped from Alaska. Why is it so popular? The fish must be soaked overnight just to make it edible the next day. It is so salty that one can hardly bear the taste without a good day's soak. Why are there no less than 365 individual recipes for the prized catch? Mesmerized by the thought of *bacalhau*, the Portuguese rave about its virtues. It can be boiled, baked, ground up into a paste, shredded, fried, steamed, eaten cold, or made into tasty fried snack cakes. It is the staple of the country. Believe it or not, there is even a Ministry of *Bacalhau* at the national government level. Though *bacalhau* is not very popular with tourists, one should try a meal of this national food. The most popular recipe is a simple dish of steamed cod with potatoes and other vegetables (*cozida*). It can also be enjoyed in several *cataplana*-style dishes that are popular in Algarve.

Caldeirada is another word that starts any Portuguese mouth to watering. It is a fish stew that requires a hearty appetite. Using any fish available at the time, the stew embellishes the fish with copious amounts of onion, potatoes, olive oil, and a few tomatoes, as well as liberal amounts of paprika to give the broth a lovely glow. A little garlic, of course, is thrown in for luck and taste. This dish and *cozida* survive the centuries as the most traditional Portuguese seafood dishes.

Sardines, although not really a dish in the same order as the salt cod *cozida* or *caldeirada*, are nevertheless of long-standing Portuguese tradition and reverence. Actually, the sardines sold fresh and whole are not very small. About six to eight inches in length (only the tail portion of the fish becomes the canned sardine), the silvery beauties are usually served grilled. Look for *sardinhas assada* on the menu. In the beach areas you will note many restaurants, cafés, and itinerant cooks grilling sardines to order. The procedure is a simple one. The fish is dredged through coarse salt and placed on a charcoal brazier for a few minutes on each side. A cold beer or chilled bottle of *vinho verde*, a salad, hard bread, and grilled sardines must be served daily in heaven!

There is a trick to eating these fish. You will reveal yourself as an amateur if you use a knife and fork. Some people try to be sophisticated, wielding a fork deftly to lift the tender meat from the bones. But it really looks awkward. To the purist, the meat loses some of its flavor as well. The proper method to eat a sardine is to address the fish, as it lies on its side, facing left. Gently pinch the meat from tail to gills and from top to bottom. A gentle lift will separate the entire filet from the bone. Depending on the size of the fish, you can slip the filet into your mouth or parcel it out into several morsels. Turn the fish over and repeat the process. Don't pinch too hard. Remember, this is a whole fish. A poke, prod, or pinch in the wrong place can leave one with a messy and unappetizing plate. This is not recommended for the squeamish. If you do it right, only the bare bones will remain. The best time to order sardines is in the spring when the catches are plentiful and tasty.

Other forms of seafood not unique to Portugal but sometimes served in unusual ways are eels, squid, and octopus (*enguia, lula,* and *polvo*). The restaurants on the south bank of the Tagus River from Lisbon at Caclihas specialize in eels. Most tourists prefer not to order a plate of baby eels. They may witness nightmarish incidents in markets, where they see huge vats of live squirming eels waiting to be sold by the kilogram to eager customers.

Octopus, on the other hand is favored by many tourists, even American and British. Grilled fresh, it has a savory seafood tang. Octopus sliced cold as a snack and served with lots of beer and wine seems to be the tourists' preference. Squid can be prepared in several ways. The way the Portuguese enjoy it seems to be much too strong for most American and British tastes. The unique method of preparation preferred by the Portuguese is squid fried in its own ink. Most Americans will not like the strong flavor of the squid prepared in that manner. Fried crisp, it is much more palatable but still very flavorful.

The varieties of shellfish available in Lisbon restaurants are incredible. Oysters, however, are not to be found. The oyster beds have been depleted to a nonproductive state, and importing them is too costly. But the substitutes are many. You can enjoy steamed, raw, or grilled *lagosta,* or crayfish. Look for the restaurants with stacks of these little beauties in the window. The *lagostinos* or Portuguese lobsters offer another taste treat. Try spider or rock crabs, which are usually served whole. Eat a plateful of prawns or shrimps (*camarões*) in any of the dozens of specialty restaurants in Lisbon, Cascais, or Algarve. Try the tasty little mussels called *mexilhões* or the little clams called *améijoas*. These shellfish are often presented as ingredients in other dishes such as *cataplanas* or the pork and clams dish indigenous to Alentejo. The *percebes* is one seafood item rarely served outside of Portugal. They are a form of barnacle and are served by the tons in Lisbon drinking establishments.

The seemingly infinite variety of fish can be a somewhat confusing to tourists trying to read the Portuguese menu. A favorite selection is the sole *(linguado)*. Most is fresh. In Sagres, try a whole grilled sole. Order it with a crisp lettuce salad. It should be a memorable meal. Add to the fresh sole a view of the towering cliffs and red beaches for a lingering memory.

Also try the hake, or *pescada*. A favorite way to serve hake is *cozida* style: the fish, whole or cut into steaks, is steamed with boiled potatoes, cabbage, onions, and carrots. Plenty of olive oil and vinegar is drizzled over this hearty dish. Even the *Rapido* train from Lisbon to Porto serves this Portuguese staple. Don't be surprised that the rather unattentive staff can serve such an excellent meal on the train. Hake is also served with tomatoes or, better yet, grilled over charcoal.

Swordfish, called *espadarte* or sometimes *peixe espado*, maintains a reasonable market price in Portugal. Its freshness makes it great grilled. Tuna steaks are also a menu favorite. Tuna is best grilled and served in light wine sauce.

The red mullet *(salmonetes)* are considered to be quite a delicacy. They too are grilled and then served with lemon and butter.

Shark and sea scallops are rarely seen on menus. There are economic as well as legal reasons for this scarcity. In the future it is expected that shark and rays will be much more common at the market place.

Finally, it may not properly be classified as seafood, but where else does the revered snail or *caracois* belong? During the late spring when the peasants are collecting snails from the shrubs and fields by the ton, many restaurants will display the hand-painted sign, "*Ha caracois!*" This means, "We have snails, folks! Come and gobble them up!" The snails one sees here are not the giant escargot of France. No, they are small ones that require about fifty or sixty to fill a plate. Steamed and served hot, they are eaten by pulling them out of their shells with a pin. When snails are in season, everybody sells them. One can even order them as a pizza topping. One day as we passed a beach cafe displaying the big sign "*caracois!*" I asked my teenage son if he would like a plate of snails. His reply was classic, "I make it a point never to eat anything that leaves a slimy trail. Thanks anyway!"

Fruits and Vegetables

The fruits and vegetables of Portugal are fewer in variety than in the United States and Britain. The cost of these food items, however, is quite low while quality remains high. Quality means taste, texture, and freshness, not outward appearance. Most of the fruit and vegetables in the supermarkets or shops are grown in small orchards and vegetable gardens cared for by an individual farmer and his family. Agriculture in Portugal is more labor intensive than capital intensive, so there are few costly chemicals used, such as pesticides. The result is that the produce may be scarred, bruised, or otherwise not as pristine as Americans have come to expect. Beneath the imperfect wrapper are some of the best apples, oranges, pears, and other fruit one can find. Because of the huge capital outlays necessary for long-term storage and long-range marketing, in Portugal the "storage facility" is the tree, vine, or bush on which the produce is grown. In other words, fruit and vegetables are ripened on the vine or tree and marketed fresh. Naturally, when a crop is ready for harvest, there are tremendous supplies. At other times of the year, one must settle for dried fruit, imports, or preserves. When found in the stores, fruit is truly fresh, not having been stored for weeks or months in a warehouse.

During the autumn, nuts and dried fruit seem to be available in incredible supply. Portuguese nuts, though abundant, are not inexpensive, particularly almonds from the Algarve. The price is kept relatively high by the export markets. A handful of freshly roasted almonds with a dab of salt is well worth the price. Most of the more expensive hotel bars and lounges supply each table with a dish of almonds and raisins as munchies to accompany port wine or liquor. Peanuts, however, are even more expensive than almonds. Since they are not produced in Portugal, all peanuts and peanut products must be imported. Peanut butter is available, but it is very expensive and of low quality.

As noted earlier, many of the heartier soups and recipes originating in the rural areas call for cabbage (*couve, repolho,* or *lombarda*). The three types include ordinary cabbage, savoy, and kale. Kale is considered cabbage throughout Portugal and is an important constituent in *caldo verde* and other old recipes. Kale is grown in nearly every available space. Very mature kale plants reach four or five feet in height. Aged maybe six years, their leaves are continually harvested as the long stem continues to produce new leaves. It is a perfect plant for the cool but mild Mediterranean winters.

Other greens served and consumed fresh include several varieties of lettuce. Iceberg or head lettuce, so popular in the United States as a salad green, is unknown in Portugal. The lettuce produced is a sweet, tender variety that is simply called lettuce (*alfaçe*). Always a green salad contains onions and tomatoes. A surprise, at first, may be the tomatoes. They are not red ripe as Americans prefer them. Expect them to be served green and quite firm. It is the preferred way to eat tomatoes in a salad. When the fruit is red and ripe, it is considered suitable only for sauce or cooking.

Potatoes are used in many traditional rural recipes. Potatoes form the base for several soups, are always in the *cozida* recipes, and are served with nearly every meal in one form or another. If they are not served boiled, then they are served French fried. In fact, French fried potatoes seem to be a national standard. Nearly every lunch plate has French fries. They are more popular in Portugal than in the United States or France. Baked potatoes are not served, nor are hashbrowns or cottage potatoes.

Like French fried potatoes, olives seem to be a part of every meal. Used as garnish, they appear in every salad, every plate of appetizers, and generally decorate most lunch plates. In the more expensive restaurants an entire bowl of olives will be on the table. These are not the green kind traditionally added to a martini. These are the beautiful dark brown or black olives produced throughout Iberia and the Mediterranean. Buy them by the kilo at the market, rinse them, add fresh water, a clove of garlic, a bay leaf and enjoy them by the handful. The fresh water tends to freshen them up, washes the very salty brine from them, and cuts the sodium a bit. The garlic sweetens and livens the taste, as does the bay leaf. Olive prices remain relatively low.

Turnips and carrots are common vegetables that play an important role in many Portuguese meals. They are used not only as filling additions to recipes but also as flavor and aroma enhancers.

Wine and Other Beverages

The wines of Portugal are highly underrated. With the exception of the ports and Madeira, little is known of this country's sublime offerings of the vine. Most Americans are familiar with Mateus and its unique bottle. And, certainly, everyone knows of Lançer's and its opaque terra-cotta-colored bottles. But beyond those, the wines of Portugal are relatively unknown outside of the country. Yet Portugal's wines are so important economically that almost one-quarter of the population depends upon wine production in one way or another. Wine is a way of life in this small country. The question is, Is it any good?

Before answering that question, consider some facts. Portugal is Europe's fourth largest producer of wine. The most important wine region lies in the northern two-thirds of the country, north of the Tejo River.

Allegedly, Portugal, relative to its size, produces a greater variety of wines than any other country in the world. The Portuguese claim that their abundant sunshine and obdurate granite soils give a particular character to their wine. Many of these wines are appreciated by connoisseurs the world over. From the internationally known port wines of Porto to the refreshing "green" wines of the Minho, every region of the country has its characteristic wine. Those regions have been officially designated by type as *Região Demarcada*, by the *Justa Nacional do Vinho* (National Wine Council). Take for example the granitic area around Viseu. That region produces the aromatic, mild, and velvety wines of the Dão. Around Lisbon, the cities of Colares, Buçelas, and Carcavelos produce wines of an unmistakable taste and bouquet. Setúbal produces a generous, aromatic, fruity wine. Another great wine-producing region is that around the Bairrada, with its full-bodied and satisfying red wines. Also in that zone, you find a natural sparkling white wine.

From Torres Vedras to Ribatejo some excellent table wines are produced for the popular taste. In the Alentejo and Algarve, too, the wines are fruity and velvety. The rosés come primarily from the *Douro* region. Yet none of these excellent wines have enjoyed the popularity outside of Portugal that French or Italian wines have. The reasons for this unfortunate situation are complex, but it is basically the result of years of economic isolation, dictatorship, and lack of entrepreneural expertise. The wines are good; some could be called great. Only the Portuguese and visitors to Portugal know for sure.

How did it all begin? The story of Portuguese wine is believed to have begun when Henry of Burgundy, father of Portugal's first monarch, Afonso Henrique, brought grape vines from France in about A.D. 1100. The vines flourished, and the fruit eventually became the raw material for the great port wines of today.

Port wine grapes are now grown in the officially demarcated region of the Douro River in northern Portugal. Ruby, tawny, and white ports tend to come from the lower part of the valley, whereas the vintage character of finest ports originate further up the river in the Alto Douro region. For reasons of climate and soil, the grapes here are of better quality. Hence wine is invariably higher in quality. The Alto Douro region produces the late-bottled vintage, the old tawnies, and the crusted and vintage ports. These fine and generally expensive wines are produced only on the finest estates and farms, called *quintas*.

The principal grape varieties used in port production are *Touriga Naçional, Touriga Françesa, Tinta Barraea, Tinta Çāo,* and *Tenta Roriz.* The grapes are harvested in late September and early October. As one can imagine, this is the peak labor period in the Douro region. Entire families are sometimes employed in the harvest of the grapes. Hard work, long days, and tremendous effort in the harvest is accompanied by much singing, hearty meals, and heavy sleep.

The collected grapes are transported to the wine-making centers where they are crushed both by traditional foot stomping and by the machines used in larger, more modern wineries. The stalks are partially removed. Fermentation in huge vats begins and continues for thirty-six to forty-eight hours. Adding pure-grade brandy stops the fermentation. The critical decision to halt fermentation depends upon the proper proportion of sweetness remaining in the grape. That decision is based upon data collected by modern methods as well as testing done by experienced human palates. The alcohol content at this point stands at about 20 percent. This wine is known as "young port" for obvious reasons.

After it is allowed to rest for four or five months following the harvest, the young port is transported down the Douro River to the city of Vila Nova de Gaia, across the river from Porto. Today the conveyance is by conventional rail or truck tankers. In days not too long ago, the traditional and very picturesque boats, *barcos rabelos,* sailed down river with their precious cargoes. Some wineries display the old boats as reminders of the colorful tradition.

The business of wine making continues. At the city wineries the young port is transferred to "pipes," 534-liter casks or barrels. Here the wine rests for at least three years. Some is aged for as long as fifty years.

Note that most of the port labels have British names. It happened that the modern port industry was originally founded and promoted by the British. For many centuries the Portuguese had produced the wine, but only for local consumption. Through word of mouth, trade, and travel, the English became more and more attached to the port wines. English monarchs have considered port to be *their* drink for many centuries. To keep the product flowing to the British Isles and to control standard quality, the British themselves became involved in the business. Soon they established their own bottling and export companies, chose the grapes, oversaw their fermentation, and built great "lodges" for the aging of the wine. Thus in 1703 an agreement between Portugal and England was reached. The Methuen Treaty gave England priority in the choice of Portuguese wines while the Portuguese were given priority in English wool. Look for the names Dow, Cockburn, and Sandeman on port bottles. These are the same companies, named for their founders, that were established in the 1700s.

There are two types of port wine: wood aged and bottle aged. The tawny, ruby and white ports are aged in oak casks or large wooden vats. To arrive at fine balance and flavor, the wines are usually blended and bottled after only three years of aging.

Vintage character ports are four to five years old when bottled. The vintage wines, too, are blended, but only with ports of specific years to reflect the quality of a vintage wine—full flavor, deep color, and smoothness.

The old tawnies are ten, twenty, thirty, or even forty years of age. The tawnies take on a new character as they are aged again in oak casks for that length of time. In fact, the tawnies change color from the deep red of their youth to the classic amber shade. This aging and consequent color change gives them their name.

Vintages are declared every so often, depending upon the quality of the grapes at the time of harvest. This is serious business and not taken lightly by the vintners. Only when a vintage is declared can the late-bottled vintage ports be produced. These wines are produced by the same vineyards that, when a vintage is declared, can legally produce a vintage port. The late-bottled vintage wines are bottled after the fifth year of aging in wood, and they tend to mature more quickly.

A second aging method is bottle aging. There are three great wines produced by that mode of aging. Crusted port is made by blending the wines of different years and bottling the wine at a young age. In time, the wine will form a deposit or "crust" in the bottle. After only three or four years it is said to be aged sufficiently and can be sold for consumption.

A "single *quinta*" port, as its name suggests, is the product of a single farm or estate. These wines are made in good years but when a vintage is not declared. They too are bottled young, and then the aging process commences.

"Vintage" refers to the outstanding wine of an outstanding year. Perhaps only three years in ten does the weather cooperate to produce a grape suitable for the declaration of a vintage. The produce from the vintage can be bottle aged, but it is usually aged in wood for two to two and a half years before being bottled. Vintage is the pride of each of the port companies. The anxious consumer can purchase vintage port immediately after bottling without further aging. The true wine connoisseur will allow the wine to age and mature for many years in order for it to develop its unique character.

The bottle-aged ports are bottled unfiltered, and as part of the natural aging process, a deposit, or crust, forms in the bottle. Before serving, the bottle should stand upright for several hours. This allows the sediment to settle. The cork should be carefully drawn and the wine decanted. The crust remains in the bottle. But the wood-aged ports are filtered before bottling and are, therefore, ready for immediate consumption without the worry of crust. There is no sediment and decanting is not necessary. Some experts suggest that it may, in fact, improve the wine if one allows the wine to "breathe" after decanting.

Of the wood-aged wines of moderate price range, some favorites are Sandeman Tawny, Presidential Tawny, Cockburn's *Açordo,* and Cockburn's Special Reserve. The very old bottles and the vintages are expensive. Most casual tourists do not buy them for everyday consumption. Good places to sample some of the better and older wines are the hotel bars or the very comfortable *Solar do Vinho do Porto* in Lisbon's Bairro Alto.

Buying true port in the U.S. has been rendered easy. To distinguish real Portuguese ports from domestic port wine, the Portuguese wines are officially labelled for the U.S. market as *"Porto"* or *"Vinho do Porto."* The domestic ports are simply called "Port."

Portugal's second most famous wine is produced solely on the island of Madeira, from which it takes its name. Madeira was a very fashionable wine in colonial America but has gradually lost its popularity on this side of the Atlantic. The Madeira grapes are crushed like the port grapes. After fermentation, the young wine is also fortified with brandy. Interestingly, and unlike port, it is matured in "hothouses" for several weeks. This practice originated in the early days of trade when the long ocean voyage in the warm holds of sailing ships was credited with giving Madeira wine its special, smooth, characteristic taste. Today Madeira wine is used primarily as an aperitif and is also widely used in French cuisine.

Muscatel wine, produced in Setúbal, is probably one of the most intriguing of the sweet Portuguese wines. Another sweet wine is produced between Lisbon and Estoril in the town of Carcavelos. The British also found this wine and adopted it as a favorite. Carcavelos wine is sherry-like and ranges from dry to dessert quality.

Portugal's best kept secrets are the *vinho verdes*, or "green" wines. They are not really green in color; "green" refers to wines' age. They are young, fresh, white wines from the Minho region of the country. The Minho is the extreme northwest of Portugal, where the climate enhances the cultivation of light grapes. What is nice about the *vinho verdes* is that they are truly light, low in alcohol content (8–9%), and inexpensive. Enjoy a bottle, always chilled, with lunch, a snack, dinner, or as a refreshing drink on a warm afternoon. Unfortunately it does not ship well and has a short shelf life. As a result, it is rarely found outside of Portugal. The Lançer's brand imports *vinho verde* to the United States, but it is hard to find and, because of the cost of importation, the market price is significantly higher than in Portugal.

Vinho verde is definitely the Portuguese national drink. Whereas most port is exported, most *vinho verde* stays at home. The wine is popularily purchased in returnable two-, four-, or five-liter bottles and jugs. Once opened, the wine must be consumed within a day or so; it does not keep well. Most grocery stores have dozens of brands. Pick any bottle and you will probably be satisfied. There are, of course, some differences in quality. By consensus, the best *vinho verdes* are *Casal Mendes*, with a green lacelike label; *Aveleda*, with an interesting pictorial label; and *Casal Garçia*, with a blue and white lacy label.

The white, red, and rosé table wines are honest and straight forward. Quality is variable, more variable than in the *vinho verdes*, but the prices make up for it. It is surprising how inexpensive wines can be in Portugal. For red or white wines, the *Dãos* are the best. The Dão region near Coimbra produces several brands. Rely on the opinion of your wine steward or the waiter. One extremely popular brand among the Portuguese, however, is *Gatão*. Also look for *Colaris* and *Bucaços*. The fine wines of the F. M. da Fonseca winery of Azeitão are numerous and pleasing. This winery produces the famous Lançer's brand so popular in the United States. Also available is *Branco Seco*, an extra-dry white wine that is said to be unique to Portugal. A full-bodied *Periquita* will please your nose and palate. The types and brands seem limitless.

Some of the liqueurs and spirits produced in Portugal have a unique quality. *Licor de Améndoa*, or almond liqueur, is very soothing. Enjoy it often after dinner. This liqueur is an excellent example of Portuguese spirits, a good one to bring home to share with your friends.

Also try *Ginginha*, or cherry liqueur. It is made mostly in Lisbon and sold under several brands. Price varies considerably, and you get what you pay for.

A specialty liqueur of the province of Algarve is the sweet and easy, ever so smooth *brandymel*. This is a luscious dessert brandy that warms the innards and lifts the spirit with a combination of brandy and honey. The best *brandymel* is made with the honey from almond blossoms. At least that is what the Portuguese like to believe. Most tests, however, cannot identify a bottle so labeled.

Another drink produced in Algarve is the very powerful *Aguardente de Medronha*. This will curl your hair (or make it fall out!) Frankly, it is too acrid for most Americans and Britons, but it is a popular drink in the local cafes.

Straight brandy is sold, too, by the large port producers under the wineries' labels. Try the moderately priced *Maçieira* Royal Old Brandy.

The best, and perhaps most special, of the Portuguese liqueurs is that produced at Castello Branco. The name is *Licor Beirão* and it is sublime! The taste is slightly licorice with a creamy sweet afterglow. The Portuguese recommend it highly. The spirit is very popular as a drink to offer honored guests as they enter a Portuguese family home. This one, too, is worth bringing home.

Imported spirits such as Scotch, vodka, and bourbon are very expensive. There are some locally produced spirits, but their quality matches the low price.

Beer (*cerveja*) is all locally produced. There is one brewery, and it is a government monopoly. This fact does not mean the beer is bad. In fact, *Sagres cerveja* is considered to be, at least, good. The *Sagres* brewery also produces the slightly more expensive *Sagres Europa* and *Cristal*. Both are good to excellent. Additionally, the *Sagres* organization brews and distributes two other popular European beers of excellent quality. Under a Danish license, *Carlsberg* beer is brewed in Lisbon. Another Danish license allows *Tuborg* to be brewed in Portugal. With only those five brands from which to choose, ordering a beer is easy. Beer is always served cold in the U.S. fashion and in the fashion of the British lagers.

Bottled mineral water is a common mealtime beverage. Served very cold, the water is excellent and refreshing to the taste buds. There are several brands, but usually restaurants offer no choice. The critical choice is either with gas (*com gas*) or without gas (*sem gas*). The natural sparkling waters tend to be very inexpensive and as palatable as the famous French brand. Note that most Portuguese diners will consume both a bottle of water and a bottle of wine at mealtimes.

Soft drinks are certainly available anywhere. The popular U.S. brands, like Coke and Pepsi, are everywhere. Schweppes has also invaded the market, but *Sumol* is the domestically produced soft drink brand. *Sumol* offers a wide range of refreshing fruit drinks. The *Lemonada*, or lemonade, is particularly good.

Coffee (*café*) is, like *vinho verde*, a national treasure and way of life. Every restaurant or snack bar has the classic espresso coffee maker. You may have had espresso in France, Italy, Austria, or Spain, but the Portuguese coffee is truly head and shoulders above all others. By comparison the Spanish coffee is bitter and the French is insipid. Generally agreed, Portuguese espresso is without peer. The reason is this: Although it would seem logical that the Portuguese would import rich Brazilian coffee beans, this is not the case. Most coffee brewed in Portugal comes from Africa, the home of coffee. Centuries of colonial ties and economic trade with Africa have promoted the flow of rich, savory African beans to the grocers of Portugal.

For each cup the dark roasted beans are ground and then brewed by the espresso method. Each cup, therefore, is tiny but potent.

Bica is the popular term for the small cup of coffee. It is a slang word literally translated as "jet" or "spout." The term obviously comes from the sound the espresso machine makes as it forces hot water through the coffee grounds and thence the tiny spout. This process produces coffee of sublime perfection. Most Portuguese drink their *bicas* with much sugar. It is traditional to start the day with that potent shot of caffeine and sugar. Midmorning is yet another time for a *bica*. After every meal, coffee is traditional. During intermission at the movies or a bullfight or while waiting for a train, people consume *bicas* in larger numbers. Two or three sips will empty the cup, so there is always time enough for a *bica*. This very strong coffee seems to be consumed at all hours of the day.

There is one other way to serve coffee in Portugal. It is called the *galão*, which translates as "gallon." The term is descriptive of the drink. Compared to a *bica*, it is very large. Coffee is simply mixed half and half with heated milk and served in a four- or five-inch-tall glass. It is a popular midmorning drink if one is not in a hurry.

Coffee is a Portuguese pleasure. Remember it is served strong, concentrated, and powerful. What do the Portuguese think about our coffee and the way it is served, by comparison? They find our coffee weak, watery, and virtually tasteless. When American or British coffee is mentioned, the Portuguese laugh smugly.

Desserts

For dessert the tradition is *pudim flan*, or flan pudding. Served in every restaurant and Portuguese home, it is an egg custard with a topping of caramel. The recipe is simple. If you plan to make it at home, you can buy flan cups designed specifically for the preparation and molding of the custard.

Ovos moles is a simpler version of flan. It is merely sugar, egg yolks, and water heated and then allowed to set up. Usually it is served with a light syrup in a fancy dish to give the simple item a bit of flare.

The *pastelerias*, or pastry shops, sell a little tart filled with custard and sprinkled with cinnamon. It is called a *"pasteis de nata"* or simply *"nata."* Ask for it by the short name and everyone will know what you want. The pastries are not very original or very fancy, but they are good. You cannot compare the pastries with the light and airy ones of eastern Europe or with fancy Swiss and Dutch pastries. Portuguese pastries are good, wholesome, tasty, and substantial food but not fancy. There are some very elaborate pastry shops in the Chiado district in Lisbon. These up-scale shops are clever in design to please their up-scale clientele, but generally the pastries are merely embellished standard varieties.

A favorite midmorning snack is a simple *bola*. You can get this little round pastry *com creme*, with cream filling, or *sem creme*, without cream. Either way, it satisfies a midmorning craving. Temptations are everywhere. The aroma of fresh coffee very much adds to temptation and the enjoyment of Portuguese pastries. A *bica* and a *bola* seem to be a logical combination. Anything would taste superb accompanied by that agreeable coffee potion.

In addition to pastries, the Portuguese of long ago developed several methods for preserving the profuse fruits of the country. Dried fruits and figs are very commonly sold and consumed. Fresh fruits are always a dessert option at any restaurant. One of the better fruit products is the *marmelada*, made famous by the nuns at the convent of Odivelas. The old convent and girls' school can be visited by prearrangement only. Our friend's grandmother had attended the school as a young girl and arranged for us to see the interior of this famous institution. This is no usual tourist excursion. In fact, without having our valuable connections, we never would have been allowed inside while school was in session. The giggles of the young girls alerted everyone to our presence as we wandered the halls and courtyards. We were shown the huge *azulejos*-lined kitchen where the nuns produced their ambrosia-like marmalade from the fruit of the quince. We were also shown the revolving hatch where the nuns could sell their product to the public but not come in direct contact. Now, of course, the *marmelada* is produced under several brands and can be purchased anywhere. It preserves well and lasts a long time. Portuguese children grow up with *marmelada* much as American children grow up with peanut butter.

The grocery stores also feature a wide range of fruit preserves, jams, and jellies produced within Portugal. The orange preserves are particularly enjoyable. Occasionally you can find an unusual offering like the chocolate-covered orange peels in Évora or the decorative and sometimes comical shapes of the marzipan candies of Alentejo and Algarve. The almond-flavored marzipan of Algarve is, by far, the best sweet treat in Portugal.

Types of Establishments

In most countries there are restaurants, and there are restaurants. In Portugal there are *pastelerias, confeitarias, cervejarias, adegas, churrasqueiras, tabernas, marisqueiras, cafés,* and *restaurantes.* The number of places in Lisbon where you can be served a meal is incredible. In the Greater Lisbon telephone directory "Yellow Pages," there are no fewer than six thousand eating establishments! Those are just the ones that have telephones! There are countless others in Alfama, Bairro Alto, Rato, and elsewhere that have no need for telephones. Add maybe another two thousand small establishments and you have an accurate picture of the importance of eating and dining in Portugal and the reason why the two-hour lunch is a tradition. Consider that Lisbon is Europe's smallest capital city. A city of fewer than a million people, it still supports eight thousand eating establishments.

Most of these restaurants (using the inclusive term here) are rated as "1," "2," "3," "4," or *"Luxo."* That is, the owners have chosen the restaurant's classification and paid for the license accordingly. To understand the meaning of this rating system you must realize that if a restaurant displays its "3" rating, for example, it cannot offer food or service or cleanliness *below* that level. The higher the number, the better. Look for the standardized placard near the entrance. If it has none, that means that there are no standards and anything goes. Curiously, a lack of a rating does not mean bad food or horrid conditions. It simply means that the owner chose not to play the game. Lack of a rating does mean, however, that you have no assurance of quality at any level. You will note that cleanliness is seldom a problem in any restaurant. The Portuguese restaurant is impeccably clean, so there is no need to worry about sanitation. But look for the rating. It is a good indication of the quality of the food and, hence, its cost. The *"Luxo"* or deluxe restaurants are expensive. As an example, the *Avis* in the Chiado district of Lisbon is probably the best restaurant in the entire country. It can stand up to any of the fine European restaurants and is correspondingly expensive. Fourth-class restaurants are many and usually associated with hotels in resort areas. You will find the third-class restaurants to be the best bargain and most numerous. Third-class establishments are mostly simple places that offer typical Portuguese fare at moderate to low prices. Pick a street, any street, in Lisbon and you will find restaurants in this class offering good, wholesome, and hearty Portuguese food served with speed and finesse. Restaurants in this category are always crowded at lunchtime. ("Packed" is probably a better word than "crowded.") "Noisy" is a good description of the ambiance. Restaurants in this category are where Lisbon's professional and clerical people eat, and it is quite unlikely that anyone would be disappointed with the food or service. Also note that many of these establishments cater only to the lunchtime trade and are not open for dinner.

There is another group of unmarked restaurants in Lisbon. You would never know they existed except for their unobtrusive and plain signs. Interestingly, these signs do not indicate function, only a name. Finding and patronizing these establishments can be a problem for the casual tourist. You need a local friend who knows the territory and the language. Ask around. For example, near the Camões square, we entered an unmarked door with a sign that indicated nothing except the family name, presumably of the owner. Inside, we were surprised with the small restaurant that was humming with customers. The room was spotless and was quiet for a Portuguese lunch crowd. The moderate size restaurant was on two levels. It also had a bar and a central dessert-serving stand. It was owned and operated by two distinguished elderly women. No menus were offered, but we were told the three dinner choices: hake with clams, beef with mushrooms, and a squid dish. Service was impeccable. The cost was high, but it was worth it. We looked for other places like this and found a few. The problem with this type of restaurant is that they are more or less semiprivate dinner clubs with a clientele of mostly professional or government people. Tourists are not encouraged and rarely is English spoken. If you want to eat in such restaurants, you must meet and befriend local professional people. Then suggest lunch at one of these fascinating establishments.

You will always find the *pastelerias* and *confeitarias* to be genial places to enjoy a quick meal or a sandwich. In addition to pastries, most serve lunch plates from a limited menu. Some of the larger ones offer specialities or daily specials. You can eat well and inexpensively at most *pastelerias*. They are, indeed, interesting institutions. Years ago the café was the meeting place for socializing, arguing, politicking, and just generally hanging around. Cafés are European institutions devoted to life and living. Portugal was no exception. But after the revolution in 1974, the cost of urban land skyrocketed and the cafés could not afford the high rents with corresponding low volume of sales. A student studying for an exam, a would-be poet or novelist sipping a coffee for six hours did not pay the rent. Changes took place. The high-rent spaces were converted to high-volume restaurants or very common *pastelerias*. There are about twenty-five hundred *pastelerias* in Lisbon. They appear on every block. They are the Portuguese indoor recreation spaces. *Pastelerias* not only substitute for cafés but are akin to an indoor park. There are a few that even retain the look and feel of the cafés of the old days. They are all social and recreational gathering places.

Within the Portuguese system of socializing, *pastelerias* have a noticeable pattern of clientele. The early-morning breakfast rush sees throngs of people reaching for a pastry and quick *bica*. In midmorning, the *pasteleria* is full of young mothers with their babies and toddlers. At lunch, the *pasteleria* is a madhouse, where the cacophony of rushed diners all looking for counter space or tables space sets the tone. Incidentally, the *pasteleria* usually has two prices. If you eat at the counter, or *bar*, the price is cheaper than at the table, or *mesa*. Things quiet down for an hour or two after lunch, but then the midafternoon snack-and-*bica* crowd comes and goes in a never-ending stream. *Pastelerias*, however, are not usually open beyond the dinner hour.

Pastelerias come in all shapes and sizes. The dimly lit, former cafés of Bairro Alto are good places to watch people. The bright new *pastelerias* in the suburbs or resort shopping areas are fun places to rest for a few minutes. For the charm of the past, visit the *Brasileiria* in the Chiado district of Lisbon. Watch for the ghost of the poet Pessoa and enjoy a pastry and coffee amidst the dimly lit spaces. Note the dark mahogany bar, the brass trim, and the mirrored wall. This is still a popular place for would-be writers. Also try the *Nicola* at Rossio in Lisbon. Its interior and exterior are good examples of the art nouveau style. *Nicola* was built only in 1928, but it has not changed one bit in the ensuing years. Its builder, the architect Notre Junior, would recognize the place as he left it.

Then there is the snack bar. Don't expect the snack bar to be anything like the one at K-Mart in Des Moines or anywhere else in the United States. A Portuguese snack bar is where you can buy a sandwich or a meal. Some snack bars are like restaurants. Some are reminiscent of a *pasteleria*, and others are just a counter with service for sandwiches only. The term "snack bar" seems to be used to designate not the type of eating but its modernity. This is a popular term for a place that's "with it." Interestingly, the term "snack" is of Dutch derivation, not English or American.

There are nearly one thousand *cervejarias* in the Lisbon area. *Cervejaria* literally translated would be a "beer parlor" or "pub." But it is hard to tell whether *cervejarias* are merely drinking establishments or eateries. Most do serve food and some even have a full menu. Probably the most famous of the *cervejarias* is *Cervejaria da Trindade* on the Rua Nova da Trindade in Lisbon, just west of Rossio. It is the biggest and best-known beer hall in Lisbon. Lisboetas, while consuming piles of shellfish, imbibe tremendous quantities of beer. The *Trindade*'s average daily sales of beer is fifteen hundred liters. The stacks of plates and heaps of mussels and shrimps indicate that the shellfish consumption must be in the tons per day. In addition to shellfish appetizers, *Trindade* has a full menu as well. The recommended item happens to be the Portuguese steak. It is great with cold beer. With the noise of the crowd, the bustle, and the good fun, a guest will never notice the toughness of the beef. Midafternoon is a good time to wander in to look the place over. At lunchtime, *Trindade* is a madhouse of noise and laughter and eating and drinking. After working hours, right after the offices and shops close, it again becomes very animated.

The *Alema* is the best of the *cervejarias*. It is totally unlike any of the busy, noisy, and far from unpretentious *cervejarias* in Lisbon. Just a few blocks up Rua Alecrim from Cais do Sodré station, the *Alema* is not merely a beer hall. The only thing *cervejaria* about it is the small bar at the entrance. Strangely, the decor of the vaulted brick and wood dining area has a German flavor. In fact, the menu features authentic German fare such as bratwurst and Wiener schnitzel. The house beer, a light pilsner, is brewed specifically for the restaurant according to the owner's specifications. Order the veal with madeira sauce or a spinach souffle. Also try the *sopa de legumes*. Everything is served beautifully. Each dish is precisely arranged with flair by the professional waiters. The point is to please not only the palate but also the eye. The portions are incredible and prices are moderate.

An *adega* is a small hole-in-the-wall, often lower than street level. The *adega* seems to be a drinking place for men only. At least you never see any women in these places. An *adega* looks rather unsavory, with a bar stretching across one side of the room, no tables, and low lights. In this smoke-filled room, darkly clad figures sip wine or beer. This does not mean *adegas* are bad places for a quick visit, but they are not the sort of places to take the family. Hanging from the rafters you will see some smoked hams and sausages. Huge wine barrels are propped in place behind the bar. *Adegas* are places for serious drinking. The adventurous may try a piece of sausage or ham to wash down with the wine.

In Lisbon there are still establishments called *tabernas*. These are simply *cervejarias* with all the same characteristics. If there is anything that distinguishes a *taberna* from a *cervejaria*, it is the age of the establishment. Most of the *tabernas* predate *cervejarias* and tend to emphasize wine more than beer.

Within the broad category of "restaurants," there are, indeed, some specialty eating places. The type is indicated by the establishment's sign. For example, a *marisqueira* is a place specializing in shellfish. Look for one of these. Some of the better ones are near Rossio in Baixa or on Rua Portas Sta. Antão. There are many in the towns of Cascais and Nazaré.

A *churrasqueira* specializes in grilled items such as chicken or pork. Don't confuse these restaurants with the more chic designation of *"grille."* The new grills are usually in the hotels and are just restaurants or coffee shops with a fancy title.

Chinese restaurants are becoming more and more popular, and Indian food is available also. Italian food is not quite as popular as Chinese, but pizza parlors are multiplying in number, an indication of growing popularity. The best is the *Casa Pizza* of Monte Estoril and Estoril. If you prefer an English pub atmosphere and a decent piece of beef or steak, try the *John Bull* in Cascais. The beef is good, the Portuguese cuisine is superb, and a fun atmosphere prevails.

There are numerous restaurants in the Lisbon area that offer something special. That is, they offer something in addition to good food. For example, try the unique *Casa de Leao* right in the Castle St. George. With a wonderful view, the restaurant is particularly famous for its first-class service and vast wine cellar. It features an outstanding cold buffet, but you can also order traditional dishes from an extensive menu.

In Setúbal, have dinner at the *Pousada de São Filipe*. The view of the city, river, and ocean take your breath away. The food, as in all *pousadas*, is first rate.

Try the *Restaurante Alcobaça* in Sintra for its regional dishes and its nearness to the National Palace. If you want to dine in a palace, visit the *Cozinha Velha* in the Queloz Palace. The restaurant's location in the old kitchen of the palace makes it a unique dining experience. It is small, however, so make reservations. Traditional Portuguese food prevails here, using recipes based on generations of good cooking. Save room for the restaurant's famous pastries. The decor is intriguing, and the central buffet is loaded with mouth-watering delicacies.

Tipping in any restaurant is a matter of choice. On your check or bill note the addition of a 10 to 15 percent service charge. Most menus will indicate "T.S.C." meaning all charges, including service, will be shown on your check. If you feel the service merits more than the standard gratuity, a few more *escudos* will be appreciated. In fact, you will be pleased with the service in most restaurants. Waiters (99 percent men) are professionals. These men regard their profession highly and do not take service lightly. Waiting on tables is their work, not a sideline or a way to pay their way through college. Interestingly, many waiters were raised in families of waiters, service is their heritage. The service you receive is usually worth more than the "T.S.C." 10 percent. No matter how small the restaurant, no matter what its rating, no matter whether it is the poorest *adega* or the mighty *Avis*, a waiter will never hurry the meal. A waiter will never rush a customer and will never, ever, bring the check until asked.

In conclusion, it has been established that eating in Portugal should not be a dull experience. The basic characteristics of Portuguese cuisine include savory, substantial, succulent, abundant, and varied menu items. The geographic situation, the climate, the various natural landscapes, social customs, and cultural attributes have shaped a cuisine unique in Europe. In addition, Portuguese cuisine has been influenced by centuries of input from the people of Africa, Asia, and the Americas. The appetizing soups, the delicious and abundant seafoods and the countless ways in which they are prepared, the meat dishes, the game, the sausages, the fruit, the jams and marmalades, the cheeses, and the wines add up to an adventure in dining for any visitor.

CHAPTER 5

Language:
Benvindo a Portugal

*F*or a brief visit to Portugal as a casual tourist, you will not need to have an extensive knowledge of the language. But if you are touring by car or train for more than a week or two, your familiarity with vocabulary and grammar and your storehouse of useful phrases should be more comprehensive.

In the resort areas nearly all waiters and hotel personnel speak some English. But out in the countryside you cannot expect people to understand English. Remember, Portugal has yet to be "discovered" by hordes of tourists from the United States, so the need for the common person to speak English is negligible. You may, however, be surprised. English-speaking people are indeed fortunate that the non-English speakers of the world often study English from an early age and can use the language to communicate passably. Americans, as a group, possess far less foreign language skill than the vast majority of the world's population. Americans, as they travel, tend to expect all people to speak English. Interestingly, a significant portion of the world's population generally does. Why this is true is no mystery. English, the mother tongue of the British and the British Empire, was the *lingua franca* of colonial administration, trade, and commerce for at least two centuries. As travel and tourism blossomed in the last half of the twentieth century, the Americans, along with the British, dominated tourism on a worldwide basis. To accommodate both trade and tourism of the dollar-bearing Americans, others found it necessary to learn to use English. Because so many people spoke some form of English, there was less need to learn the languages of other countries. As a result, travelers may encounter a teenager in a small town in rural Portugal attempting an English conversation.

Unlike the French, who feign misunderstanding when a tourist attempts to communicate in French, the Portuguese will allow you much time and consideration. In fact, the Portuguese are generally pleased that someone is interested enough to try the difficult pronunciations. Even if you make a glaring error, you will be accepted with a smile and maybe a polite correction. When communication does result, the unabashed pleasure of the Portuguese will be obvious.

The unusual sound of the language is one of the interesting sounds of Portugal. It is surprisingly unlike Spanish, even though many of the spellings and grammatical constructs are quite similar. Clearly, Portuguese is related to Spanish, but it may actually have been the base of the Spanish language rather than the reverse. It has been hypothesized that spoken Portuguese may be closer to the sound of the original Latin language, from which it emerged, than any of the other Latin-based languages. The likely reason is that service to the Roman Empire was often rewarded by grants of land when honored soldiers or public servants chose to remain in outpost areas. Many Latin speakers, not all of who spoke pristine Latin in grammatically correct form, probably settled in Portugal. Unlike the many other areas of Roman occupation, the region to become known as Portugal was isolated for centuries and lay out of the mainstream of European development. As a consequence, there developed a distinct language with Latin roots. The sounds of the language heard today may, indeed, be a mixture of intonations similar to the utterances of the Roman legions of two thousand years ago.

It is important to have a working knowledge of the language if you plan a prolonged stay. Before leaving for Portugal, you can study Portuguese at the accelerated level at a university or college. Language study can and should be augmented with tape cassette lessons to improve pronunication and extend vocabulary.

Such preparation is useful to be sure. But no matter what language skill or wealth of information and knowledge a tourist possesses, he or she will soon learn how little is really necessary. At times tourists become frustrated by not being able to use the Portuguese they have learned. Portuguese politeness and willingness to please results in Portuguese speakers lapsing into English for the tourists' benefit.

Strange and amusing things can happen because of language smugness as well. There is the example of an American from Florida who spoke impeccable southern American English and prided herself on her ability to deal with the confusing array and contracted use of Portuguese pronouns. Portuguese pronoun structure is difficult. She was also a whiz at sentence construction. Her major problem was pronunciation of the Portuguese words; a Florida accent does not mix well with Portuguese. The result was delightful and incredible convolutions of otherwise standard Portuguese vocabulary that no one understood, despite the perfect grammar. Interestingly, however, the Portuguese are able to understand the spoken southern American English drawl better than some northern American accents. At any rate, a little language knowledge can often get in the way of otherwise normal cross-cultural communication.

Misunderstandings are often the result of what one thinks one hears. Unfortunately, what one hears is often not what is said. Spoken Portuguese is very difficult to grasp because of the number of "sch" or "zh" sounds that tend to substitute for the expected "s" sound. There are also many nasal tones that are not used in English. If a tourist can acquire a tape cassette with Portuguese pronunciation practice, it is worth the time and effort to tune the ear to separate sounds and, hence, words.

Note, however, that there is a major difference between spoken Brazilian Portuguese, and Continental Portuguese. Generally Brazilian pronunciation is slower. The unstressed vowels are clearer and the final "e" is sounded much more frequently than in Continental Portuguese. Those visiting Portugal should avoid Brazilian tapes and phrase books. Brazilian is understood in Portugal just as American English is understood in England, but there is a big difference in accent and word usage. Brazilian soap operas appear on Portuguese television, and Portuguese people enjoy mimicking the Brazilian pronunciation of certain words.

Tourists who speak Spanish will have no problem reading Portuguese and probably will be adequately understood if they speak

Spanish. They will, however, find it difficult to understand what is being said in reply. Portuguese people traveling to Spain can understand what is said in Spanish but cannot communicate easily. This is often taken to be Spanish snobbishness and reluctance to recognize another Iberian language. It is not. The truth is that for the Spanish listener there are too many sounds, too many unfamiliar tones, and too many missing vowels and unspoken syllables when the Portuguese speak. The person trying to understand Portuguese must not only be familiar with words, grammar, and syntax, but also must be able to recognize sounds and meaningfully reconstruct those sounds into language.

This chapter lists the phrases and words with which travelers should be familiar. They are shown with phonetic pronunciation symbols. But no adequate English symbols can represent with accuracy the complexities of Portuguese sounds. In fact, no attempt is made in this book to do so. For complete and detailed transcriptions, consult a good dictionary or text book. A problem in trying to symbolize language is that many letters take on different sounds depending upon their position in a word or the relationship to surrounding letters. There are also nasal sounds of vowels and diphthongs that are difficult to symbolize. This book's meager review of the Portuguese language does not pretend to be comprehensive. The serious student of language must take courses or consult professionals for a more comprehensive approach.

An in-depth study of the language reveals that although spoken Portuguese sounds complicated, the written form is remarkably clear, concise, and uncomplicated. Most concepts and ideas, when translated to English, seem precise and direct. When one translates between any two languages, there are many ideas and words that are not translatable, however. For example, there is no Portuguese word for the English concept of "worry". There is a Portuguese word for "home" as used in English, but it is rarely used in the spoken language. The commonly used word for "home," "house," or "residence" is simply *casa*. The single word seems to be adequate for all uses. Minor items of that nature tend to simplify the language to the advantage of the learner.

Portuguese is a Romance or Latin-based language. This means that it is related not only to Spanish but also to French, Italian, and Rumanian. Familiarity with any of these languages will make understanding the grammar and the vocabulary of Portuguese a little easier. Languages of common origin usually have words that are similar in meaning as well as spelling. Such words are known as cognates. There are even cognates among languages of dissimilar origins; for example, the English word "institute" translates to a very familiar *instituicão* in Portuguese. The knowledge of cognates can be very handy. The tourist who speaks no Italian can get by in Italy with certain Portuguese phrases. If the driver of a Roman taxi is trying to impress an American with driving maneuvers reserved only for Italians, the tourist can scream: *"Mais devagar, por favor!"* ("More slowly, please!") Somehow the driver will understand, because the words are close to the Italian equivalent.

To master a language you must concentrate on combining sounds into words. For example, to bargain for some object you can't live without, listen carefully to the words of the seller. Repeat them several times. If you are familiar with the language's number words and monetary system, you will eventually understand and communicate. The fun and satisfying part of learning a new language is being able to understand what is said and then communicate another thought in response. The tourist who makes no attempt to communicate in the language of the country is missing an intriguing and gratifying aspect of travel.

Need to Know

To begin you will need to know the following words and phrases at a minimum. For more complex constructs, purchase a comprehensive phrase book and a Portuguese/English dictionary. Phrase books can be especially useful since you do not need to know grammar. All you need to know is how to read and speak the words with the proper pronunciation.

Yes, No. *Sim* (seen), *Não* (nown). Nasalize the final "n" sounds.
Please. *Faz favor* (fash fah-vohr), *Por favor* (poor fah-vohr).
Thank you. *Obrigado* (oh-bree-gah-doo)-masculine speaker, *Obrigada* (oh-bree-gah-dah)-feminine speaker. (When one says thanks, one must be aware of one's own gender. The female's "thanks" has the feminine ending—*obrigada;* the male's "thanks" has the masculine ending—*obrigado).*
Thank you very much. *Muito obrigado (a)-(mweento-bree-gah-doo, -ah).* Note that the two words are often run together in the spoken form. The tourist tends to be very precise with pronunciations and articulate each letter syllable. When lis-

tening, you learn that, like spoken English, not all words are pronounced as spelled nor are all letters and syllables sounded. The vernacular pronunciation for "Thank you very much" is *"Tobregad"* (tow-bree-gahd).

Very good. *Muito bem* (mweetoo-behn). Here again is an example of run-together and shortened forms in common usage. When a waiter asks if you liked the squid fried in its own ink, you respond, *"tobem"* (tow-behn), meaning "very much." There is a feminine form of this also, *"tabem"* (tah-behn).

Good morning. *Bom dia* (bon dee-ah).

Good afternoon. *Boa tarde* (boh-ah-tard).

Good evening. Boa noite (boh-ah-noit).

Good-bye. *Adeus* (ah-day-oosh). Note the pronunciation of the final "s."

Good-bye, So long until next time. *Até logo* (ah-tay-lo-goo).

Excuse me *(I'm sorry)*. *Desculpe* (desh-koolp).

Excuse me *(to pass)*. *Com licença* (kon lee-son-sa).

Don't mention it; You're welcome (in response to "Thank you"). *De nada* (day nah-dah). In practice, the usual response to *"Muito obrigado"* is *"Nada."* The *"de"* is rarely used.

Do you speak English? *Fala Inglês?* (fah-lah een-glaysh). This is a very handy phrase to pull out when one's vocabulary fails or one just can't think of the right thing to say.

Please speak slowly. *Faça o favor de falar devagar* (fah-sa oo fah-vohr day fah-lar day-vah-gar).

Please write it down. *Faça o favor de o escrever* (fah-sa oo fah-vohr day oo ish-cre-vay).

I don't understand. *Não compreendo* (nown com-pree-an-doo); *não percebo* (nown per-say-boo).

Can you help me? *Pode ajudar-me?* (pod ah-zhoo-dar-me).

I am looking for . . . *Procuro. . .* (proo-koo-roo).

My address is . . . *A minha direcção e . . .* (a mee-hja dee-re-sown e).

Where is the American [British] consulate? *Ande e o consulado Americano [Britanico]* (on dee e oo kon-soo-lah-doo ah-mer-ee-cah-noo [Bree-ta-nee-koo]).

Where can we have something to eat? *Onde podemos comer?* (ond poo-day-moosh koo-mayer).

Where is the station? *Onde e a estação?* (on dee ay ah esh-ta sown).

One beer, please. *Uma cerveja, por favor* (oo-nah ser-vay-zha, poor fah-vohr). This phrase can be an integral part of a tourist's survival kit. The kit includes the next three prhases, usually spoken in order after short intervals.

How much? *quanta?* (kwan-tah).
One more, please. *Uma mais, por favor* (oo-mah-maysh, poor fah-vohr).
Where is the toilet? *Onde é a toilette?* (ondee ay ah twa-let). "Where is the toilet?" is very important and should be committed to memory. One rule that should be tattooed on the back of the hand of all travelers is this: "Never pass a toilet without using it. You never know when you may find another." In Portugal the "bathroom," "toilet," or "restroom" is generally indicated as the "W.C." When all else fails, just ask, *"Onde é W.C.?"* Remember there is no "W" in the Portuguese alphabet, so it is pronounced "duplo oo".
Where is the post office? *Onde é o correio?* (on-dee a yoo koo-ray-yoo).
What time is it? *Que noras são?* (kee o-rash sown).

Days

The days of the week are expressed uniquely in Portuguese. In addition to the usual Saturday *(sábado)* and Sunday *(domingo)*, the days are numbered, beginning with Monday. The interesting aspect is that the numbers originally kept track of fair days. So Monday is *Segunda-feira* (second fair day after the principal fair day, Sunday). In general practice, a less formal form is used. That is, usually the speaker will indicate the number only and omit the "feira".

The days of the week are thus:

Sunday - domingo (doo-meen-goo)
Monday - segunda-feira (say-goon-dah fay-ee-rah)
Tuesday - terça-feira (tayr-sah fay-ee-rah)
Wednesday - quarta-feira (kwar-tah fay-ee-rah)
Thursday - quinta-feira (keen-tah fay-ee-rah)
Friday - sexta-feira (saysh-tah fay-ee-rah)
Saturday - sábado (sah-bah-doo).

Time

Time of day is expressed on the twenty-four-hour clock instead of the American A.M. and P.M. Hence, 3:00 P.M. becomes 15.00 hr. or *quinze horas* (kenz o-rash), and so on. It makes the system simple and expands vocabulary. You must be able to count to at least twenty-four.

1. *um; uma* o (oon; oo-mah) Feminine form is used for time.
2. *dois; duas* (doh-ush; doo-ash)
3. *trés* (traysh)
4. *quatro* (kwah-troo)
5. *Cinco* (seen-koo)
6. *seis* (say-aesh)
7. *sete* (set)
8. *oito* (oh-ee-too)
9. *nove* (nov)
10. *dez* (desh)
11. *onze* (onz)
12. *doze* (dohz)
13. *treze* (tray-ze)
14. *catorze* (kah-tohrz)
15. *quinze* (keenz)
16. *dezasseis* (de-zah-saysh)
17. *dezassete* (de-zah-set)
18. *dezoito* (de-zoh-ee-too)
19. *dezanove* (de-zah-nov)
20. *vinte* (veent)
21. *vinte uma* (veent-ee oo-mah)
22. *vinte e duas* (veent-ee doo-ash)
23. *vente e tres* (veent-ee traysh)
24. *vente e quatro* (veent-ee-kwah-troo)

Places

While traveling around the country, learn to pronounce the name of places properly. That skill makes buying tickets or asking directions much more enjoyable and less frustrating.

The major cities and tourist destinations are listed here in alphabetical order:

Alcobaća (al-koo-bah-sah) - site of a monastary.
Algarve (al-garv) - southern Portugal.
Alentejo (ah-len-tay-zhoo) - region rich in olives and cork.
Arrábida (ah-rah-bee-dah) - natural park near Setubal.
Aveiro (ah-vay-ee-roo).
Batalha (bah-tie-lya) - site of a monastery.
Beira (bay-ee-rah) - region.

Braga (brah-gah) - city in northern wine country.
Bragança (brah-gan-sah) - city in northeast.
Cascais (kash-kysh) - town with name mispronounced more than any other.
Coimbra (koo-een-brah) - university city.
Douro (doh-roo) - region of port wine production.
Estoril (esh-too-reel) - community near Lisbon; pronounced "shto-reel" in general usage.
Évora (e-voo-rah) - beautiful town in the Alentejo region.
Faro (fah-roo) - Algarve city.
Fegueira da Faz (fee-gay-ee-ra da fosh).
Guimarães (gee-ma-rynsh).
Lagos (lah-goosh) - city in Algarve.
Lisboa (leezh-boh-ah) - If you pronounce this correctly, the people of Lisbon will love it.
Minho (mee-nyoo) - region of northern Portugal.
Nazaré (nah-zah-ray) - beautiful fishing town.
Olhão (oh-lyown) - town in Algarve.
Peniche (pe-neesh) - seafood town.
Porto (pohr-too) - Portugal's second city.
Queluz (kay-loosh) - royal palace.
Sagres (sah-greesh) - far southwest but should not be missed.
Santarém (san-tah-rem) - fishing and industrial city.
Sesimbra (se-zeen-brah) - fishing village of good character.
Setúbal (se-too-bal) - most often pronounced as "stu-bal."
Sintra (seen-trah) - lovely setting for palaces near Lisbon.
Tejo (tay-zhoo) - major river (anglicized name: Tagus River).
Trás-os-Montes (traz-oosh-mon-tsh) - region of northeast.
Viseu (vee-shoo).

Everyday Phrases

As you move about the country, you will need to know how to say everyday things as indicated here.

restaurant. o restaurante (oo resh-tow-rant).
café. o café (oh ka-fay).
tavern. *cervejaria* (ser-ve-zha-ree-ah).
hotel. *hotel* (oh-tel).
boarding house. *pensão* (pen-sown).
train. *comboio* (kon-boy-oo).
train station. *estação* (esh-tah-sown).
parks, squares, plaza. *praça* (prah-sah); *parque* (park).

basic monetary unit. *escudo* (esh-koo-doo).
menu. *ementa* (ee-men-tah).
pastry shop café. *pasteleria* (pash-te-la-ree-ah).

Menu Items

The menu is a most important concern of the tourist and traveler.
Menu *(ementa)* items are fairly standard throughout the country. If
you dine at the fancy hotels, you will enjoy a more continental
selection. But if you dine in the restaurants of the people, the cafés
or *pastelerias,* you will be served good food and inexpensive food.

In nearly every restaurant *sopa* (so-pah), or soup, is served. The
usual soups on the menu are:

Caldo verde (kal-doo vayrd) - a green cabbage and potato soup of
   hearty variety.
Sopa de Alentejana (so-pah day ah-len-tay jah-nah) - a soup from
   the province of Alentejo that is basically a garlic and coriander broth served with a poached egg and bread within
   the broth.
Legumes (le-goom-esh) - a vegetable soup.
Açorda (ah-sohr-dah) - variable ingredients but always stale
   bread soaked in broth and oil.

Every menu will list egg dishes:

Ovos (oh-voosh) - usually served *fritas* (fried) or in a variety of
   omelatas (omelettes) (oom-lay-tash).

Many restaurants will have a listing of *sanduíches* (sand-weech-esh),
or sandwiches:

Hamburguesa (ham-bur-gay-sha) - hamburgers.
Friambre y queijo (free-amb e kay-e-zhoo) - ham and cheese.
Prego (pray-goo) - literally translated as "nail," but refers to a hot
   beef sandwich.

You will always see:

Pão (pown) - bread.
Manteiga (man-tay-ee-ga) - butter.
Salada (sah-lah-dah) - salad.

Tomate (too-maht) - tomato.
Alface (al-fas) - lettuce.
Arroz (ah-rohsh) - rice.
Batatas fritas (bah-tah-tash free-tash) - fried potatoes.

Beverages usually include:

Agua (ah-gwa) - water.
Agua com gas (ah-gwa con gash) - carbonated water.
Coke (koke) - Coca-Cola.
Café (cah-fay) - coffee.
Vinho (vee-nyoo) - wine. Wines are discussed comprehensively in the chapter on food.

The following items will vary from restaurant to restaurant but in a short time one will notice each of them. Sometimes these are presented on the menu in classifications (seafood, beef, and so on), but usually they are listed as entrees or specialties of the house. For ease of reference, they are listed here by classification. Remember, these are common menu items. Variations may appear as specialties.

Seafood

Mariscos (Mah-reesh-koo) - shellfish.
Lagosta (lah-gohsh-tah) - lobster.
Lagostine (lah-goosh-teen) - prawns.
Ameijoas (ah-may-ee-zhoo-ash) - clams or mussels.
Camarões (ka-mah-roynsh) - shrimp.
Atum (ah-toon) - tuna.
Pescada (pesh-kan-dah) - hake.
Linguado (leen-gwah-doo) - sole.
Salmonetes (sal-moan-etch) - red mullet.
Lula (loo-lah) - squid.
Polvo (pohl-voo) - octopus.
Sardinha assada (sar-dee-nya a-sah-dah) - sardines (grilled).
Peixe espada (pay-eesh ish-pah-da) - swordfish.
Bacalhau (bah-kah-lyow) - saltcod.
Pasteis de Bacalhau (pass-taysh de bah-kah-lyow) - cod cakes.
Caldeirada (kal-day-ee-rah-dah) - fish stew.
Cozida de Peixe (koo-zee-dah de pay-eesh) - fish cooked with vegetables.
Filetes de Peixe (fee-laych de pay-eesh) - fried fish filets.
Eiroz (ee-rozsh) - eels.

Beef, Veal, Pork

Carne de vaca (karn de vah-kah) - beef.
Bife a portugesa (beef a phry-too-gaysh-ah) - Portuguese-style
   steak.
Vitela assada (vee-te-la ah-sah-dah) - veal roast.
Friambre (free-am-b) - ham.
Presunto (pre-soon-too) - ham.
Chouriço (shoh-ree-soo) - sausage.

Chicken

Frango na Pucara (fran-goo nah poo-kar-ah) - chicken roasted in
   a clay pot.
Frango churrasco (fran-goo chew-rash-koo) - roasted chicken.
Frango frita (fran-goo free-tah) - fried chicken.

Miscellaneous

Cabrito (kah-bree-too) - kid goat.
Rissões (ree-zoynsh) - deep-fried snacks.
Coelho (koo-ay-lyoo) - rabbit.
Queijo (kay-ee-zhoo) - cheese.

Desserts

Flan (flahn) - egg custard.
Fruta (froo-tah) - fruit.
Arroz doçe (ah-rohsh dohs) - rice pudding.
Bola (boh-lah) - cake.
Massa (mah-sah) - pastry.
Doçes (dohsh) - sweets.

CHAPTER 6

The Land:
Ancient and Aged

*T*he statistics are simple. Portugal's land area includes only 35,000 square miles (56,800 sq. km.). The country is only about 345 miles (561 km.) from north to south and about 130 miles wide (220 km.). That is smaller than many of the states in the United States and less than half the size of the United Kingdom. Hills and mountains predominate north of the Rio Tejo (Tagus River), and rolling plains predominate south of the river. The river is the major divider of climates and landforms. The climates of Portugal are varied. It is wetter and cooler in the north than in the south. These are the simple facts, but obviously this short description masks much variation in landscape, climate, and economic activity.

Portugal has a mild climate for its latitude. Lisbon, for example, lies roughly at the same latitude as New York (40° N.). Because of the effects of the massive warm Gulf Stream, which sweeps up the east side of North America and then bends eastward across the North Atlantic to warm western Europe, Lisbon is much milder than its latitudinal position would normally dictate.

The average temperatures given in the guidebooks and brochures for various locations in the world mean very little. The tourist must dress for daily weather conditions: the highs and lows of each day. Averages offer little planning information. For example, the average temperature along the Estoril Coast in January is 62.8° F (17.1° C). In January, statistics show that one can expect some days to have a high temperature of only 50° F (9° C) and the evenings can be even cooler. Lisbon is cool, rainy, and breezy in January and February. In November the people begin to prepare for winter. Usually during this period there is a marked warm spell known locally as *Verão de São Martinno* (St. Martin's Summer). This is similar to the North American "Indian Summer." Later, in March, the wet winter weather begins to break up and lovely springlike days are very common. Even in February there will be an occasional warm day. As spring ripens into summer, however, Portugal's weather is at its best. Truly mild, not hot, temperatures prevail. There is little rainfall, but the landscape seems to burst into color with the deep blue sky as a backdrop.

In the Algarve, the southernmost province of Portugal, the climate is more influenced by the Mediterranean than the Atlantic. The result is that the province is drier and less extreme in temperature. During the winter months it is extremely mild. The coastal region is the warmest area of Europe. During February, for example, Algarve is the only region of Europe that has green grass at that time of the year.

In the Lisbon area, even though the deciduous trees lose their leaves in winter, the palms remain healthy and the geraniums and bird-of-paradise flowers bloom all year. To the north of Lisbon, however, there is a significant climatic change. Topographic elevation increases and temperatures are lower. Rainfall is influenced by the Atlantic. Frosts and freezes are expected in the northern uplands during the winter months. Mountainous areas experience snow several times during the winter.

The mountains and hills of the north contrast sharply with the gentle plains of the south. This contrast is very apparent as the tourist traverses the land. Portugal is divided into two parts by the Rio Tejo (Tagus River). The river originates in central Spain and meets the Atlantic at Lisbon. Within these two major north-south geographic divisions, there are several subdivisions that reflect local topography and climate. In fact, Portugal consists of six provinces, whose designations have existed for hundreds of years, according to folk knowledge and scholarly observation. Administratively, however, the country is subdivided into eleven zones. Each administrative zone is, in turn, divided into eighteen districts.

This chapter, however, will consider only the traditional geographic divisions.

The three provinces completely north of the Tejo are *Trás-os-Montes*, *Beira* and *Minho*. The first, Trás-os-Montes ("beyond the mountains"), is the most isolated and least economically developed region of Portugal. Located in the extreme northeast of the country, it is hilly, dry, and sparsely populated. Interestingly, this region is almost totally unknown and, therefore, untouched by European tourism.

The Minho province, on the other hand, is also hilly but much rainier and very heavily populated. This is the district of the famous *Douro River Valley*, the focus of port wine production. Surprisingly, it is this province, not the Lisbon area, that is the most densely populated region of the country. Only one major city, *Porto*, lies in the region, but the countryside is densely settled. Every available parcel of cultivable land is utilized for food or grape production. In fact, pressure on the land has influenced an interesting agricultural practice known as "storied" cultivation. In this three-dimensional kind of agriculture, grape vines are grown on elaborate trellises under which the cultivation of household vegetables or cereal crops additionally takes place. The result is a unique landscape that displays centuries of agricultural adaptation. In addition, the 3-D effect is enhanced by elaborate field terraces along the river valley.

The Beira region is much larger than the other two northern provinces. Beira spreads east and west across the country and is much less mountainous than its northern neighbors. Yet Portugal's major mountain range, *Serra da Estrela* (mountains of the stars), lies within the region.

The remaining three provinces, *Estremadura*, *Alentejo* and *Algarve* share certain commonalities. Estremadura is divided by the Rio Tejo and includes the Tejo estuary, Lisbon, and the Tejo valley, which is so important to the country agriculturally. The Alentejo (meaning "across the Tejo") is the largest of the six provinces. Its gently rolling landscape is punctuated by ancient olive groves and the painfully twisted cork oaks. It is here that most of the world's cork is produced, and it is here that the great Portuguese olives are produced. The Alentejo is dry and experiences some severe temperature extremes, particularly in the east near the Spanish border.

The Algarve is physically and culturally distinct. Culturally, it has been influenced significantly by the Moors. Physically, the

Algarve is separated from Alentejo by the *Serra de Monchique* and *Serra de Caldeirão*. These mountains form an impressive barrier between the central region and the south of Portugal. Because of its climate, the Algarve is considered the new Portuguese Riviera, and many of the former small fishing towns have evolved into major tourist centers. Agriculturally, the landscape is similar to that of southern California. Here oranges, figs, and other fruits, nuts—particularly the almonds, which blossom in January—lettuce, tomatoes, and other vegetable crops are grown for the city markets.

The physical environment is varied in this small country. The rivers and watersheds of Portugal illustrate this variety. Of the ten major rivers in the country, five originate in Spain.

One of the most important rivers is the *Rio Douro*. It originates in Spain and drains a significant portion of northern Portugal, where it has historically served the commerce and trade of that region. Its steep banks, often terraced to accommodate more vineyards, are very picturesque. Of historic interest is the revival of the old river craft *Barco Rabelo*. Not long ago such craft were used to transport casks of port wine to Porto from the interior. In fact, each July the various wineries sponsor a riverboat race to commemorate that old tradition of the port wine industry.

In the Beira province there are two important rivers, the *Rio Mondego* and the *Rio Vouga*. Both flow entirely within Portugal. The Mondego originates in the mountains of the Serra da Estrela. It wanders down the mountains and through the university city of Coimbra. The water at this point is remarkably clear, and many women can be seen using the river, its stones and banks, as a convenient laundry.

The *Rio Tejo* is the most important river in all of Portugal and Spain. Called the Tagus River in English and the Rio Tajo in Spanish, it is the longest of the Iberian peninsula. This is the river that drains much of Spain's interior "mesata" (tableland) and is of considerable historic importance to both Iberian countries. Historically, its most essential function was the deposition of fertile silts, which enrich the soils for wheat, rice, and olive production in the Estremadura province in Portugal.

Certainly, the Tejo estuary is the river's most striking feature. It is, indeed, one of the world's largest natural harbors. The Portuguese refer to the vast expanse of the tidal estuary as the *Mar de Palha* (sea of straws). In bright sun it does glisten like dew-dressed straw, and it is large enough to be viewed as an inland sea.

In the south the major rivers include the *Sado*, the *Mira*, the *Arade*, and the *Gaudiana*. The Sado River was as important economically in the ancient past as it is in the present. The Sado enters the Atlantic at Setúbal. Historically, the estuary has been known for the production of salt as far back as Roman times. There are a few remaining archaeological sites where the original salt works are in evidence.

The only other river of economic significance is the Gaudiana in Algarve. Its major contribution to Portugal's economic structure is that it functions as the principal waterway for mining and shipping the copper ore of the interior.

Portugal's rugged and magnificent coastline is one of the country's greatest assets. Much of it, in fact nearly all of it, is untouched by tourist development, with the exception of the Algarve, where the beaches are wide and long. Generally, the coastal plain is narrow. The coastline is marked, in most of Portugal, by steep cliffs, and an occasional sandy beach. But the views are what tourists seek, and they are always beautiful. The coastline is spectacular from Sagres Point and Cape St. Vincent in the southwest to Cabo da Roca (the westernmost point of Europe) and north. Getting to see that great beauty is quite difficult since few roads parallel the coast for any distance and fewer still terminate at the ocean.

In north-central Portugal (the Beira Litoral), the coast is much different and departs in structure and appearance from the typical precipitous cliffs. Instead, there is a wide coastal plain extending inland for nearly thirty miles (48 km.). Reminiscent of the southeastern United States, this is an area of salt marshes and river deposits, as well as wide, undulating sand dunes. Because of the flatness of the terrain and the organically rich soils of drained marshes and bogs, the region is one of Portugal's most agriculturally fertile and, hence, productive. North of the Rio Douro, the coastal plain again narrows to a sandy strip through the Minho province.

There are many fine beaches along this vast expanse of coastline, but in the densely populated resort areas of the Estoril Coast and Algarve, there is a pollution problem. Great effort is being made by national and municipal agencies to control the pollution of rivers and coastal waters, but much still needs to be accomplished. Unfortunately, the tourist who chooses to swim at the beautiful beaches along the Tejo estuary in Estoril or Cascais, may be assuming a health risk. The beaches are used by thousands of people daily.

There have been no significant outbreaks of water-borne illnesses, but the risk remains. The Algarve also has a pollution problem at the beaches. The Portuguese government is taking positive action to control illegal contamination. Some of the problem lies in the fact that storm sewers have inadvertantly been used as sanitary sewers and raw sewage has been piped directly into rivers and the waters of the Atlantic itself. Shellfish beds near Faro have been declared unfit, and some beaches have been closed for short periods during the past few years. These incidences, however, are rarer in Portugal than in the United States.

The water may be lovely to look at, but in some instances it is not perfectly safe for swimming. Because tourism is so vital to the Portuguese economy, these problems are regarded as very serious. Remedies are being sought. For example, a sizable portion of the tax income realized from the operation of the Casino in Estoril is earmarked for public health and beach projects along the whole of the Estoril coast. This is discussed in detail later in this volume.

Agriculture and Vegetation

As the tourist traverses the countryside by train or roadway, he or she will surely note the striking changes in the agricultural activity from the north to the south. Agricultural pursuits are intimately related to the natural vegetation and soils. A great deal of natural vegetation survives, which is surprising in such an old and long-settled country. Nearly a quarter of Portugal remains forested. The soils are similar to those of most of the Iberian peninsula and are generally of volcanic origin. But such soils are not particularly productive for agriculture.

Soils in combination with climate influence vegetation. In the north one sees forests of primarily pine and oak. In the higher elevations one sees heather, yews, and birch.

In central Portugal, the climatic transition zone, there is also a vegetative transition. There are a few pines, but the predominate natural vegetation is the so-called Portuguese oak. In coastal areas the predominant trees are the graceful sea pines with their bulbous crown. These trees are also known as Italian stone pines.

New forests of the messy-looking but fast-growing imported eucalyptus are cultivated in many areas where other agricultural pursuits have proved to be marginally productive. Eucalyptus provide a fresh scent to the air, but their shaggy bark and unkept appearance mar an otherwise classic landscape. The tree is used for pulpwood, and its oils are extracted for medicinal and some industrial uses.

South of the Tejo River the cork oak is the native vegetation. Large stands are cultivated in plantations, but individual specimens and small groves permeate the Alentejo landscape. Olive trees also have been cultivated for centuries on huge plantations. The trees are appropriately knarled and bent with age. Coastal areas are again occupied by the stone pine.

Further south, in Algarve, the vegetation is strikingly Mediterranean. The natural vegetation consists of heath and gum citrus, pine and cork oak. But because of the long growing season and favorable climate, much of the landscape is given to the cultivation of figs, grapes, almonds, citrus fruits, as well as other fruits such as apples, apricots, and plums.

As noted before, soils and climate influence natural vegetation and certainly play a role in the selection of agricultural crops. Portugal is not a rich agricultural country. In fact, by western European standards, Portugal ranks ahead of only Greece in agricultural production. The soils do not seem suited to, for example, the grain crops. As a result, much grain and other foodstuffs are imported. Pastures are poor, either from poor management or overgrazing, so there is little beef production.

Grape and fruit production are most obvious as one travels about the country. In the north, the Douro Valley, grapes are grown on every conceivable inch of ground and on trellises or arbors above the ground to leave that space beneath free for food crops. The regions of central and southern Portugal are covered with fruit trees, midlatitude varieties in central Portugal and citrus in the south. Some land is given over to grape production, but unlike in the north where population densities are much higher, grapes are grown low to the ground in vast fields. Space is plentiful.

Throughout central and south-central Portugal huge plantations of cork oak and olives dominate the landscape. In fact, much of Iberia seems to be blanketed with olive trees. So prevalent are olive trees that one wonders why olives seem to be so expensive in North America. The reason is that the olive crop is harvested by hand. The process is very labor intensive and, therefore, expensive. Most of the crop is used in the production of olive oil. Because the product is too costly for the average Portuguese, most of the oil is exported to western Europe. Only a small percentage of the olive harvest is for table consumption or export to North America. What is exported bears import duties and the heavy cost of transport to U.S. markets. Hence the high price of olives at the supermarket.

Cork production is an important part of the Portuguese economy. Although the cork industry employs few people, cork is Portugal's largest cash crop. The cork oak tree deserves careful study. The cork oak's trunk is a fleshy pink or deep blood red, and a single-digit number is painted on each tree. That number indicates the year the tree was last stripped of its bark. Cork production involves a complicated agricultural system. In August, usually, the bark of the cork oak is removed. The first stripping for each tree takes place when the tree is no less than twenty-five years old. Every nine years thereafter, the trees are stripped again (thus the number indicating the year). The entire stripping process is carefully controlled by the government to ensure the health of the country's most important export crop. For example, no tree is stripped unless its trunk is at least 70 centimeters (approximately 27.5 inches) in diameter at one meter (39 inches) from ground level.

The tree itself is a remarkable botanic specimen, possessing the peculiar property of producing bark that can be easily removed without killing the tree. This is possible because it produces its cambium layer during the hot, dry months of summer. Having survived the summer, the tree can have its bark removed without damage to the living wood. Bark removal is performed by skilled workers using a tool that looks much like an executioner's axe. The job is the most critical in the entire cork process since damage to the tree must be avoided. Once the bark is stripped, it is stacked in piles near the farmstead. In the south of Portugal these cork stacks punctuate the landscape as silos punctuate an American dairy landscape.

Strangely, the factories that manufacture products from the raw cork are located primarily in the north of Portugal. This unlikely situation is the legacy of pre-1950 wage scale policies. The government, in an effort to encourage migration from the densely populated north, officially set the wage scale 30 percent lower in the north than in the south. Although this disparity no longer exists officially, the tradition remains. As a result, most of the bottle corks are produced in northern factories where labor is cheaper. Bottle corks, in fact, account for 60 percent of the total cork exports and are the basis of the nine-year stripping cycle since the bark grows only one inch in nine years. A bottle cork is approximately one inch in depth. So important is the bottle-cork product that at the producing areas, cork is priced according to its potential yield of bottle stoppers.

Once shipped to the factory, the cork is boiled, sorted, and flattened. Further processing takes place after about a two-month holding period. In time the bottle corks are punched out. They are graded, bleached or dyed, sterilized or waxed, and sold by the millions to various vintners throughout the world.

Nearly two-thirds of the cork bark is waste, in other words, not for bottle stoppers. This portion is usually not discarded but ground and mixed with glues and formed into blocks from which any size or thickness can be cut for myriad uses. Some products include gaskets, insulation, bowling-ball fillers, bulletin boards, flooring, and wall covering.

Throughout Portugal, there is an agricultural activity that occurs everywhere and on every conceivable plot of land. That is the family garden. The dominant crop seems to be cabbage. Other crops include turnips, onions, *fava* or broad beans, and potatoes. The placement of these plots is sometimes a curiosity. They are placed along the rail rights-of-way in Lisbon, on rooftops, in open fields, at the edge of the beach, in rocky crevices—anywhere there is a bit of space and soil. Public spaces seem to be prone to private or individual use as garden plots. The official level of tolerance seems to be extended in these circumstances.

Large scale agriculture, as practiced in Algarve, generally utilizes modern and efficient technology. The farming practices of the countryside off the main roads, however, is best described as medieval. Traditional Portuguese agriculture is picturesque; one seems to have stepped back in time. Pretty it is, but productive it is not. The backward nature of Portuguese agriculture accounts for Portugal's low productivity. Coupling this low-level technology with other factors—poor soils, rugged topography, climatic handicaps (low rainfall), and ancient and inefficient landholding patterns and traditions—it is understandable that the system lags well behind the remainder of western Europe.

Since 1986, Portugal has been a member of the European Economic Community (EEC), or Common Market. The association with the EEC will act as a stimulus for the modernization of agriculture. Portugal must compete with other western European countries, and to compete successfully means that Portugal must modernize. Not to improve agricultural methods and technologies will mean that Portugal will fall further behind its European nieghbors.

Presently, only about 50 percent of the total land area is utilized in crop production. Another 5 or 6 percent is pastures and nearly 30 percent is in forests. Rapid reforestation projects are tending to increase this last figure and make productive what was otherwise marginal land.

Most farms are less than three acres in size. In the north and central region of Portugal, landholdings have been fragmented over the centuries through the practice of subdividing by inheritance. This practice was introduced by German invaders in the fifth and sixth centuries. Today a typical farm may consist of scattered small plots affording no efficient means of mechanization. Southern Portugal, however, is of different historic influence. Today one sees larger estates, plantations that reflect the original Roman estate system and the later feudal system of the Middle Ages. Strangely, the landholdings are similar today. The feudal estates have essentially remained as the *quintas* and huge farm cooperatives of Alentejo.

Agricultural landscapes are often regarded by tourists as boring or of little interest. Yet if tourists look closely, they can discern much of the country's vitality and life. A typical traverse in rural Portugal would net scenes of peasant agriculture that have changed little in four hundred years.

Wildlife

Portugal has been a relatively densely settled country for many centuries and, as a result, does not have an abundance or wide variety of wildlife. Generally, the wildlife is similar to that of the remainder of Iberia. In the remote mountain regions there are still a sizable deer herd, some wolves, foxes, and wild boar. Although hunting is still possible for the tourist, the country is not a hunting and fishing paradise. To obtain a license to hunt, a person must pass an exam issued by the Ministry of Agriculture. The exam includes both theory and practical sections with questions dealing with species of game, laws, dogs, arms, and ammunition. It is hoped that the exam will eliminate unlawful or uninformed hunters from the fields.

Water fowl are quite common, and game birds like pheasant and quail are found but not in great abundance. There are also rabbits and other rodents and the usual predatory birds to control their population.

Trout and salmon are caught in the north. The trout season extends from March 1 to July 31. The best fishing, however, concentrates along the coast. Deep-sea, big-game fishing is available in Portugal. There are charters in the Algarve town of Portimão and Vilamoura. One should not expect hot and fast action because this is an overfished region. It is a fishery that has been exploited, not always efficiently, for many centuries. There are also fishing boats accommodating 20–50 persons departing from the Cascais Marine Club and from Sesismbra near Lisbon. They offer a less expensive alternative to Portugal's marine fishing. One can catch swordfish, skate, bluefish, mackerel, and tuna. Each year large schools of tuna make their way around Gilbraltar to spawn in the Mediterranean Sea. As they pass the Portuguese coast, they are fairly close to shore so the game-fishing action can be good at these times. Other fish caught include grouper, dolphin, wrasse, brime, rock bass, and conger eels.

The apparent reason for the richness of the deep-line fishing experience is that Portugal's continental shelf is narrow (50 to 100 miles, 80 to 160 kilometers). The bottom fish, it is said, emerge from the deeper waters to feed on the shallow shelves. So within a few hours' boat travel from shore, one can catch a wide variety of fish to tantalize even a blasé angler.

Beach fishing, rock fishing, and fishing from small boats in-shore are also popular and inexpensive. Many tourists simply choose an area by watching the other fishermen and fish where others are fishing. The sea birds will not indicate good fishing because there are few of them. There are a few gulls but no pelicans or petrels. Interestingly, there are also no porpoises near shore.

In general, one should not regard Portugal as a wildlife haven or a bird-watcher's delight. The Iberian peninsula was at one time the home of some unique species because of its geographic isolation. The separation from Europe by the Pyrennes Mountains and from Africa by the Strait of Gibralter has given the peninsula a unique character. At one time the Portuguese territory was almost completely covered with dense forests in which bears, boars, lynx, wolves, and roebuck were abundant. With development, of course, came the alteration of the flora and, hence, the disruption of the fauna. As a result, there are no bears or wild mountain goats left. The continued threat to wildlife in Portugal is typical of all Europe, but the government is taking measures to halt the invasion of wild lands. There is also an active private organization called ADN *(Acção em Defesa da Natureza)* that aims to promote links between various organizations and individuals interested in preserving nature and wildlife. It is a beginning. The movement is akin to the Sierra Club in the United States and takes much of its inspiration therefrom. For those interested in contacting the organization, the address is: Movemento ADN, Rua Dr. Antonio Jose de Almeida, 35, 2 Direito, Venda Nova, Amadora, Portugal.

CHAPTER 7

A Peek at the Past:
A Clue to the Present

Portugal's past is as colorful as its present. The people take pride in their history, keeping the past alive today by recalling historic events and revering bygone days of glory. In fact, it seems that the Portuguese possess more than the expected dose of national pride. This pride is manifest as a patriotism that is not public-spirited flag waving and fireworks. It is mainly a nostalgic allegiance to an idealized past. People and events are not forgotten in Portugal; they are continually enhanced in the theater, the arts, and literature. History is romanticized as a symbol of national pride.

It all began many years ago. The name "Portugal" is derived from the Roman town *Portus Cale*, where the modern city of Porto lies. The country surrounding it, or *Portucalense*, was first recorded in the ninth century A.D. as the administrative area on the frontier of Leon, a part of Spain. This region between the Rio Douro and the Rio Minho was the core area from which the Portuguese state eventually emerged before the end of the thirteenth century.

It seems almost an accident of history that such an independent political entity, exposed and peripheral to other cultural hearths, developed in that region. It had no distinctive natural borders and no apparent ethnic cohesion. Its language had a common root to

Spanish Galicia to the north of Portugal. But independence resulted despite the odds.

Portugal, the nation-state, exists today primarily because of the early development of its colonial empire, an extraordinary relationship with England, and Spain's preoccupation with more urgent matters than Iberian unification. The eventual selection of Lisbon as the national capital tied Portugal's future to the Atlantic, making a Portuguese, in the words of the Spanish writer Salvador de Madariaga, "a Spaniard with his back to Castile." Throughout its history, Portugal has had an ambiguous relationship with Spain. Absorption and loss of national identity were resisted in spite of repeated efforts by Portugal and Castile to achieve dynastic union. Ironically, in order to maintain its independence from Spain, Portugal became, for a time, an economic dependent of England.

Portugal was the first European nation to establish an overseas empire. The small country ensured its continued existence by its ability to remain in and exploit far-flung colonies. But the story begins at an earlier time. Going back far in time one can better understand the roots of present day Portugal.

Lusitania

To imply that Portugal's culture was rooted in Roman times would be incorrect. Certainly a civilization of sorts had existed for many thousands of years on the west flank of the Iberian peninsula. Scholars debate over the origin of the earliest inhabitants, as well as subsequent migrants. But the evidence points to a common southern Mediterranean Paleolithic culture emanating from north Africa.

Compared with adjacent areas of Europe in prehistoric times, the territory lying within the geographic confines of modern Portugal was an isolated backwater. During the third millennium B.C., the so-called Iberians spread over the peninsula that came to bear their name. They provided the genetic base for the populations of both Portugal and Spain. They differed greatly among themselves, however. In some areas a sophisticated urban society emerged, supported by a prosperous agriculture. By contrast, the Iberians who settled in the region bound by the Rio Tejo and the Rio Minho were primitive. Called *Lusitanians*, they have been described as a loose, quarrelsome federation of tribes, living behind walls of fortified villages in the hills, engaging in banditry as their primary occupation, and carrying on incessant tribal warfare.

The Lusitanians seem to have assimilated Celtic culture by their contact with the Celtic herders and metalworkers who settled in the northern half of the peninsula after about 900 B.C. Similar though they were in many ways, even in language, there was nonetheless a clear dividing line at the Douro between the patriarchal bandits of Lusitania and the matriarchal pastoralists of Galicia. Also, apart from several Phoenician and Carthaginian trading stations exploiting the salt basins and fig groves of the Algarve, there were no substantial settlements of these two civilizations as there were elsewhere in Iberia. The Carthaginians, however, did hire the bellicose Lusitanians as mercenaries, some probably serving under Hannibal during his Italian campaign in the third century B.C.

Roman armies invaded Iberia in 212 B.C. to cut Hannibal off from his source of supplies and reinforcement. Resistance by the Iberians was fierce and prolonged, and it was not until 19 B.C. that the Roman Emperor Augustus was able to complete the conquest of the peninsula, which the Romans renamed Hispania. The people south of the Rio Tejo, Mediterranean in outlook, were docile in the face of the Roman advance, but it took seventy years to subdue the Lusitanians. Native chieftains, such as Viriato, hassled army after army and occasionally did some damage. Viriato, the first of the Hispanic world's popular military leaders, remains one of Portugal's folk heroes. Once the people were subdued, though, the process of pacification was so complete that no troops were permanently garrisoned in Lusitania. Roman towns of some size were established at Baracara Augusta (Braga), Portus Cale (Porto), Pax Julia (Beja), and Olisipo (Lisbon), which according to legend had been founded by Ulysses. Although Lusitania played no significant part in the history of the Roman Empire, it was for five hundred years part of a cosmopolitan world empire, united by the Roman road, a common language, and a common legal system. Evidence of the Roman occupation can still be seen today at Evora's Temple of Diana and the ruins of Conimbriga near Coimbra.

Christianity, although introduced in the second century A.D. made little progress in the Lusitanian countryside until the late fourth century. In fact, the bishops were the leaders who maintained order after the Roman government had collapsed in the fifth century. About the same time the *Swabians*, along with the *Vandals*, crossed the Pyrenees into Hispania and settled in Galicia and Lusitania. The Swabian farms were dispersed. Single small holdings were divided among heirs in smaller portions, a pattern for landholding that persists in the Douro-Minho area. But times were not good. Violence and disorganization permeated the land. In A.D. 415, the Emperor Honorius commissioned the *Visigoths*, the most highly Romanized of the Germanic peoples, to restore order to Hispania. The Swabian kings and their Visigothic overlords governed in the name of the Roman Emperor, their kingdoms remaining, in theory, a part of the Roman Empire. Latin remained the language of government and commerce. By the middle of the fifth century, the region's people had accepted Christianity. The Swabians lost their autonomous status within the greater Visigothic state at the end of the sixth century, but by that time they had come to identify their interests entirely with those of the Visigoths. A small, quiet reminder of Portugal's Visigothic past can be seen in a bas-relief sculpture on the north exterior wall of the Cathedral of Lisbon.

Moorish Invasion

An army of *Moors* (Arabs and the Morrocan Berbers whom the Moors had conquered and converted to Islam) crossed to Hispania in A.D. 711. The invaders were allies of Visigothic nobles who had rebelled against Roderic, their king. After killing the king in battle, the Moors returned home but attacked again the next year intent on annexing Hispania to their domains. By A.D. 715, *al-Andulus*, the name for Islamic Spain including its western provinces, was reorganized. In Lusitania, land was apportioned among the Moorish troops, but the Moors preferred the familiar dry country below the Rio Tejo, especially in the Algarve (from the Arabic *al-Garb*), where the Moorish heritage remains today. The Christian Luso-Roman urban and landholding classes retained freedom to practice their religion and remained largely self-governing. Called Mozarabs (Arab-like people), they were profoundly affected by Islamic culture, adopting social customs, dress, language, and artistic styles.

For two hundred fifty years, a united al-Andulus flourished, until the eleventh century when rival claimants to the throne, military commanders, and opportunistic aristocrats staked out and claimed various independent regional city-states, among them Lisbon and Évora. Active resistance was limited to small groups of Visigothic warriors who took refuge in the mountain vastness of Asturias in the old Swabian Kingdom. Within fifty years of the Moorish conquest, the Christian kings of Asturias-Leon, who claimed succession from the Visigothic monarchs, had retaken Braga, Porto, Viseu, and Guimaraes in the Douro-Minho area.

Portugal emerged as a separate nationality at the same time as the expulsion of the Moors. Substantially autonomous counts, appointed by the kings of Leon, ruled the desert zone between Galicia and the Moorish territory. In 883, the term *Provincia Porticalense* (Province of Portugal) was first recorded to designate the Douro-Minho region. By the mid-eleventh century, the frontier had moved southward to Coimbra.

The House of Burgundy

In 1096, the counties of Portugal and Coimbra, part of the dowry of *Teresa*, illegitimate daughter of *King Afonso VI* of Castile-Leon, were given to a crusader named *Henry of Burgundy*. When Henry died in 1112, Teresa was left as regent for their son *Afonso Henriques*, but her allegiance appeared to be more toward her kinsmen in Castile. Afonso Henriques seized the throne from his regent mother in 1128 and defeated the Moors at Ourique (ca. 1139), a battle acclaimed in legend but whose site is unknown. It seems that Afonso, like Constantine, experienced a vision of the sign of the cross in the heavens and so gained assurance of victory on the field of battle. The Portuguese coat of arms commemorates the seven Moorish strongholds Afonso captured—Lisbon, Sintra, Santarem, Leiria, Palmela, Évora, and Montemor.

When his cousin, *Alfonso VII* of Castile, demanded Afonso Henriques' homage as a vassal, he was refused. It was perhaps the coincidence of historical timing that prevented Castile from chastizing the usurping vassal. At the time, Castile was absorbed in a renewed Moorish offensive. So Afonso Henriques assured recognition of Portuguese political independence by swearing fealty to the Pope. According to some authorities, this act qualifies Portugal to claim itself the oldest continuous European nationality. Portugal benefited from one hundred fifty years of strong leadership by the line of kings descended from Afonso Henriques, who in his long

reign of fifty-seven years laid a firm foundation. Using their en-
trenched royal power, his successors founded towns, compiled the
law, and carried forward the distinctly Portuguese Reconquest that
Afonso Henriques had begun on the field of Ourique.

The Moors called the Portuguese "the bravest of the Christians,"
but the Portuguese Reconquest regularly relied on the aid of
Crusaders. In 1147, when Afonso Henriques succeeded in taking
Lisbon, as many as fifteen thousand English, French, Flemish, and
Danish crusaders were his allies. Some remained as settlers on the
land they had helped to conquer. When the Algarve fell in 1249 to
Afonso III, the Portuguese phase of the Reconquest was completed.

Lisbon became Portugal's capital in 1298. A predominantly
Christian city, even under Moorish rule, Lisbon was already the
economic, social, and cultural center of Portugal before being
chosen as its political center. One Crusader described its buildings
as "crowded together with great skill." But the city, surrounded by
the country's most productive area, grew at the expense of the
countryside. Lisbon also was not part of the Portuguese northern
core and heartland and so remained remote from it.

Portuguese was introduced as the official language in place of
Latin under *King Dinis.* Known as "The Farmer," he encouraged his
nobles to cultivate their lands, reassuring the warrior aristocracy
that "no baron shall lose caste by dedicating himself to the soil."
The crops of the new lands in the south stimulated Portugal's
export trade, but, despite increased production, Portugal remained
a poor country even by medieval standards. Besides promoting
agricultural production, King Dinis was also fruitful with his own
children, legitimate and illegitimate. In fact, the offspring of most
Portuguese kings were plentiful. The daughters of prolific monarchs were married well, extending Portugal's political contacts to
England, Flanders, Burgundy, France, and Denmark, as well as
establishing dynastic connections with other Hispanic states.

Fewer limitations were placed on the authority of the Portuguese
monarchy than in other medieval kingdoms. The king's government was administered by a centralized bureaucracy. The Portuguese *Cortes* (houses of parliament), composed of representatives
of three estates—the church, the nobility, and the towns—have a
continuous history beginning in 1254. The stronger the king, the
more willing were the *Cortes* to provide the funds that he re-
quested. The weaker the king, the more demands were made on

him by the estates through their representatives in the *Cortes*. All governmental and judicial power was vested ultimately in the crown, but in time it was delegated to landlords acting as the king's agents on their property. But as the origins of jurisdictional grants were obscured by the years, the lords assumed further jurisdiction, thus increasing their powers.

In spite of the fact that Portugal's borders with Castile were stabilized in 1295, the threat of war was a constant concern. A legendary result of this instability is the tragedy of *Pedro*, heir to the throne of *Afonso IV*, and his beautiful Castilian mistress, *Ines de Castro*, lady-in-waiting to Pedro's wife *Constança*. To keep the tenuous peace, the king ordered the murder of Ines in Coimbra on suspicion that she was involving Portugal in Castilian politics. When Dom Pedro became king as *Pedro I*, he proclaimed Ines his queen and forced his court to pay homage to her corpse, clothed for the occasion in the robes of state. When he died, Pedro was buried with Ines at the Abbey of Alcobaça. His tomb is embellished with the scene of her murderers in hell and placed opposite Ines' tomb so that on Resurrection Day their first sight would be each other.

During the period since the twelfth century, Portugal had conducted a profitable trade with England and Flanders in grain, salt, olive oil, wine, honey, cork, and leather and was Europe's chief producer of broomstraw. But tragically, depopulation caused by the Black Death, which claimed the life of one in every three Portuguese in 1348 and 1349, put once-productive land to fallow.

Unfortunately, Portugal did not enter fully into the intellectual development of medieval Europe either. In the twelfth and thirteenth centuries, monastic development was geared toward promoting the Reconquest rather than furthering scholarship. Dinis had founded a university in 1290 at Coimbra, but it was not highly regarded. The best of Portugal's scholars studied and made their reputation abroad. For example, the only Portuguese to become pope, *Pedro Julião* (John XXI), was an eminent teacher in Paris, and *Anthony of Padua*, the great Franciscan saint born in Lisbon, is identified with his adopted Italy. The Portuguese church during this time suffered from its very low standards of clerical education. Morals were relaxed, and concubinage among the clergy was common. The hierarchy and many religious houses grew enormously wealthy, and their wealth often implied great political power.

House of Aviz

When *Fernando*, last of the House of Burgundy, left no male heir, it was intended that the offspring of his daughter and her husband, *Juan I* of Castile, should inherit Portugal. In 1385, *João*, Pedro and Ines' son and Grand Master of the Military Order of Aviz, was proclaimed king by a *Cortes* called in Coimbra. To uphold the rights of an as yet unborn Castilian heir to the Portuguese throne, a Castilian army invaded Portugal. Not only the future of the House of Aviz but, even more so, the independence of Portugal was decided at the epic battle of *Aljubarrota*. Under *Nuño Alvares Pereira*, Portuguese infantry fought beside English longbowmen and shattered the Castilian's heavily armored cavalry. In 1386, the *Treaty of Windsor* confirmed the alliance between Portugal and England with a pact of perpetual friendship. The alliance is represented by the oldest unbroken treaty in existence. The two countries celebrated its six-hundredth anniversary in 1986.

John of Gaunt—Duke of Lancaster, son of Edward III, and father of Henry IV—landed in Galicia in 1387 with an expeditionary force to press his claim to the Castilian throne. He failed and returned to England but left behind his daughter *Philippa of Lancaster* as wife of João I to seal the Anglo-Portuguese alliance. Philippa reformed the morals of the Portuguese royal court and imposed uncomfortably rigid standards of behavior. More important, she provided royal patronage for English commercial interests—cod and cloth—in return for wine, cork, salt, and oil. Philippa also became the mother of six princes, who, according to the poet Luis de Camões, were the "marvelous generation." The future of the Aviz dynasty seemed assured by this extraordinary line of royal princes, but the king also provided for his illegitimate children as he had been provided for by his father. João conferred on his bastard son *Afonso* the hereditary title of Duke of Bragança. The house of Bragança accumulated wealth to rival that of the crown and assumed leadership of the aristocracy in opposition to Aviz. Eventually, João and Philippa died and were buried in the monastery of Nossa Senhora de Vitoria at Batalha. The monastery was commissioned by João in gratitude to the Almighty for his victory at the Aljubarrota.

The Portuguese Expansion

Throughout most of the fifteenth century, attention was focused on Morocco rather than on exploration and colonization of unknown territory. In 1415, the Portuguese seized Ceuta in Morocco, the western depot of the spice trade. They began building strongholds that, by the end of the century, enabled them to control most of Morocco's western coastline. Several factors seem to have impelled Portugal, a marginal country in the European context, to become the first European nation to expand its territory outside the continent. First, the continuation of the crusade against the Moors in Morocco was viewed as a necessary preliminary move to the reconquest of Spain. Second, these strategic considerations were interlocked with concern for profits. There was nothing ambiguous about obtaining material gains from crusading. Third, there was a deeply felt religious and cultural motivation. Finally, the overseas enterprise provided an outlet for the restless military aristocracy and the pursuit of personal honor and adventure.

One of the princes of Philippa and João I played such an important role, not only in the reconquest of Ceuta but in the entire Portuguese exploratory movement, that he became known as *Henry The Navigator.* Although he himself was not well traveled, he commanded a permanent military force and had access to substantial resources. At his villa on the promontory of Sagres in Algarve, astronomers, seamen, mapmakers, and scholars combined experience and imaginative minds to develop new navigational principles. They also invented the *caravel,* the first ship that could be maneuvered and sailed safely and efficiently in a crosswind.

Henry prodded his mariners to explore further and further beyond Cape Bojador on the extreme west coast of Africa. He believed it was not the outer boundary of the knowable world. In the decade of the 1420s, Portuguese seamen discovered the islands of Madeira and the Azores. In 1434, *Gil Eanes* rounded the Cape of Bojador and reported back to Henry that it, indeed, was not the end of the world. Eanes' succeeding voyages further south to the Cape Verde Islands produced material gains, such as exotic animals and slaves for Henry's estates. Although Henry's motives were obviously many and certainly not altruistic, the explorations he sponsored were well planned and organized and began to be profitable in slaves and even gold. By midcentury, Portuguese mariners had ventured far enough to map the curve of the African continent.

For several years during this period the voyages ceased, but under *João II,* official patronage of exploration and trade was renewed. Priorities were set after some conflict over expansion in

Morocco versus overseas trade. The first comprehensive plan for overseas expansion and the idea of rounding Africa as a trade route to India are credited to this grandson of João I. The crown, of course, took its royal share of the profit, assumed direct management of trade, and reaped most of the benefits.

The Portuguese conducted their expeditions in great secrecy. The advantages from advanced ship design and navigational devices, as well as information from earlier voyages, were carefully guarded. In 1484, Christopher Columbus, married to a Portuguese, recommended a westward approach to the Indies. Local legend claims that a Portuguese fisherman from Cascais first discovered the New World after his boat was swept westward from Madeira. Supposedly, he returned and told Columbus, who was living at that time on Madeira, of the discovery. Truth or legend, the Portuguese did reject Columbus' proposal, since they had an accurate measure of the earth's circumference that committed them to finding an eastward route. Instead, Queen Isabella financed Columbus' explorations for Spain.

New discoveries followed rapidly along the coast of Africa to the Cape of Good Hope, although it was another decade before *Vasco da Gama* rounded the Cape in 1497 and sailed up the east coast across the Indian Ocean to India. After Columbus' initial discoveries in America, *Pope Alexander VI*, a Spaniard, divided the world between Portugal and Spain, supposedly to thwart conflict. At first, Portugal had title to all lands east of a line passing near the Cape Verde Islands. A year later the line was redrawn in the *Treaty of Tordesillas* and moved a thousand miles westward, perhaps more than coincidentally granting Brazilian land to Portugal. Speculation persists that the Portuguese were aware of Brazil's location before the Tordesillas agreement but kept its discovery under a blanket of secrecy.

The African route to the East was the main concern, however. Since the Asian spice trade had been controlled by Arabs, military means were required to break that monopoly and allow Portuguese traders to do business. So, in 1503, Vasco da Gama sailed in a convoy with an escort of warships, with which he defeated the Arabs. Subsequent victories in the East confirmed the Portuguese as the dominant power in the Indian Ocean in the early sixteenth century. Portugal itself was weak militarily, with a rudimentary domestic economy. It had few warships and sailing men. Yet the ships it possessed were better ships and had better guns, winning a psychological advantage over Asian adversaries. The myth of the near invincibility of the Portuguese men-of-war sustained their superiority after the actual power to defend their interests had diminished.

Afonso d'Albuquerque, as the Portuguese viceroy in the East, was perhaps the single greatest strategic planner in the history of European imperialism. He established a center for operations at Goa and constructed military and commercial bases that protected an expanding trade network and secured a line of communications back to Portugal. The Portuguese probed the Mekong Delta, and in 1513 were at Canton in China before making contact with Japan. They obtained the enclave of Macao, one of many intended for warehouses, repair depots, and trading posts. Increasingly self-sustaining, Portuguese trade within its colonial system assumed a greater importance than trade with Europe. So intent was Albuquerque to maintain and strengthen the eastern colonies that he had ordered his men to marry in Asia. Therefore, generations of Portuguese, Eurasians, and Asian converts identified with a Portugal they had never seen.

The very successful commercial expansion overseas allowed João II and his successor, *Manuel I,* to operate the government without subsidies or consent from the *Cortes.* In addition to being an astute politician, Manuel was a man of taste who used Portugal's new wealth to embellish his court with art and literature, theater, and architecture. Under his patronage, the church and monastery of the Jeronimites at Belem was built. The site, near Lisbon, was the harbor from which da Gama had sailed. He also built, nearby, the beautiful Tower of Belem in the style now known as Manueline.

In Portugal the church was the only institution outside the control of the crown. Because it was not influenced by the Protestant Reformation and yet was removed from the mainstream of sixteenth-century Roman Catholicism, standards of clerical discipline were low. Remarkably, parts of the Algarve and the Alentejo remained missionary areas. In addition there was prodigious effort put forth by Portuguese missionaries in Brazil, Asia, and Africa. A small Jewish community had been protected by the crown, and in 1492, more than fifty thousand Spanish Jews were accepted as refugees on condition that they pay for their transportation out of Portugal within eight months. Four years later, after an alliance with the Spanish monarchs Ferdinand and Isabella, Portuguese Jews refusing to become Christians were to be expelled and restrictions were to be placed on those new Christians who did convert. The Portuguese inquisition was established by the crown in 1531 as a political instrument, forcing many Portuguese Jews and new Christians to emigrate to northern Europe or colonial Brazil, rather than be among the more than one thousand persons to burn at the stake.

The first half of the sixteenth century was the golden age of the Portuguese seaborne empire built on the spice trade with Indies. The *Casa da India*, established in 1503, regulated a tight monopoly on the trade. Gold from Guinea was traded for the spice and pepper taken to Portugal that was reexported to European markets. Manuel, "The Grocer King," and his court were able to operate on a level far beyond what Portugal's domestic economy could support. Yet the economic benefits of the passage to India, the yearly voyage of the commercial fleet, had little effect on Portuguese society outside the restricted circle of the court and a few merchants in the city. Indeed, success in overseas trade had its detrimental effects. Rather than stimulate the domestic economy, overseas trade tended to depress it because cheaper, more efficiently produced wares and food were purchased abroad. And, unfortunately for the home economy, continuous expansion of trade was necessary for success of the monopoly.

By 1560, however, the Casa da India faced hard times. It had to turn to foreign investors for survival. The result was an increasing share of spice-trade profits distributed outside Portugal.

A new king, *Sebastian*, grandson of Manuel and Charles V of Spain, was a bumbling fanatic who launched an ill-advised military campaign in Morocco, where Moorish counterattacks had actually reduced Portuguese holdings. His fourteen thousand ill-equipped troops were destroyed, Sebastian was presumed killed in battle, and large numbers of nobility were killed or captured. And so, as Morocco was the setting for the commencement of Portuguese expansion, it was where Portuguese glory collapsed as well. The natural leadership was depleted, the treasury was emptied, and the government was at a standstill.

House of Hapsburg

For the next sixty years (1580–1640), Portugal was united with Spain. It had become obvious that Sebastian lacked the inclination to perpetuate his dynasty, so the succession of a Spanish Hapsburg king had been anticipated. Actually, the union between Portugal and Spain had been promoted by dynastic marriages for generations. The two countries even shared an heir apparent for a few years at the end of the fifteenth century. Yet in Portugal, *Phillip II* and his successors ruled as kings of Portugal; the government and currency remained Portuguese. For two years (1581–83), Phillip II made Lisbon his capital. In later years it was not Spanish oppression that his Portuguese subjects complained of, but rather neglect by a distant king.

Resistance among the masses in the countryside took the form of an almost mystic cult preoccupation with the "hidden prince," Sebastian, who they believed did not die in battle but would return again. Several so-called false Sebastians claimed the throne and were actually supported by popular sentiment. Some scholars have seen this nostalgic longing for the unattainable as the basis of much of Portuguese art and literature, and a continuing feature of Portuguese political and social life.

As part of the larger Hapsburg Empire, the Portuguese were forced to be involved in European religious and dynastic wars for which the Portuguese had little sympathy. In protest in 1640, the Duke of Bragança was installed on the Portuguese throne by Portuguese nobility. Popular in the countryside, in Brazil, and in the urban merchant community, *João IV* also was supported by the powerful Jesuits. Unfortunately, peace with Spain's enemies did not result; the Dutch returned none of the Portuguese holdings they had taken in the East or in Brazil, and took more territory after 1640. Peace was not made between Spain and Portugal for twenty-eight years; Portugal had chosen to protect its overseas empire rather than participate in a common Hispanic nation-state. This choice, it has been suggested, may have condemned Portugal to be a small, underdeveloped country dependent for a time on England for survival.

House of Bragança

The dukes of the powerful House of Bragança had been leaders of the Portuguese aristocracy, their wealth and land equalling that of the crown. João IV was no exception. Essentially a businessman in outlook, João IV had profitable interests in the Azores and Brazil and, at one point, had contemplated selling Portugal back to the king of Spain. His sons, however, were another story. His son *Afonso VI* was a degenerate whose brother, *Pedro II,* seized control of the government and imprisoned Afonso in 1667 with the aid of Afonso's wife.

But the empire somehow survived and the affairs of state continued. Despite losses suffered during the Hapsburg period, Portugal at the end of the seventeenth century was responsible for an empire focusing political concern and commercial interests on Asia, Africa, and Brazil. Goa remained an administrative center for Portuguese interests in the East Indies and East Africa. Portuguese Goans had gained prominence in Mozambique, where traders had settled in the mid-sixteenth century. In search of the reputed "River of Gold," the Portuguese had established a chain of depots on the coast of West Africa that through the seventeenth century yielded not only gold, but slaves and ivory as well. Angola, first settled in 1575, offered such an abundance of slaves that at one point in the seventeenth century Africans accounted for 10 percent of the population of Lisbon. The expansion of the coffee plantation economy in Brazil compensated for losses in Asia. Brazil played an increasingly important role in domestic political considerations. Portugal became, in fact, dependent on its colony of Brazil after the discovery of gold in Brazil in 1687.

England sheltered the rich but vulnerable Portuguese empire after João IV renewed the Anglo-Portuguese alliance and particularly after the marriage of Catherine of Bragança to the English King Charles II in 1661. That union added prestige to the fledgling royal house. More important, English troops served with Portugal against the Spanish. But Portugal's weak domestic economy remained static.

The several generations of initiatives for domestic development were destroyed. Brazil's wealth in gold and then diamonds assured Portugal of the means to pay for imports. Brazilian gold also encouraged England to update its commercial relations with Portugal. Unfortunately, English imports rose by 120 percent in Portugal while Portuguese exports to England, mainly wine shipped through English merchants at Porto, rose by less than 40 percent.

Pombal

The eighteenth-century Portuguese government had a highly centralized bureaucracy managed by powerful ministers responsible only to the king. *João V* directed ambitious works such as the aqueduct in Lisbon, the monastery at Mafra, and the University of Coimbra's library, but when he sank into melancholy, he turned his government over to inept ecclesiastical advisors. His successor, *Jose*, was indolent, eager to reign but not eager to bear the burden of ruling his country and empire. A diplomat, *Sebastião Jose de Carvallo e Melo*, later *Marquis of Pombal*, directed the government. He was praised for his accomplishments, but at the same time he was criticized for the methods he used to achieve them. In time, Pombal became the veritable dictator of Portugal. The most authoritarian regime known in eighteenth-century Europe existed under his hand.

Ironically, Pombal was thrust into prominence after Lisbon's worst natural disaster. On November 1, 1755, All Saints Day, an earthquake followed by fire and tidal waves destroyed all but a portion of Lisbon, killing sixty thousand Lisboetans. In the aftermath, Pombal's direction to "bury the dead and relieve the living" was the first step in rebuilding the city. He restructured the administration of state, stimulated industry, and regulated the export of gold and the production of wine to keep prices high. Opponents of his enlightened despotism were arrested, tortured, and some executed. Only the church retained a degree of independence from state control and continued to oppose his sometimes harsh reforms. In retaliation, Pombal intervened in ecclesiastical affairs, confiscated church property, and expelled the Jesuits. But with Jose's death, Pombal's dictatorship quickly collapsed, suspending his restrictive monopolies on all things economic. After Pombal, a class of independent merchants brought relative prosperity to the country at the end of the century and permitted Portugal to pass through the revolutionary 1790s unscathed.

Constitutional Monarchy

The continental blockade imposed in 1804 by Napoleon Bonaparte against importation of British goods was obviously resisted in Portugal. So Napoleon sent an army supposedly to liberate the

Portuguese people from British economic domination. The royal family, *Maria I* and her son *João VI* (who acted as regent during her long mental illness that began in 1779), retreated to Brazil, where a government in exile was established under British protection. The French withdrew from Portugal, but the royal family remained in Brazil, and in 1816 João VI succeeded to the Portuguese throne while still in Rio de Janeiro. Discontented, the middle class, the merchants, and the army officer corps called for a constitutional government, believing that a responsible parliamentary government could cure the country's economic and social ills. In 1820, the army demanded the reestablishment of the *Cortes* and the drafting of a workable constitution.

João VI accepted his status as a constitutional monarch, returned from Brazil, and left his heir *Dom Pedro* behind as "co-king." The first *Cortes* elected under the 1822 Constitution attempted to reassert Lisbon's economic control over Brazil. As a result, Dom Pedro, with British support, declared Brazil an independent state, installed himself as emperor, and let it be known that he was still heir to the Portuguese throne. In Portugal, opinion was polarized between militantly anticlerical radicals and the traditionists who were hostile to the urban, middle-class *Cortes*. Calling for a return to absolutism, the traditionalists supported *Dom Miguel*, younger son of Joao VI, to succeed his father in Portugal. When João VI died in 1826, Pedro reluctantly returned to Portugal, pressured by the British to leave his prosperous Brazilian empire for an impoverished country with an unstable constitutional regime. Backed by the army, Pedro demanded return of executive authority to the king as outlined in the Compromise Charter of 1826. After the charter was adopted, Pedro returned to Brazil, leaving his young daughter *Maria da Gloria* as heir to the Portuguese throne and Miguel as regent, provided he accept the new constitution. After duly swearing to abide by the settlement, Miguel seized power, abolished the charter, and appointed an absolutist government that offered him the crown. Leading an expeditionary force, Pedro abdicated his Brazilian throne, landed near Porto in 1832 and defeated Miguel, with substantial British assistance, in a civil war of liberals against traditionalists. The church had overwhelmingly supported Miguel; as a consequence, the religious orders were abolished, and in 1834 church property was expropriated and sold below market value. The sale resulted in a shift in ownership of more than one-fourth of all land and created a new class—wealthy landowners—who influenced political life of the country throughout the rest of the nineteenth century.

Anticlericalism, economic freedom achieved through unregulated trade, and new bourgeois aristocracy in the *Cortes* were the realities of nineteenth-century Portugal. In spite of confidence that national honor could be restored through constitutional government, the new governments came to office through manipulated elections. Revolts by an activist army divided in its political sympathies were regular occurrences. British and French intervention was required to forestall civil war and protect investments.

An artificial two-party system of Regenerators and Progressives developed in the *Cortes* by midcentury. Both parties agreed on policies and political tactics, which were actually the most cohesive forces in keeping the party system functioning.

After 1856, "Rotativism" was instituted. It was the practice of alternating parties in power at regular intervals. Rotativism produced relatively stable governments that nonetheless failed to solve Portugal's underlying social and economic problems.

Lacking domestic capital, skilled labor, technology, and raw material, Portugal's economy did not become industrialized. The level of agricultural production had not been affected by the changes in landholding after 1834. Up to 80 percent of the country's trade involved reexport of colonial goods. Half the state income went to service the debt owed to foreign creditors. Dependent on outside investment, public works projects designed to stimulate the economy led the country deeper into debt. Despite these chronic economic problems, socialism and republicanism had little appeal, and the crown, respected and admired, exercised considerable political influence within the framework of the constitution.

After a serious confrontation with Great Britain over territory in southern Africa, the Portuguese government withdrew many of its African claims in 1890. The government's retreat in the face of a British ultimatum was loudly denounced by the new Republican Party, with propaganda playing on fears of Portugal's becoming a British colony or a province of Spain. The advisors to *King Carlos* insisted he rule by decree. The king, an artist and distinguished scientist, flatly refused.

In 1900, *João Franco*, a conservative reformist in the *Cortes*, was summoned by Carlos to form a coalition government. Both the Regenerators and Progressives were unwilling to cooperate, so the Republicans were the immediate beneficiaries of Franco's program.

With the encouragement of greater participation in political debate, they turned on a well-meaning king, blaming him for the corruption of the political parties that Rotativism had made inevitable. The splintering of the established parties, the lack of approval of Franco's legislative program, and the ceasing of the parliamentary process, lead Carlos, in 1907, to dissolve the *Cortes* and grant Franco authority to rule by decree. In February, Carlos and his heir *Prince Luis* were assassinated at Terreiro do Paço in Lisbon, leaving the eighteen-year-old *Manuel II* as king. In an effort to save the young king, Franco called for an election and stepped down as prime minister. The Republicans became the party of urban, middle-class radicalism. It was nationalistic, libertarian, and intensely anticlerical in temper. In October 1910, troops in Lisbon refused to put down a mutiny aboard two warships, and some went over to the dissidents. With no one willing to take charge of the situation and his appeals for advice unanswered, Manuel II fled with his royal family to exile in England. A provisional government was formed under the presidency of the historican *Teofilo Braga* and the political direction of *Afonso Costa*.

The Parliamentary Republic

The 1911 Constitution, which formally inaugurated the Portuguese Republic, provided a parliamentary system of government, guaranteed individual civil rights and vested authority to a cabinet and a president, chosen by the parliament. In 1913, Costa's party, the Democrats who were radical and uncompromisingly anticlerical, gained a dominant position in the *Cortes* by eliminating illiterates from voting rolls.

But the rest of the world was embroiled in war. Afraid that a German victory would mean loss of the African colonies, Portugal sided with the Allies in 1916. Nevertheless, there was a genuine lack of enthusiasm for the war, which brought food shortages and inflation. Leftist army and navy units mutinied. In reaction, a parliamentary coup, backed by the military, succeeded in overthrowing Costa's government in December 1917. A new government was formed under *Sidonio Pais*, a diplomat known for his pro-German sympathies. Pais was the Republic's first leader to command mass popular backing. Yet, a wave of terrorism swept the country as extremists took to the streets and troops protested being sent to the front. Pais was murdered in a train station in December by a politically motivated assassin. A clamor arose in the leaderless country for a dictatorship, but the *Cortes* restored the 1911 Constitution and the Democrats regained their majority for seven more years.

The war debt was insurmountable. Portugal received almost none of the German reparations and no territory. Successive governments in the early 1920s developed no comprehensive programs for fiscal and economic recovery. Military intervention in politics increased, about half the prime ministers after 1919 coming from the armed forces. Official anticlericalism, including the seizure of church property, the abolishment of religious orders, and the exiling of bishops, made it impossible for many to accept the Republic. The apparitions at Fatima in 1917 occurred at the height of Costa's anticlerical campaign and fueled Catholic resentment of it. The parliamentary government was finally dissolved in June, 1926, after a popular military coup in Braga.

The Salazar Era

In order to restore order and revive the economy, a military government held the country, although a gradual institutional transition to an authoritarian republic was envisioned. *General Antonio Oscar de Fraguso Carmona* was named president and held that office until his death in 1951. The new military government, recognizing the most serious problems to be economic, appointed a university professor and leading conservative economist as minister of finance. *Antonio de Oliveira Salazar,* however, wanted free reign to manage the economy, so he resigned until 1928 when he was granted the power of veto over all fiscal matters. In 1932, this indispensable and powerful figure was named prime minister and introduced a civilian government. Salazar came from a peasant background, having studied for the priesthood before turning to economics at Coimbra University. He earned a reputation as a scholar and writer, as well as a leader in Catholic movements. He retained his professorial style as prime minister. Austere and ascetic in his tastes, he was a skillful political manipulator with a capacity for ruthlessness. He was feared rather than loved as a public figure.

With the adoption of the 1933 Constitution dictated by Salazar, the New State was created. Salazar was head of government, exercised executive and legislative functions, controlled local administration and police, and was leader of the National Union, the only legal political organization. A legislature, the National Assembly, restricted to members of the National Union, could initiate legislation but only concerning matters that did not require government expenditures. Women were given the vote, but literacy and property qualifications continued.

In 1945, Salazar introduced so-called democratic measures, including an amnesty for political prisoners and a loosening of censorship that liberals believed to be a move toward democratic government. But the New State was Salazar's and not a forum for a party or ideology. Politics in Salazar's Portugal consisted of balancing power blocks within the country—the military, business and commerce, landholders, colonial interests, and the church. All political parties were banned. The National Union, officially a civic association, had no guiding philosophy apart from support for Salazar. The regime was satisfied to direct public enthusiasm into "*Fado, Fatima,* and *futebol*"—music, religion, and sports. Although he was a devout Catholic, Salazar's policies were aimed essentially at healing the division caused within Portuguese society by generations of anticlericalism. Although the church had consistently supported Salazar, the regime was increasingly criticized by progressive clergy, resulting in the expulsion of the Bishop of Porto in the 1960s.

Whatever the criticism of his political methods, his program of economic recovery succeeded. In a few years Salazar achieved a solvent currency, a favorable balance of trade, and surpluses both in foreign reserves and in the national budget. Yet the majority of the Portuguese people remained among the poorest in Europe. Outside the cities, traditional patterns of life were not altered. To create an unrealistic atmosphere of rising expectations, Salazar argued, would return the country to the pre-Salazar chaos. Priority was given, however, to colonial development. Salazar insisted that the overseas territories be made not only to pay for themselves, but also to provide trade surpluses required by Portugal so that it might import the essentials it could not produce itself.

In the years before World War II, Salazar cultivated good relations with all major powers except the Soviet Union. Initially intent on preserving Portuguese neutrality during the Spanish Civil War, he supported Francisco Franco's nationalists when Soviet activity in Spain persuaded him to send twenty thousand Portuguese volunteers. Likewise, Salazar found German Nazism repugnant and protested the invasion of Poland in 1939. Although Portugal was not a combatant during World War II, the Anglo-Portuguese alliance was preserved. Bases in the Azores were granted to the United States and Great Britain, and Portuguese colonial products—copper and chromium—were used in Allied war production. Portugal became a charter member of the North Atlantic Treaty Organization (NATO) in 1949. Admission to the United Nations was prevented by the Soviet Union until 1955. Soon afterward new troubles began. In 1961, Indian armed forces invaded and seized Goa, a Portuguese territory since 1510. Also in 1961, armed resistance to the Portuguese colonial administration broke out in Angola and, by 1964, had spread to Mozambique and Guinea. Portuguese forces contained the insurgencies and seemed to be capable of sustaining military activity in Africa indefinitely. Instead of interrupting colonial production, the wars promoted economic development in Angola and Mozambique, both with large settler communities.

Marcello Caetano

After completely dominating Portuguese government and politics for nearly forty years, Salazar suffered an incapacitating stroke in June, 1968, after a freak accident. He died, still in a coma, more than a year later. President Tomas appointed *Marcello Caetano*, a teacher, jurist, and scholar of international reputation, to succeed Salazar. Considered a moderate, he had taken unpopular stands in opposition to Salazar, such as protesting police repression of student demonstrations at Lisbon University by resigning as rector of that institution. Unlike Salazar he had come from the upper middle class, was ebullient and personable, and sought contact with the people.

It was obvious that Caetano was a different type of leader. He spoke of "evolution with continuity." He introduced technocrats into the government and eased police repression. The elections in 1969 were the freest in decades, but his regime remained authoritarian. Caetano advocated an expansionist economic policy without, however, supplementing the means of production. The consequence of this liberalization was rampant inflation. Though powerful, Caetano lacked Salazar's skill as a politician and econo-mist. On April 25, 1974—known since as the *"Day of the Red Carna-tions"*—the officers and men of the Armed Forces Movement ousted Caetano and Tomas, paving the way for a junta under *General Antonio de Spinola* to take command of the Portuguese Republic.

Post-Revolution

The fall of the Carmo Convent barracks where Caetano was beseiged with his loyal National Republic Guards marked the tri-umph of the revolution. In one night a handful of junior officers toppled Europe's longest-surviving police state. The forty-eight-year-old dictatorship, often called the "Neo-Inquisition," collapsed. It brought to an end the thirteen years of colonial war in Africa. It also brought a new freedom unknown in Portugal in modern times. Thousands of people poured into the streets, decorating the tanks and soldiers with red carnations. They danced and sang songs that had been banned for nearly fifty years.

In the anarchic months that followed that jubilant evening, ten-sions built. Interrupted television broadcasts became the alarm signal for a series of coups and countercoups. The tension fed on fears that leftist or rightist extremists would assume power and forever snatch away that hard-won freedom. Neither extreme today has much influence in the country. In the years since the revolu-tion, the history of the country can be written only in economic terms. No less than sixteen governments have held the reigns of leadership since 1974, but all governments have come and gone on the issues facing Portugal's economic future. As will be discussed later, Portugal's economy is a precarious one. The democracy is immature, struggling but relatively stable. In a recent election, the Communists lost more of their seats in the national assembly. The Portuguese people constantly express the wish to see no ex-tremism.

The 1974 revolt to topple the rightist dictatorship was stirred by opposition to the colonial wars. Those wars had exacted a bitter toll. More than a million men, a tenth of the total population, were drafted into the unpopular conflict in Africa. People still remember that more than twenty thousand families suffered the loss of a husband or son in Africa. The war was fought against Russian- and

Chinese-backed guerrillas. This too is remembered. But abandoning the colonies was costly. The domestic economy was heavily dependent upon colonial trade. Many people blame decolonization for Portugal's political and economic woes of today, but decolonization is only a part of the story. Successive government collapses, spurred by inexperience in finance, have also strained the economy badly. The one bright hope for Portugal's economic future was the entry into the European Economic Community in 1986, but these issues will be discussed in the following chapter.

In the years since 1974, Portugal has experienced political freedom, free speech, increased prestige in the world, and a gradual decrease in its conservative attitudes toward life and living. It has become a true democracy and is a safe place to visit. Its efforts at freedom are respected throughout the world. The 1990s will surely see a stronger economy and healthier politics.

CHAPTER 8

The Economy: Never Too Late

The single most important event in the modern economic history of Portugal is the country's accession to the European Economic Community (EEC) or Common Market. With that act, Portugal's lagging economy may gain some headway. There are attendant problems to be sure. For the past few years the prospect for and then the reality of membership has created a sort of euphoria regarding Portugal's future economic prospects. After centuries of isolation, Portugal is coming, finally, into Europe's economic mainstream. It took eight years of negotiations, but a happy prime minister announced that "Portugal will be a completely different country within five years." That was in 1985. At the same time, there was no general jubilation among the people. There was, in fact, deep concern about the real costs and some skepticism about the benefits. The politicians are focusing upon the political stability the decision will lend to the democracy that emerged in 1974. Since that time Portugal has faced serious economic problems and many government changes.

Industrialists are concerned about the consequences if industry and agriculture fail to compete successfully with other European countries as the protective barriers come down. The people fear that the immediate impact of membership could aggravate the hardships that already exist. For example, the experience in other European countries has been an immediate increase in the cost of living, increased taxes, and some inflationary trends. Portugal already suffers from several years of 30 percent inflation. Many feel it cannot bear any more inflation.

Government leaders who negotiated the accession (notably Mario Soares) argue that despite the costs, Portugal must modernize and be ready to meet the challenge of European competition. They are asking the Portuguese people to realize that every step toward modernization has its social costs but that these costs are necessary for the future of the country. This sort of talk does not spark great enthusiasm in a country where recent austerity programs aimed at reducing inflation and the foreign-debt load have increased unemployment and the incidence of bankruptcy.

Apparently, the sharpest impact was felt during the first two years of EEC membership (after 1986) when prices rose and noncompetitive industry and agriculture failed to meet European competition. It is difficult for the average person to look toward the long-term benefits, to realize that membership is vital to Portugal's economic future, or to think in terms of fifty-year benefits when the costs affect the purse in the present.

This chapter looks at the present day economy and then future prospects for economic development. In 1974 when the band of army officers overthrew the Caetano regime, there were immediate economic repercussions. For fifty years under Salazar the economy had lagged behind Europe in general. The colonial wars drained the coffers badly, and there were fundamental weaknesses in the system that made Portugal Europe's poorest country.

During the years following 1974 until the present, Portugal's democracy has struggled with economic problems of a severe nature. For example, nearly 26 percent of the labor force is employed in agriculture. Compare that to 2 to 3 percent in the United States and other developed countries and you have at least an indication of Portugal's level of development. Roughly 37 percent of the work force is in the industrial sector. Combined, the figures constitute a slightly larger proportion than is seen in the more developed countries where generally the service sector dominates.

Over the years, Portuguese agriculture and industry tended to complement each other. Agriculture provided the raw materials for the traditional industries of food processing, cork producing, wine making, and wood processing. The newer industries that have developed during the past two decades have become heavily dependent upon foreign imports. Both sectors were and still are in need of investment capital. Agriculture in particular has not kept pace with the remainder of Europe.

Modern industry in Portugal focuses upon shipbuilding, chemicals, electrical equipment, machine tools, fertilizer, and paper. The major growth industries during the 1970s and 1980s were textiles, clothing, and footwear. Most of the industry is concentrated in the Lisbon-Setúbal area or in the region surrounding Porto in the north. Most of Portugal's heavy industry is located in the Lisbon area, while Porto is primarily a light-industry region. One reason there is a concentration of industry at the two major ports is that modern manufacturing depends on imported raw materials, fuel, and equipment.

Growth in industry has been slow. Although there are a few large and modern enterprises, Portugal's economy is still characterized by many small enterprises using obsolete technology.

After the coup in 1974, the industrial sector received a breath of fresh air. There was promise of access to more investment capital, but more than a decade and a half after the revolution, instability remains. Today, there are an estimated one hundred thousand workers employed full-time in state-owned or privately owned industry whose pay envelopes are empty or contain only a small portion of their rightful salary. Portuguese employers owe tremendous sums in back salary and wages to workers who sacrificed their pay in an attempt to help industry cope with the recession of 1982–83. They survived but have yet to be fully compensated. This is one of Portugal's serious economic problems. The recession was the worst of the post-revolution economy. To be working, even if not paid in full, was a better alternative than to be unemployed, with the attendant uncertainties.

During the Salazar years, the dictator feared the rise of an organized working class and was able to depress industrial growth deliberately by drawing on the immense resources of the colonies. Since then there has been some improvement, but industrial development lags far behind Portugal's European counterparts. For example, an interesting project developed before the revolution was the new industrial complex at *Sines*. The plan survived the revolution, was completed in the late 1970s, but never has been a success. Sines is about ninety miles south of Lisbon. The plan was based upon the idea that the location was an ideal point at which to refine middle-east oil for European markets. The project included an oil refinery, associated petrochemical and fertilizer industries, rail-car manufacture, and various light industries. A deep-water port was constructed to accommodate supertankers. New housing for the workers was constructed. Rail service was extended to Sines. Today, most of the refining capacity goes unused, the housing units are empty, rails are rusting, and few ships call at the port. The scene is depressing. As government officials speak optimistically of the future, the present is bleak. The reasons for the near failure of the scheme are many and complex. Basically, the reasons are related to location, timing, and lack of investment capital. In terms of location, Sines offers no particular advantage as a transshipment, or break-in-bulk, point. Also, the timing of the huge project was bad. Begun during the oil crisis of the early 1970s, completed during the oil crisis of the late 1970s, and operating in the oil glut of the 1980s, the project never received serious attention outside Portugal. Because of other economic problems, investment capital was in short supply and many of the details of the project's infrastructure were never completed. Additional problems emerged. For example, a huge seawall built by Italian engineers was breached by a storm in 1981. It has yet to be repaired for lack of funds. In effect, the port and industrial complex is grossly overbuilt, in need of repair, and under utilized—a capital liability to Portugal. To the Portuguese who saw promise here, it is a sad sight—modern factories sitting empty, new apartment developments windblown and dusty.

The political successes and evolution that have taken place in the years since 1974 have not, in short, been matched by economic progress. Portugal is at the bottom of every European statistical table dealing with social and economic well-being, from infant mortality and health care to agricultural productivity. The truly depressing aspect is the realization by the political leaders that the economic system must first absorb the failures before it can get better.

Education in Portugal has also been in a state of transition since the revolution. It is generally recognized that Portugal has never had a strong educational tradition. Despite the fact that the University at Coimbra is Europe's oldest, it has never commanded the same respect achieved by other European universities. Today, Coimbra is the best of Portugal. It is difficult to get into and hard to stay in. In addition to Coimbra, there is a nationwide network of universities associated with the larger cities. The largest of these institutions are the University of Lisbon and the Technical University of Lisbon. To accommodate the rapid increase in demand for a university education during the 1970s and early 1980s (partly due to high levels of youth unemployment), the New University of Lisbon was formed. Occupying formerly unused structures such as army barracks, palaces, and office buildings, the system seems to accommodate huge enrollments at virtually no cost to the student. Standards, however, are low and most faculty is recruited on a part-time basis. Serious students, if they can afford it, try to go to the University of Lisbon or Coimbra.

A system of public secondary schools was established in 1821. The system struggled for a century and lagged seriously behind all of Europe. In the 1960s, public education improved vastly and was able to accommodate most pupils. The post-revolution picture is varied. In the first two or three years after the revolution, education was again neglected because of a scarcity of funds. Subsequent improvements and reorganization during the late 1970s brought public education standards back to acceptable levels by the 1980s. Church-operated schools receiving state funds account for significant secondary level enrollment and provide a needed service to the country.

The future of Portugal's economy is difficult to predict. Headlines in the newspapers continue to read: "Lisnave Jobs to Be Cut" (Lisnave is the shipbuilding and repair facility in Lisbon); "More Jobless"; "Inflation up to 30.4%"; "Bread, Milk, Petrol Go Up"; "Purchasing Power Down." Such messages are not encouraging. Yet there is much evidence that despite discouraging headlines the Portuguese are better off economically than they were prior to entry into the EEC.

The keys to economic development are education and agricultural and industrial modernization, as well as immediate austerity. To accomplish this will be difficult. Portugal faces a serious foreign debt that creates more obstacles to progress. Politically, there have been sixteen governments since 1974. One major obstacle to political success has been the complicated and unwieldy leftist-oriented constitution of 1974. It not only sets forth the principles of nationhood but also deals with the day-to-day details of government, tying the hands of those who would initiate creative political change and progress. All major political parties except the

Communists are in favor of cleaning the constitution of its complexities. None, so far, have succeeded.

Compounding the above is the fact that the Portuguese are already heavily taxed. Portugal, with a 31.3 percent tax rate, ranks just between Switzerland and the United States in terms of tax burden. Additional taxes would be difficult to enact or to collect.

A partial solution can come from aid offered by the United States and the EEC. Other foreign investment and tourism are obvious helpmates. Presently tourism accounts for a significant amount of Portugal's foreign exchange and eases the burden on the debt. Recent tourist figures indicate there are nearly 10 million tourists visiting Portugal each year. This represents a major increase from previous years. This can be explained partly by the relative strength of other currencies against the *escudo*, but travelers have also realized that Portugal is Europe's last tourist bargain. This fact is recognized by more Europeans than North Americans, however. For example, the Spanish account for the largest number of tourists, nearly 7 million. The British were next most numerous (700,000). Germans accounted for about 400,000, while the French accounted for about 350,000 tourists. Only about 200,000 Americans visit Portugal each year. This is particularly surprising despite the aggressive advertising of the past several years. For Americans in Portugal, the cost of living has actually decreased in the past few years. The reason, of course, is that even the value of the faltering dollar has outstripped inflation and cost-of-living increases in Portugal. The real cost of goods and services is less in Portugal than in the United States. One reason is that the average cost of labor is only 12 percent that of the United States and only 30 percent that of Spain. Because of these circumstances and the favorable exchange rate, travel in Portugal offers a considerable advantage to Americans, who are now using premium-yielding dollars.

CHAPTER 9

Art, Architecture, Crafts, and Culture: A Rich Land

The visual texture of a country is not created by only terrain and other topographic features. A country's architecture, building styles, art, and artifacts finish and refine the landscape. In many countries regional styles transform various parts of the country to create different looks. That is why New England has a different appearance than Texas, Oregon, or Iowa. Even small countries like Portugal have distinctive regional styles of architecture and art. For example, the Algarve is quite different in appearance from the Minho province. But before reviewing details of the cultural landscape, this chapter discusses Portugal's literary and artistic heritage. Literature and art reflect the life and thought of the time in which the works were produced. They represent distinctive achievements of a country and should be reviewed critically to gain insight into a society and culture.

Literature

The literature of Portugal contains a wealth of lyric poetry. The lyric form is somewhat of a Portuguese tradition, and even today modern poets have returned to the style. Its popularity can be attributed to the fact that spoken Portuguese verse projects a delightful tonal quality that seems to enhance the drama of the work. Portugal has also excelled in its nurture of historical writers and has produced a small number of novelists. Few Portuguese authors, however, have received any attention beyond the borders of the country. Except for the well known *Luis de Camões*, author of *Os Lusiadas*, Portuguese writers are virtually unknown outside of Portugal. It has been suggested that the reason Portuguese literature is not highly regarded beyond its own cultural realm is that the themes and characters presented in Portuguese literature are not understood by non-Portuguese readers. In fact, the typical Portuguese theme, "*Saudade*," tends to pervade the literature. The word *saudade* itself is not easily translated, but it refers to a longing, a yearning, an unrelenting nostalgia for a gilded past. Other observers have noticed this feeling, too, in the everyday life of the Portuguese. The present economy, politics, and employment are all precarious. The present, therefore, is uncertain. The future is unpredictable. The people's refuge becomes the past. Unfortunately that glorious Portuguese past is unattainable and not re-livable. The country's literati nevertheless seem to possess a double dose: they are nostalgic about nostalgia.

Within the country too, local recognition of the literature has had its difficulties. For many centuries, illiteracy was a problem, and an obvious spin-off of illiteracy is a lack of interest in literature. In the twentieth century, censorship by the Salazar regime nearly destroyed the literary spirit. Coupled with a weak economy and the high cost of books, the situation led many writers to become frustrated in their own milieu. The written word has had a tough time in Portugal.

The earliest known literary works still in existence are the manuscript collections of the *Cancioneiros* (song books) that contain the *cantigas* (lyric songs). These date from the twelfth century. The songs are the most ancient of Portuguese literature, but they are obviously based upon an even older oral tradition. Most *cantigas* were composed in very courtly and formal language by professional court troubadors. Some were composed by aristocrats and clerics who assumed they possessed some poetic talent themselves.

Portuguese prose originated from anonymous chronicles dating as far back as the fourteenth century. These chronicles were apparantly written by members of the royal court. The first of the great chroniclers was *Fernão Lopes*, who compiled a detailed record of the rise of the House of Aviz. Lopes' well-told and detailed stories recounted how the Aviz dynasty was indebted to the artisans and townspeople for their support against the old aristocracy. Lopes' successor was *Gomes Eanes de Zurara*, who went on to chronicle the stories of a changing political atmosphere and the rise of nationalism in the fifteenth century.

Sixteenth-century chronicles focused on the development of the empire and the Age of Discovery. Large numbers of books were written about the new and intriguing colonies. Like travel books, they were widely read. Some inspired the imagination and some were mere description, but all are now valuable historic documents.

Portuguese *theater* was first organized by *Gil Vincente* (ca. 1470–1536). At the time, Vincente was merely a court poet, but some say he was as significant to Portuguese theater as William Shakespeare was to English theater. His plays were of the medieval tradition and possess little or no plot. Most were farces or religious dramas. The majority of his characters were stereotyped into good and evil, virtue and vice. All of his plays, in the tradition of the day, focused upon a moral lesson. Vincente, however, toyed with satirizing the clergy, women, and courtiers of the time. The end of the sixteenth century, however, saw the demise of the secular theater and the beginning of a period of church censorship of even Vincente's religious dramas.

Also during the sixteenth century, Portugal's literary giant and most beloved author lived and wrote. The adventurer-poet *Luis de Camões* composed his famous *Os Lusiadas* (*The Lusiads*, 1572). The work is held in the highest regard in Portuguese literature. A lyric chronicle of Vasco da Gama's voyage, it also focuses on the Portuguese national story. *Os Lusiadas* additionally reflects many of Camões' experiences during his quarter century of travel in the Orient and Africa. Camões is now revered as a national hero, and the poem is regarded as the national epic. Camões' poetry actually introduced new words and expressions, enriching the Portuguese language. The revered poet left his lasting mark on the language and the literary heritage of the country.

In the seventeenth century, Castilian was the preferred language of literature in Portugal. The outstanding talent of that century was *Francesco Manuel de Melo*. A poet, historian, statesman, and writer, he served both the Hapsburgs and the Braganças. De Melo cleverly wrote in Portuguese, Castilian, and French to broaden his potential audience.

The eighteenth century was, to some critics, a literary wasteland. Only a few authors published and none were outstanding. In the nineteenth century, the poet *Manuel Maria Barbosa du Bocage* was the rising star that outshone all other poets. His works stood well above anything produced in the previous one hundred years. He is often called the critics' choice in the nineteenth century. In his time, Bocage was jailed as a radical, and he cleverly capitalized on this image to produce some very popular but somber and brooding poetry.

Two literary greats, the poet-playwright *Visconde de Almeida Garrett* and the novelist *Alexandre Herculano*, dominated Portuguese literature in the first half of the nineteenth century. The public loved them. Their works were regarded as the benchmarks for comparing the works of other writers. Both very prolific writers, they also enhanced their image with political activism aimed at bringing Portuguese society into the European mainstream.

The decade of the 1870s saw several writers achieve artistic maturity. The best known and one of the "Generation of 1870" was Portugal's most original and forceful novelist, *Eça de Queirós*. In his earlier social novels, his realism exposed the vices of the middle class and clergy and concentrated on the foibles of women. *The Sin of Father Amaro* (1875) and *Cousin Basilio* (1878) are considered the best of his novels. Most of Queirós' works have been translated into English. As a diplomat Queirós lived most of his adult life abroad. He claimed that the distance between himself and his homeland allowed him to look objectively at his country. This resulted in novels of incisive criticism and value judgments about Portuguese life at the time. His insightful and often biting observations left many people uncomfortable. But the theme of disillusionment with Portuguese society pervaded all the works of the "Generation of 1870." Others, such as *Ortigão*, became defeated by life. *Antonio Duarte Gomes Leal*, fascinated with the sins of society and the failures of the church in his early works, reconciled with the church in his later years and vigorously argued for its support.

Later in the century, Portuguese readers found and loved the nostalgic poetry of *Fernando Pessoa* (1888–1935). He is recognized as the greatest Portuguese poet since Camões. Pessoa's influence was full and intense. Not only was he immensely popular with his readers, but his followers paid him the highest compliment. His works, moods, and ideas were models for the poets of the 1940s and 1950s. The introspection, subjectivity, and intellectual quality of Pessoa's verse were matched in widely read novels such as those of *Raul Brandão*. Brandão's stories were essentially philosophical meditations and conversations with himself.

Aquilino Rebeiro authored more than seventy novels, stories, and other works. His early works were based upon the rustic life of Beira. A contemporary and another author with a regional focus was *Miguel Torga* from the province of Trás-os-Montes. While both of these writers dwelt on the harsh existence in rural Portugal, Torga took it one step further with his criticism and ridicule of the seemingly futile rural existence.

Under the influences of Steinbeck, Hemingway, and Dos Passos, the Portuguese novelists *Jose Maria Ferreira de Castro* and *Fernando Namora* developed a style focusing on social issues and the realistic portrayal of workers, migrants, and peasants. Ferreira de Castro won international acclaim for his novel *The Jungle* (1930) and its treatment of migrant workers in Brazil. Namora is best known for his *Fields of Fate*, a narrative dealing with the hardships of the peasants in Alentejo.

Thus far in the twentieth century, no publication has attracted more attention than the *Nova Cartas Portuguesas* (New Portuguese Letters). Likewise, no Portuguese writers have attracted more notoriety than the three "Marias": *Maria Teresa Horta*, *Maria Isabel Barreno*, and *Maria Fatima Velho da Costa*. The trio compiled an exchange of stories, letters, poems, all with a common theme. The theme lamented the repression of women by men and the social institutions created by man. Some critics call it a landmark of feminist literature, and it has received some attention outside of Portugal. Within the country the book was immensely popular.

Music

The music of Portugal was dominated by the church through the seventeenth century, since all formal musical training was under the tutelage of the clergy. Later, in the eighteenth century, the courts of *João V* and *Jose I* boasted of, apparently, the liveliest musical life in all of Europe at the time. Both lavished money and attention on composers, teachers, and virtuosos. During this period, *Carlos Seixas*, perhaps the best known Portuguese musical figure, composed his scores for organ and keyboard. King Jose's musical tastes also influenced the opera, which flourished under his patronage.

Opera remains the most popular serious musical form in Portugal. Lisbon is a regular stop on the itineraries of the major European touring opera companies. The center for the opera is the *National Theater (Teatro São Carlos)* at Rossio. There are smaller local opera companies that perform at the smaller *Teatro da Trindade*. The repertoire of the *Portuguese Opera Company* includes primarily Italian operas, but at least one Portuguese opera is performed each season.

The *Lisbon Philharmonic* is alive and well and performs at the *Teatro Municipal de São Luiz*. *The Gulbenkian Orchestra and Chorus* performs at the Gulbenkian Foundation's main auditorium.

Painting

Painting, as an art form, arrived late in Portugal. Its early development occurred as late as the fifteenth century under the influence of Flemish artisans. The dominance of the Flemish primitive style was confirmed by the sizable contingent of Portuguese craftsmen who worked as apprentices in the workshops of Flanders. The bright panels these painters produced portrayed daily life with accuracy and precision. The patronage that determined the taste in Portuguese painting until the mid-sixteenth century was made possible by the profits from trade in colonial goods with Flanders and its great markets of Ghent and Antwerp.

Probably the most famous and finest result of the Flemish influence is the magnificent *Adoration of St. Vincent,* by *Nuno Gonçalves.* His contempories produced some sensitive and tasteful works but none to match his in terms of execution and style. Other artists in the years following Gonçalves have matched his standard of excellence.

During this period, charts, maps, and atlases were produced as high art. Corresponding to interest in the new world, discoveries and commensurate curiosity about the world in general, maps became an extremely popular form of artistic expression. The most famous were those of mapmaker *Fernão Vaz Duorado.* He is credited with raising the craft of cartography to a significant artform. Today, replicas of those splendid spatial renditions are still popularly displayed in many public spaces and private homes.

Times change and tastes change as well. Portuguese taste shifted to Italian styles and modes after the mid-sixteenth century. When this shift was made, Portuguese artists failed to move with the flow and lost any gains of the previous century. In comparison to the blossoming of artistic achievement in Spain, Portuguese painting lacked imagination and originality. The so-called "Portuguese School" (actually two factions centered on Évora-Lisbon and Viseu) produced repetitious, Dutch-influence canvases and panels of little interest to the critics and patrons of the arts.

Into the nineteenth century, *Domingos Antonio Sequeria* was the only Portuguese painter to attract any attention outside of the country. Some critics compared his portraits to those of Spanish master Francisco Goya, although the two artists apparently never met. Sequeira's greatest works were his charcoal drawings, produced a few years before his death in 1837.

Portuguese artists in the nineteenth century tended to lag further and further behind their European contemporaries. Little inspiration or originality is offered in the popular paintings of *Silva Porto, João Malhoa,* and *Sousa Pinto.* Probably the best known painter of the era was *Columbana Pinheiro.* Pinheiro's works evoke some positive response, and many are worth a second look. The works of these painters are well represented in the galleries of Lisbon, but they are virtually unknown outside of the country.

During the twentieth century as the result of Salazar's advocacy of a so-called "national style," nothing of note was produced. Portugal's most promising artists left the country because of the oppressive atmosphere in the arts. For example, *Maria Helena Vieira da Silva*, Portugal's most gifted artist of the era, left in 1929. Others with any promise also sought inspiration elsewhere. During the first two-thirds of the present century, the Portuguese public was reluctant to accept contemporary twentieth-century art. After the revolution, however, attitudes changed and a less conservative and critical public allowed, and even embraced, the trends of the late twentieth century.

Exhibits are found everywhere—the Casino in Estoril, restaurants, *Tourismo* offices, private galleries, and so on. The most well known post-revolution artists include *Noronha da Costa, Eduardo Nery, Manuel Baptista, Antonio Palolo, Fatima Vaz,* and *João Abel Manto. Jose de Guimarães* is Portugal's most prestigious artist of today. His work is widely recognized throughout Europe.

Architecture

The architecture of Portugal is richer and more flamboyant than its heritage of the canvas and brush. In fact, the creative architectural legacy began in the twelfth century. This was the castle-building era. Many fine examples of the fortresses built in that era still stand today. Castles, like any architectural form, had style. Some were fancy, some plain. Others followed fashion and were copies of trend-setting castles elsewhere. The largest castle in Portugal still dominates the city of Bragança. The great fortification at *Amieira* is modeled after the Crusader castles in Syria. The Lisbon fortification, Castle St. George, is similar to Italian models of the same period. Throughout the entire country, one can find numerous impressive structures built during that time period. The imposing, majestic, and stately styles of the world's castle builders all exist in Portugal. For the student of castle construction, Portugal is an excellent classroom.

During this flurry of castle building in the twelfth to fourteenth centuries, cathedral building also flourished. During that era, construction commenced on the four great Romanesque cathedrals at Lisbon, Porto, Coimbra, and Évora, as well as hundreds of smaller village and town churches.

The religious order of Cistercian monks played the most influential role in early architectural styles. The French friars' style was rather austere in appearance. For example, in their monasteries the monks cultivated a functional architectural style that served the monastic life well and eventually, because of its pleasing form, became the basis of the architectural mode of Portugal. The best example, the *Monastery at Batalha*, reflects the simplicity of design and the simple beauty that inspired many ecclesiastical structures thereafter.

The earliest Gothic structures date from the late thirteenth century. Although all styles of architecture common throughout Europe can be found in Portugal, few examples remain in their original state. Most of the medieval church buildings have been changed or embellished over the centuries as kings and queens vied with their forebears to leave individual imprints on the nation's great buildings.

Portugal's most original contribution to European architectural expression was the so-called *Manueline* design. The style was named for King Manuel, under whose reign the style developed and flourished. *Jeronimos Monastery* at Belém is the prime example of Manueline expression. Elsewhere the style was used to embellish porches, portals, and windows. Its development coincides with the Age of Discovery and Portuguese colonization. The style, therefore, has been deemed an expression of that age. Manueline design has been described as sonorous, exuberant, opulent, and sometimes mellow. Many of the details of Manueline decoration, in keeping with the great adventures taking place during that age, are of nautical motifs, sea life, figures of angels, and knights in armor. The first use of the Manueline concepts was in the *Church of Jesus* at *Setúbal*, but clearly the *Tower of Belém* stands as the most striking and visible example. Other exemplary Manueline-style structures include the *Convent of Christ* at *Tomar*, and the unfinished cloister at *Batalha*. The latter's detail is so intricate that it rivals the Moorish carvings at the Alhambra.

Renaissance style became vogue in Portugal from about 1550 through the seventeenth century. Because of the patronage of its bishops, the city of *Braga* became a center of baroque architecture in the early eighteenth century. Probably the most extravagant products of the period were the monastery and palace at *Mafra*. Constructed in the baroque style, the immense complex of buildings must be seen to be appreciated.

After the 1755 earthquake, the *Marquis de Pombal* dictated the reconstruction of central Lisbon in a severe Neo-palladian architectural style set in a rectangular-grid street plan. Known now as the *Pombaline* style, it was favored for twenty years and was considered the only acceptable style of bureaucrats and military engineers.

Into the nineteenth century, a new age of construction unfolded. Many of structures remain in Lisbon. The city itself is a collection of eclectic imitations of past styles. Throughout the city, there are myriad examples of the building boom of the nineteenth century.

Twentieth century architecture has seen little encouragement in innovation. Apartment and office buildings since the 1950s have all had a similar international-style look. Truly innovative designs are few. A good example of elegant innovation, however, is the *Gulbenkian Foundation* complex. Another project worthy of note is the *Infante Santo* project in Lisbon. Newer apartment-hotels along the Estoril Coast and in Algarve are showing some interesting variations of Mediterrean designs.

Sculpture

Examples of sculpture produced by Portuguese artisans are, to say the least, rare. The tombs of *Pedro and Ines* at *Alcobaça* (ca. 1360) are two of the best of the few examples of Gothic-style sculptures remaining in Portugal. These are outstanding, detailed sculptures with superb artistic rendering. Most early ecclesiastical sculpture was, however, accomplished by English and French sculptors.

The Manueline epoch saw few sculpted works despite its great architectural achievements. An exception was the work of a gifted artist named *Machado de Castro*, who helped design the statuary at Mafra and created the equestrian statue of *King Jose* in *Praça do Comerçio* in Lisbon. De Castro was the product of the "Mafra School," a group of imported sculptors commissioned not only to embellish the basilica and monastery but also to teach their art to promising Portuguese artists.

In the nineteenth and twentieth centuries, the preference in sculpture was definitely neoclassical, romantic and heroic. Two of the more prominant twentieth-century works are the *Monument to the Discoveries* at Belém (1960) and *Christo Rei* overlooking the river at Almada.

Without doubt, the height of Portuguese artistic achievement is in the form of ceramic tiles. These functional as well as decorative tiles of Portugal are known as *azulejos*. Their history is formidable.

More than three centuries of development and refinement makes the *azulejos* a distinctive national art form.

Tile making became a nationwide industry in the late sixteenth century. Eventually, the art of painting tiles evolved and was uniquely cultivated in Portugal. The art form was probably introduced by the Moors during their domination of the Iberian peninsula, but not until Delft tiles were imported and Flemish craftsmen produced similar tiles in Portugal did the painted-tile industry actually develop locally. Most production centered in Lisbon, but there were also factories in Coimbra and Porto. For the past two hundred years, Portuguese *azulejos* have been a part of exterior and interior environments. They have become a vital expression of art and ornament of the Portuguese people. The tiles inform and entertain the beholder. The tiles expressed a message and a feeling from the maker. They are a Portuguese treasure. Their decorative concepts are unique, far surpassing Spanish *azulejos* in their original purpose and application.

Azulejos have a varied appearance, each according to the tilework's intended use. Some designs are purely geomoetric or stylized with the singular purpose of embellishing a surface. Some tiles have been painted with scenes of everyday life or even a written message for advertising. They have been placed on every conceivable surface, both interior and exterior. As you travel through the country, look for them. It is this surprise of purpose and application in the most unlikely places that often makes them noteworthy. Some panels of tiles cover entire church facades of public buildings. Some smaller panels are garden centerpieces or religious pictures. Each is one of a kind. The *azulejos* remain as a distinctive and discrete feature of Portuguese architectural design.

The Portuguese also found wood an amenable medium of artistic expression. Abreast of the fantastic artistic achievement in painted tiles, wood carving reached a high level of development. The Portuguese skill in woodworking flourished in the fifteenth century when the fine woods brought from Madeira (which means "wood") and the Orient, as well as Brazil, were used to create entire carved interiors to cover bare Gothic walls. Still found throughout the country are altarpieces, ceilings, and ornate baroque ornaments of the seventeenth and eighteenth centuries. The craft reached its climax in the eighteenth century. To view the best of the best, visit the Dominican *Convent of Jesus* at Aveiro (1725). The carved wood apse of the church is considered to be a masterwork of the wood carvers' art. The baroque carvings include altars, columns, and a coffered ceiling. The chancel is of particular interest to anyone who studies the rich and elaborately carved decoration. An added touch of intertwined exuberance is the positioning of the *azulejos* panels depicting the life of Santa Joana.

Handicrafts

Portuguese handicrafts have not been overshadowed by industrial standardization. In fact, the folk traditions of Portugal are alive and well. There is an extraordinary wealth of folk handicraft. The myriad items reflect a regional variation, each with a distinct character. Markets are everywhere in Portugal, and at these markets you can find authentic pieces of folk art: multicolored ceramics in fanciful forms, glazed earthenware, quilts, rugs, carvings, wine-cask spigots, peasant clothing, traditional costumes, religious items, and filigree jewelry. Such treasures abound. Even if you cannot visit a market, you can enjoy and purchase the handicrafts of Portugal in the many tourist-oriented shops in the cities and towns.

In the northern region of Portugal, the predominant handicrafts are of gold and silver. The typical gold jewelry of the town of *Viana do Castelo* includes necklaces and earrings, often in heart designs. The famous gold and silver filigree articles are produced at *Gondomar*. Highly prized and reasonably priced examples of this artwork can be found in Lisbon at many shops. It is genuinely an art. The artisans shape gold or silver strands into intricate metal lace in the form of hearts, ships, butterflies, or anything they fancy at the moment of inspiration.

In the north also look for the costumes and aprons with embroidered pockets typical of the Viana do Castelo area. Also look for damask silk and merino shawls. Here you can find embroidered shirts and great woolen fisherman's sweaters and jerseys from *Póvoa de Varzim*. These can be purchased in Lisbon, too. For pottery, go to *Barcelos*. The glazed and painted earthenware objects and figures are well known. Best known is the famous *Barcelos rooster*, which has become a symbol of Portugal. No tourist should leave the country without buying one of these brightly painted, stylized cockerels. They come in all sizes, but the decoration is standard.

The Portuguese are happy to tell the legend of the Barcelos cock, and the tourist will probably hear it many times. The story is an interesting one. It seems that a pilgrim on his journey to the town of Santiago do Compostela was stopped as he was leaving Barcelos and accused of thievery. Despite his innocence, he could not muster a reasonable defense and was found guilty and sentenced to hang. Invoking the aid of St. James and noticing the judge was about to have lunch of roasted rooster, the pilgrim made one final plea. He declared that if he was innocent, St. James would make the roasted bird come alive and crow. A miracle did happen, and the cock crowed. After the man was set free, the judge built a monument in memory of the strange occurrence. Today the little birds are ubiquitous.

In addition to the everpresent rooster, look for earthenware figurines in the shape of oxen, religious figures, and the well-known brass-band musicians. You can collect an entire miniature band. In *Vila Nova de Gaia*, look for the painted figurines. The glazed plates of *Prado* are also worth a look. In the north is the town of *Espinho*. Here you can buy the characteristic painted furniture and decorated and carved ox yokes. In addition, the entire region is rich in basketwork, clogs, and local statuary carved from granite.

South of Porto to just north of Lisbon, the area known as the *Costa de Prata* (silver coast) is noted for the famous potteries of *Alcobaça* and *Caldas da Rainha*. The Alcobaça pottery stresses shades of blue, while that from the Caldas da Rainha area is made into fanciful shapes and colored to resemble cabbage leaves, vines, and fruit. Tourists find these dishes, plates, and other functional items irresistible. At *Aveiro* look for the faience wine jugs with elaborately painted decorations. In *Vista Alegre* note the handsome ornamental porcelain. There is excellent glassware made in *Marinha Grande*. In *Nazaré* you can buy articles of fishermen's traditional costumes, such as hats, socks, shirts, kerchiefs. Also, be sure to look for the small handmade replicas of the local fishing boats. They are a good buy.

The full-size genuine fishing vessels of Portugal are masterpieces of boat building. The boats can vary in size and type, but they all share some common characteristics. Most are made from yellow pine. The frames are sawed rather than bent to shape. Natural crooks in the wood are used for pieces such as breasthooks, knees, and stems. Guardrails and bilge keels are applied to the frame rather than to the hull planking. All the boats are brightly painted and usually have names of religious origin. The overriding and important characteristics of Portuguese fishing boats are their extreme strength and fine workmanship.

The city of *Peniche* is one of the best areas for the purchase of bone lace. Some excellent workmanship and exceptional buys are available. Since much of the lace is produced by the women of the city in their homes, many pieces are displayed for sale at individual family residences. A visitor can usually negotiate the best bargains in the homes. Someone intent on a purchase need only look carefully for a sign with the word *"Renda"* (lace). This town is also a good place to study the fishing boats.

The most tradition-bound and least modern area of Portugal is in the northeast. In the area known as *Beira Alta* you will find baskets and mats of incredible variety. Wrought-iron objects are found throughout the region. You can buy mirrors, doorposts, and even spiked collars worn by the sheep dogs of the region. In the area known as *Trás-os-Montes*, furniture is carved and painted in characteristic form. In *Viseu* look for beautiful brass and exquisite cabinets. For linen go to *Guarda* and *Pinhel*. Also note the typical heavy serge costumes worn by the peasants. Some people will find the fastidiously embroidered linen tablecloths and napkins irresistible, while others will buy the woolen and cotton quilts. You can even buy straw capes, silk hoods, and rare and delicate black pottery at *Bisalhais* and *Moledos*.

In the vicinity of Lisbon, you will see glazed earthenware at *Mafra* and *Ericeira*. Miniature windmills are interesting tourist curio items in the region as well as baskets and ceramic statues. The marble objects at *Pero Pinheiro* and *Montelavas* are worth a look. Be aware of the choice wooden objects and oil paintings in *Sintra*, *Cascais*, and *Estoril*.

South of Lisbon on the plains of *Ribatejo* and *Alentejo*, look for the green and red caps typical of the bull herders. The peasant wear of the Alentejo includes fox-collar jackets, sheepskin vests, and leggings.

Arraiolas rugs are the most famous of all handicrafts in Portugal. These beautiful, expensive, and high-quality rugs are produced in the town of the same name. The weaving of the delicate patterns in these rugs flourished in the eighteenth century and fortunately continues today. The product is, indeed, world renown and highly regarded. You can choose from a selection of ready-made rugs or select a pattern or color combination to be woven to your own specifications. Tourists should be prepared to pay approximately $100 per square yard. These rugs are not cheap souvenirs.

The art of the shepherds can be seen in the form of wooden spoons, interesting decorative pieces, and puzzling objects such as chains carved from a single piece of wood. Cork is produced in this southern region, and you can find many items made from the product. Almost anything imaginable can be fashioned from cork. Most of these cork artifacts can be purchased in shops specializing in the medium. Copper kitchen utensils are also good buys and made of high quality materials and unsurpassed workmanship. Antique cow bells, and crystallized fruit are popular items at Évora. Less durable but equally interesting are the painted paper images of the saints.

The Algarve is famous for articles made of cane and wicker. Look for baskets and rush mats at *Loule, Albufeira,* and *Silves.* Algarve is also famous for its ornate chimneys. Miniatures of the intricate designs are available. Copper and brass utensils are of good quality in *Porches.* In *Monchique* you can purchase chestnut-wood chests, spoons, and other kitchen utensils. Straight-backed chairs, stools, saddles, earthenware, fishermen's floats, and the very interesting *cataplana* pan are all superior craft buys in Algarve.

There are certain craft items that seem to be ubiquitous in Portugal. They include inexpensive but high quality woolen goods. Shop around for low prices. Prices tend to be lower in nontourist centers. Cork objects of every design are found throughout the country. Pottery, either glazed, unglazed, or painted can be purchased everywhere. Regional variations make this pottery interesting. *Azulejos* tiles are commonly sold in the shops of Lisbon and other cities and towns. Authentic antique *azulejos* are available in Lisbon and Porto. Antique *azulejos* are not inexpensive, but because of the relatively large supply, some good buys remain. The newer, more modern tiles are an excellent buy if you shop carefully. Some tiles are merely cheap imitations for the tourist trade.

The most popular, well-known, and highest quality crafts are generally available throughout the country. Lisbon, of course, is the center for handicraft shopping of immense diversity. The assortment is astounding. Look for shops with signs reading *"Artigos Regionais"* or *"Artesanato."*

Housing

The house types of the common people often vary from region to region and offer a study of cultural history, climate, and craftsmanship. In Portugal few houses of traditional style are constructed with more than one story. The houses of rural farm families of the north tend to have attached stables and storage buildings. The building material is granite in the northern regions of Minho and Beira. The northeastern Trás-os-Montes region produces homes with shale roofs. This is startling at first since travelers are conditioned to expect orange-tile roofs to enhance any Portuguese scene.

In the coastal areas and the province of Estremadura, houses are built of easily cut and worked limestone. Stucco is a common finish. In the bright Alentejo province the houses are always whitewashed. Traditional houses are constructed from locally produced adobe bricks. Windows and doors are small but style seems to be important here. Very common in Alentejo are the many decorative embellished additions, such as fancy chimneys and verandas. All whitewashed houses have been trimmed with a dark color to highlight each window, door, and architectural line.

In Algarve, one begins to note considerable Moorish influence in the house styles. The flat roof is definitely of North African origin. Arches are observed everywhere. One feature, the chimney, is in every respect distinctive. Today miniature chimneys are marketed as a symbol of Algarve. Some are so elaborately decorated and stylized that they have no chimney function. Truly beautiful, the slender, elegant filigree tops are always tidy and have a ball, a vase, or an ornament of some sort to finish the delicate structure with a flourish.

Modern houses are built of precast terra-cotta bricks, poured concrete floors, and a stucco finish that is tiled or whitewashed. There is no appreciable use of wood in the framing of Portuguese homes. The forest resource is long gone. Even the construction techniques of the traditional rural houses use wood sparingly. The construction of modern homes is even less extravagant with the use of wood.

Windmills and Pillories

The windmill is another noteworthy feature of rural Portugal. Many windmills built centuries ago remain in use today. The most common is the picturesque Mediterranean type. The tapered cylinder of the tower is usually constructed of durable mortared stones covered with a finish of stucco. Always painted white, the tower is capped by a conical roof from which the mast protrudes. Usually the mast holds four triangular sails. When spinning with the wind, doing the work for which they were intended, the mills are a winsome sight indeed. Some farmers attach small clay jugs to the sail ropes. The small jugs whistle in the wind as the mill performs its task. Alas, each year there are fewer and fewer functioning windmills as modern technology provides easier ways to pump water or grind grain. Cleverly, many abandoned mills are being purchased by wealthy city people and converted into country weekend cottages.

The pillory is one item noticeable in nearly every Portuguese village or town. Usually located near the town hall, pillories were ancient symbols of government power. Portuguese pillories are pillars of stone, not the more familiar wooden frames. Originally, they were plain pillars to which wrongdoers or thieves were chained or bound. But during the middle ages, pillories took on a more ornate appearance, often capped by intricate stone carvings. Today they are gathering places for teenagers in the center of small towns. Look for them; they are not difficult to find. Now they are at the heart of the fun, having lost all of their ominous function of days long past.

Mosaic Sidewalks

Mosaic sidewalks are another feature seen in most cities and towns, helping to make this small Iberian nation unique and engrossing. The mosaic pavement is called *calçada* in Portuguese, and the small black and white cubical stones are known as *brita*. Most *brita* is quarried near Sintra and Mafra. The practice of paving sidewalks and roadways in this manner dates back many years. Unfortunately, some of the uneven surfaces of the primary roads are being repaved with asphalt. The result is a rough and noisy ride. But on sidewalks, the mosaic effect is magical. Sometimes the elaborate designs cause an interesting optical illusion. For example, the wavelike pattern on the *Av Dom Carlos* in Cascais in front of the Cascais town hall provides an intriguing visual experience.

This age-old mosaic paving method is the job of the *calçeteiros*. These men are the skilled workers often seen busily setting each precut block 3 in. by 3 in. in place, according to a predetermined template design. Sometimes a good fit is achieved only by precise shaping or trimming of the stones. The designs can be quite elaborate and intricate, so shaping the *brita* is an important task.

After the stones have been set in a sand base, more sand is sifted over the new surface, which is then tamped and swept to produce a reasonably uniform surface. The art form is at its highest on the sidewalks of the *Avenida da Liberdade* in Lisbon.

There are advantages and disadvantages to this paving method. The advantages include their unique beauty and charm and the ease with which it is possible to excavate beneath the pavement. No heavy machinery is required to remove or replace the pavement. The disadvantages are many, however, if the pavement is uneven or has missing blocks, as is so often the case, walkers must beware at all times. As mentioned earlier, tourists unaccustomed to the uneven pavement are amazed at the ability of local women in high heels to negotiate the uneven pavement so easily. On the other hand, tourists can easily slip or trip as they gawk at some outlandish sight or turn to look at something worth a second glance.

Even with the problems attendant to the paving method, Portugal without the sidewalk mosaics is unimaginable. How dull the sidewalks would be! How dull Alfama would be if the streets, lanes, alleys and *largos* were covered with concrete or asphalt! The thought is repugnant. Fortunately for Portugal and the world, the custom seems to be here to stay as long as the cost of labor remains relatively low and this attractive addition to the urban scene is appreciated.

Cultural Miscellany

Visitors to Portugal, particularly those planning extended stays, must endure much: menus they cannot read, lines at the post office, autos having the right-of-way, taxi drivers with no fear, and, of course, the uneven pavements. Some would argue that such is a small price to pay for the myriad positive attributes of Portugal.

There are many enjoyable aspects of the country, but one of them is not graffiti. It seems that some slogan or message is painted or scrawled on every available private or public wall. It is epidemic and seems never to end. As one slogan fades, another replaces it. There are still remnants of the revolutionary slogans dating back to 1974. Who does the writing on the wall? To be sure, it is a small minority, but that minority seems to have a huge supply of paint. It is not nearly as bad as in the New York subways, but most urban scenes are interrupted by graffiti. Fortunately, churches seem to have been spared, as well as trains and other public transport. But all other structures constitute canvases awaiting the graffiti artists.

Some of the more common slogans include: *"Greve Geral!"* (General Strike!); *"Governo Rua!"* (Government Out!); *"Não Pagaremos!"* (We will not pay!); *"PCP No Governo!"* (PCP party [communists] into the government!); *"A Luta Continua!"* (The struggle continues! This dates from 1974); *"Reagan fora de aqui!"* (Reagan out of here!); *"Carter fora de Portugal!"* (Carter out of Portugal!); *"EUA fora de Grenada!"* (USA out of Grenada!); *"Unir o pova!"* (Unite the people!). From this sample, it appears to the casual observer that Portugal is anti-American, pro-communist and very revolutionary. Not so! The small minority with the huge paint supply gives the impression of wide support, but the politics of the government and the people are very much pro-U.S.A., pro-west, and pro-NATO. There is discontent, however, with rising prices and the continuing economic problems. One of the wall slogans that does have wide support is this: *"Os ricos que paguem a crise!"* (Let the rich pay for the crisis!)

Posters, a European passion, are also a highly visible part of the urban environment. Posters advertising plays, art exhibits, political rallies, political opposition, charities, fairs, and festivals are pasted on most available space. Unfortunately, they tend to deteriorate and peel, leaving hundreds of unsightly ads dangling from the walls until the next poster onslaught arrives. The trend is to paste not just one poster but dozens at a single location. With the increasing cost of posters, this practice is losing out to the graffiti artists in most Portuguese urban areas.

Portuguese cemeteries are morbid. Stop in a small village cemetery next to a church or visit the immense cemetery in Lisbon, the *Cemetério do São João* near Madre de Deus, for a glimpse. There is a strong emphasis on entombment and on visible remembrances. For example, many burial sites will have pictures, locks of hair, or

personal possessions on display. Some of the crypts even offer a
view of the coffin inside. Cemeteries are solemn places, and picture
taking is not regarded favorably. Note the tall stately pinnacles of
the everpresent cedar trees. Cemeteries are the only places where
these trees are grown in Portugal; they always denote cemetery
locations.

More pleasant surroundings are the gardens of Portugal. Lisbon
is a city of great gardens: *Estufa Fria, Jardim Botanica, Estrela,* and
others. What the Portuguese lacked in the art of paintings, sculpture, and music, they made up wholeheartedly in *azulejos,* wood
carving, and landscape gardening. The people seem to have an
inherent ability to design public and private open spaces that are
appealing and have consummate style. Open space is precious in
the big cities, but wherever there is space, you can find flower
gardens, landscaped nooks and crannies, and *azulejos* fountains. In
Cascais there is a particularly pleasing space called *Guimarães Gardens.* The park lies attached, incidentally, to one of the noble residences open to the public, which is on the coast road beyond the
old fort. The house's interior is spectacular, but people are drawn to
the gardens, the manicured and tastefully laid out landscaped
areas. There is a delightful but small aviary deep in the enchanting
park. The centerpiece, however, is the genteel *azulejos* fountain.
The garden is typical of those in Porto, Évora, Lisbon, Braga,
Setúbal, and other places in Portugal.

There are more utilitarian gardens too. Vegetable plots seem to
occupy all available growing space. The nature of the economy
dictates that families grow as many vegetables as possible to sup-
plement their income and diet. The result is that rail rights-of-way,
terraces in apartment buildings, empty fields, side yards, and any
sunny spaces are converted to vegetable production. Most popularly produced are greens, particularly cabbage and kale. These can
be produced year-round. Crops of beans, tomatoes, and lettuce are
lovingly cultivated in the most unlikely spots. Watch for them. You
will be amazed at how cleverly small plots can be utilized.

There are many traditional features common to most of Portugal.
In combination, they leave a favorable impression on the observer.
These include orange-tile roofs, lace curtains hung neatly in tiny
windows, birds in cages, tile floors imitating rugs, small doors with
oriental-style cornices, well-scrubbed entryways, jacaranda trees,
wisteria vines, jade trees of incredible size, geraniums flourishing
everywhere, and exotic shrubbery growing in unattended crevises.

A careful look at each train station reveals a small garden for flowers and shrubs and perhaps even vegetable plots maintained by the employees.

Watch at the train crossings. Note that there are few automatic lights or gates. In rural areas each crossing has a hut or small home, a manually operated gate, and a person on duty at all times. The function of these individuals is to close the gate and signal the oncoming train with a green flag if the crossing is clear. A red flag is used until all traffic is stopped. The speed of most modern trains in rural areas has rendered the system obsolete. It is unlikely a train could be stopped in the distance and time allowed with the use of these visual signals. The system is archaic and probably unsafe, but it is interesting to watch. In exchange for twenty-four-hour vigilance, the crossing keeper occupies the small house gratis. Fortunately for the safety of the traveling public, the system is changing. Within the next decade Portugal will convert to an automated, computer-assisted rail system that will be much safer. Some of the rural charm will be lost to modernity, but in this case, safety wins.

CHAPTER 10

Events and Things to Do:
Never a Dull Moment

What can a traveler do between visits to museums, monasteries, and castles? There are myriad activities to occupy one's time. Many tourists prefer to relax at a beach café, reading or trying to decifer the Portuguese lottery system. Others will surely prefer to be more active as they contemplate the wonders of the next museum or anticipate the next savory Portuguese meal.

What about a swim? Hotels outside of the city of Lisbon generally provide well-maintained swimming pools *(piscina)*. The water at the beaches along the Estoril coast, although clear and pretty to view, may not be entirely safe for swimming. But all of the major resort hotels along the Estoril Coast have swimming pools. Guests of hotels, of course, have pool privileges, others can also pay to use the hotel pools. The cost is minimal: a few hundred *escudos* per day.

The large *Hotel Estoril Sol* in Monte Estoril has the largest and best pool. The *Tamariz Restaurante, Café,* and *Beach Club* in Estoril also has a saltwater pool. The Tamariz facility, across the road from the casino and right on the beach, meets nearly every need for sun and water activities: cabañas, umbrellas, lounge chairs, showers, private sunbathing areas, lockers, sailboards, refreshments, and shops. Al'' ough the restaurant and café are open all year, the pool and other popular facilities are available only from April to November. If one takes the train from Lisbon to Cascais, Tamariz is on the left as the train stops at the Estoril station. The Hotel Estoril Sol is at the very next stop (*Monte Estoril* station).

The smaller hotels, such as the *Hotel Paris, Hotel Atlantico, Angleterra, Londres,* and others in the Cascais–Estoril resort area have smaller but less-crowded swimming pools. These too are available for use at a nominal charge.

The Estoril Coast beaches, as mentioned, are attractive but may not be entirely safe for swimming. These beaches are located at the mouth of the Tagus (Tejo) River, which drains much of the Iberian peninsula.

Riding the train from Lisbon to Cascais, one will note many beaches. Some are attractive and some are not. Beyond the station called *Paço de Arcos*, the river technically ends, the estuary widens, and the Atlantic Ocean begins. There is a noticeable difference in water quality. It is not suggested that the tourist use any of the beaches east of Paço de Arcos station. Even beyond *Oeiras, Carcavelos, Parede,* and *São Pedro,* the beaches are questionable. The first truly lovely beach to consider is the beach at *São João,* but the next two stops, *Estoril* and *Monte Estoril,* are definitely the preferred beach areas.

Beginning at the Estoril station and the Tamariz facility, there is a beautifully constructed, spacious, and pleasant seawall prominade that meanders along the beach to Cascais. The two kilometer (approximately 1.2 miles) walk is relaxing and scenic as it passes rocky shoals and four small crescent-shaped sandy beaches. The vistas of sea and shore are spectacular. This is the favorite haunt of strolling English tourists. On Sunday afternoons the prominade is brimming with Portuguese families enjoying the sun and fresh air. This is where old fishermen gather in the spring to catch the abundant *pescado* (whiting). This is where young and old stroll to catch a glimpse of the topless sunbathers. Visitors can stop for an ice cream, a beer, a glass of wine, or a soft drink at the several itinerant cafés along the way.

At the end of the prominade in Cascais, one is rewarded with a

view of the harbor from above one of the smallest but most picturesque beaches in all of Portugal. To find it one walks beyond the
very elegant *Hotel Albatroz* and through a parking area; one cannot
miss the captivating little *Praia da Rainha* (Queen's Beach). It is a
beautiful spot to view the Cascais harbor and catch a breath before
entering the busy shopping streets of Cascais. There is a rather
fancy restaurant at this point that offers the view but at fancy
prices. Instead, many tourists buy a snack or beverage at a nearby
pastelaria and savor that special space for a few quiet minutes.
Tourists from around the world gather here in small numbers to
meet, chat, and exchange travel stories. It is, after all, a quiet haven
from bustling Cascais shopping. To approach Praia da Rainha via
the principal pedestrian shopping street in Cascais, one merely
follows the street to its terminus.

Beyond the shopping district in Cascais, one can continue the
walk from the fishermen's beach along the shore to the omniously
named *Boca do Inferno* (Hell's Mouth). This is a place of great beauty
but offers no swimming beaches. Here one can relax and enjoy the
sound of the ocean waves crashing into the caves and blowholes.
This is a popular tour-bus stop and as a result the area is crowded
with vendors of Portuguese handicrafts. Nearly all popular items
are available here, and one should not hestiate to bargain for a
lower price. The buyer should never accept the first price tendered.

Beyond Boca do Inferno, along the *Sintra* coast the beaches
improve in quality. *Guincho,* for example, is highly praised for its
wide expanse, heavy surf, and light sands. Most travelers need a
car to get to Guincho. Although it would be a long hike from Boca
do Inferno, some hearty visitors might enjoy the walk along the
cliffs.

Returning to Cascais from Boca, one passes the many mansions
of deposed European royalty, international jet-setters, and old,
moneyed Portuguese families. The view of Cascais harbor toward
the east from near the old fort (now a Portuguese Army training
center) is the best view of the Estoril coast. One can see in the
distance to the castle beyond the Tamariz restaurant in Estoril. If
one prefers to walk, this is the return destination. One could stop
again at Praia da Rainha for a captivating glimpse of the changing
light and its play on the golden cliffs. The return walk to the east
along the seawall prominade is equally impressive. When tide
turns, a new shoreline will emerge or be inundated with the

incoming water. The destination, the Tamariz Café, is just a pleasant walk past the sunbathers, vendors, and swimmers. There is no
rush on the prominade.

Tennis is popular among the wealthier people and English expatriates as well as the diplomatic community. There are, however,
no public tennis courts. Many tennis *(tenis)* clubs and courts are
part of condominium or hotel complexes. These facilities in resort
areas throughout the country have a nominal cost and are generally excellent. The *Tenis Clube,* in Estoril near the Casino, for example, is a lively place frequented by the English and other interested
tourists.

The Casino is a must stop for any Lisbon area visitor. Located in
Estoril, the Casino occupies a surprisingly large piece of land.
Much of the site is occupied by rather elaborate formal gardens.
The gardens are pretty as a whole, but some details are lacking.
Most visitors would agree that the Casino gardens are not the best
in Portugal. The Casino complex is, however, a landmark in Estoril.
All roads lead to it. It is the most important tourist attraction along
the coast.

The Casino is a multi-entertainment facility. The movie theater,
showing first-run American films with Portuguese subtitles, requires the purchase of reserved seats for each showing, but tickets
are very inexpensive by American and British standards.

The Casino also has a nightclub dinner show, Las Vegas style.
For one relatively low price the visitor can enjoy a fine European
meal and an entertaining musical show in an elegant room of
massive proportions. This is a popular place, but because of its
size, reservations are rarely needed. In addition to the main dining
room, visitors can enjoy a drink at one of the two bar lounges in the
Casino building.

The Casino is also the most favored place for Portuguese artists
to exhibit their works. Contemporary artists vie for the attractive
exhibit space. Some worthwhile paintings and sculptures can be
purchased here at reasonable prices. There are additionally several
boutiques or shops that remain open until 1:30 A.M. (0130 hr.)
Other displays of art or handicrafts are often in the lobby area as
well. During the summer months theme exhibits may focus on
regional handicrafts or Portuguese industrial products.

Without doubt the main attractions of the Casino are the gaming
rooms. There are three: the slot-machine room, the main gaming

room, and the bingo room. The bingo room is the scene of an interesting, fast-paced game in which a player can lose money very quickly. Language can be a problem here since the numbers are called only in Portuguese. The called numbers are displayed on TV monitors to enable players to keep track, however. There is no entrance fee to this room, but entry is permitted only during the interval between games.

The slot machine room (*maquinas automaticos*) requires a small entrance fee. The slots are 5$, 25$, 50$ and 100$. The machines are old mechanical one-armed bandits. On any Saturday night, this room is full of Portuguese couples seeking their fortunes.

Entry to the main gaming room requires that one shows one's passport and pay an entrance fee of about five dollars. The featured games include black jack, roulette, French bank, chemin de fer, baccarat and craps. The tables have a low minimum (usually 200$), and a cashier in the room can change currency if one runs low on *escudos*. There is an interesting and original Portuguese dice game called *boulé*. For the uninitiated, it is difficult to follow. The betting is very fast, and one must study the system carefully before entering the betting frenzy. Few tourists are seen at those tables.

Betting outside of the Casino is also common in Portugal. There is an elaborate and difficult-to-understand nationwide lottery (*Lotaria Totoloto*) that is usually not for tourists. It is too complicated to bother with. Another betting system that is fun and understandable is *Totobola*. This is legal betting on the outcome of international soccer (*futebol*) games. Game cards for this weekly lottery are purchased at most tobacco stores (*tabacarias*). The game is played thus: the player indicates winning team choices on a preprinted weekly game card and returns it to the clerk with the appropriate bet (50$ to 500$). Results appear in the newspaper or on television. Winning game cards are cashed at the place of purchase.

Portuguese television is, frankly, not worth watching. The two channels, RTP-1 and RTP-2, are both government supported and managed. The Portuguese Constitution actually prohibits private broadcasting. The one redeeming quality of Portuguese TV is that there are few commercials. There are some, but usually they are bunched together every hour or so. Broadcasting is supported by an annual tax levied against radio and television owners and payable through utility bills. Given the quality of TV programming, it is no wonder that this tax is resented by many Portuguese.

Program schedules seem to be flexible. That is, shows seem to start whenever it is convenient for the person in charge to press the button. Programming consists of old American sitcoms, old English movies, Brazilian soap operas, and locally produced game shows or documentaries of questionable quality. If one is practicing language comprehension, it is good to watch the evening news at 7:00 P.M. (1900 h.). This is the only program one can be sure will start on time. The news stories are short, concise, and numerous. Unfortunately, one cannot expect a serious weather report. To the tourist this can be frustrating. It is very difficult to acquire accurate weather forecasts for Portugal. The evening news gives only the briefest computer-graphics sketch for the northern, central, and southern regions of the country. It is generally so brief that little meaningful information is given or received. During the winter months, in particular, an accurate weather report can be a valuable aid in travel planning. Limited transmissions of *Europa TV*—a few hours everyday—broadcast programs from Italy, Holland, West Germany, and other European countries. Although its programming is limited, this service does have a good weather forecast, focusing on central and northern Europe. Some people suggest this television service may be the catalyst needed to break the state television monopoly. The daily newspapers give some weather forecasts, but they too are not detailed and offer little help in planning.

There is one Portuguese-language newspaper that visitors must consult to know the entertainment possibilities for the week. It is "Sete" or "7." This weekly is available each Wednesday afternoon and lists all the movies playing throughout the country. Weekly TV and radio schedules are given, as well as listings of all other entertainment events. It is a valuable, comprehensive, and understandable source of information.

For the English-speaking visitor there is another weekly newspaper of excellent quality: the *APN* or *Anglo-Portuguese News*. Every Thursday, *APN* hits the newsstands with information on Portuguese news, who's who in the international community, club meetings, happenings and events for English-speaking audiences, church services, classified ads of incredible interest, and articles pertaining to life and living in Portugal. For example, *APN* offers a column entitled "For Your Diary." The column lists upcoming social, sports, club, and church events by month and day, usually with a month's advance notice. Some excerpts include:

Feb. 28—Tagus Golf Society Meeting and Dinner, Estoril Golf Club, 8:00 P.M. American Women of Lisbon Coffee Morning for Arraiolos group, Clubhouse, 10:30 A.M.
Mar. 8—Oporto Ladies' Guild trip to Viana do Castelo.
Mar. 14, 15—Sports Festival, St. Julian's School, Carcavelos.
Mar. 21—Charity Bridge Association Bridge Weekend. Hotel do Mar, Sesimbra.
Apr. 8—Royal British Legion, British Embassy Club, 5:30 P.M.

There are at least two dozen such entries in each issue of *APN*. Published by Nigel Bately in Monte Estoril since 1937, the *APN* is a treasure. It is an indispensible periodical for English-speaking guests on an extended visit and offers an interesting taste of international living for those on a short visit to Portugal. *APN's* audience is composed primarily of British expartriates living in Portugal. The wealth of information helps to compensate for the sometimes frustrating aspects of living in a foreign land.

Golf is an important part of life for many people. If one has the time and the propensity to play a round in the Lisbon area, the best course is the *Golfe Estoril Sol*. The club is located on the Sintra Road between Sintra and Estoril. In Algarve, where the weather is suitable for golfing year round, there are many clubs for the visitor's convenience and pleasure. Some include the *Penna Golf Club* in Montes de Alvar, the *Dom Pedro Golf Clubs* in Vilamoura and Quarteira, the twenty-seven-hole *Golf Club of Vale do Lobo,* and the *Golf Club of Quinta do Lago,* which also has twenty-seven holes. There are a number of smaller courses along the Algarve coast, so a good round of golf is never far away in Algarve.

Portugal's main sporting events include auto racing, soccer *(futebol),* bicycling and, since the 1984 Olympic gold medal win by Portugal, the Lisbon Marathon. Auto racing is very popular in Europe, and it is no less popular in Portugal. Estoril's *autodroma,* or race track, is where Europe's finest drivers compete on the oval and road tracks. Two important racing events occur in Portugal. In March racing fans seek out the *Rallye de Portugal do Vinho de Porto.* The event is a week-long road-rally race that winds throughout the entire country, beginning and ending at the *Autodroma* in Estoril. It is considered by true rally buffs as the world's best. Attracting worldwide attention, the event is at least interesting if not exciting to the average American. The rally attracts millions of Portuguese as they watch the racing vehicles career over their country's highways and byways. This is a exceedingly popular form of racing in Europe but receives little attention in the United States.

Better known in the United States is the Portugal Grand Prix "Formula I" motor race held in the summer on the road track at the *Autodroma*. When Portugal entered the Grand Prix circuit a few years ago, the race went through streets of Lisbon. But crowd control and the inherent dangers of city-street racing prompted officials to move the race to the track. Today the race is growing in prominence in the world of auto racing.

Far and away the greatest spectator sport in the country, and that which grips the attention of most Portuguese, is *soccer*, or *futebol*. The *futebol* teams, as elsewhere, have serious and loyal fans. Many local games are televised, and there is avid interest in all European soccer teams as well. It is impossible to describe the general feeling that the populace holds for this game. Only a true fan could understand. When an important game is to be played (apparently all games have great importance), all work stops. People's ears are glued to their tranistor radios. Bus drivers are oblivious to traffic, old men don't notice young ladies, waiters spend more time in the kitchen than serving customers, and office workers or shoppers gather at store-window television sets or radios. Nothing much is accomplished until the game is won or lost. Attending a game in Lisbon or Porto is worth the effort. It is serious business, so the tourist must choose the team to cheer for carefully.

Professional bicycle racing is also a very popular sport. There are heroes and villains in the world of bicycling just as in auto racing. But what is amazing is that many races take place on weekends on the regular roads and streets amidst the traffic and confusion. Crowds gather to cheer their heroes while life about them goes on as usual.

In Portugal there is no horse racing as known in the United States or Britain. There are no race tracks as such. There is one minor exception in suburban Cascais. One of the condominum associations has established a small track for races on an experimental basis. Time will tell if the experiment is successful. The English love horse racing, and with the large British population and large number of British tourists, it is quite possible it will catch on.

Horse shows and equestrian events other than racing are popular among the British and wealthy Portuguese. There are many and varied events to please the equestrian aficionado. Many of these events are held at the Casino in Estoril. Most of the shows attract a select audience and are not touted to the tourist. For announcements of the various events throughout the country, visitors must see the *APN*.

Dog shows, likewise, are local in scope but unusually well attended by the British community. These official-sounding events are sponsored by the various kennel clubs in suburban Lisbon and the Algarve region.

Other major entertainment events include the many and varied offerings of the highly regarded and respected *Gulbenkian Foundation*. That institution is discussed at length elsewhere in this volume, but for now, it should be known that the Gulbenkian offers top-notch concerts, theater, ballet, and lectures for the visitor's enjoyment. In Lisbon one can also attend the performances of the National Opera Company in the *Teatro National* at Rossio. There are, additionally, small theater groups in Cascais, Porto, and Algarve towns that present plays, musicals, and revues for every taste.

If one becomes very lonely and in need of an English-speaking friend or if one has exhausted all entertainment possibilities, one can check out a book at a quaint and unusual lending library, the *Anglo-Portuguese Library* on Av. Sintra 3, in Cascais (about two blocks from the Hotel Estoril Sol and near the train station). This venerable institution has no signs to indicate its existence, so one must seek it out. The entrance is in the rear of the building off the garden and former laundry area of the villa in which it is housed. It is unique in its basement location, and the staff is an entertaining group of British expatriates trying to keep the English language alive.

In the same building is *AWOL—American Women of Lisbon*—who invite all English-speaking visitors to their clubhouse. This is a good place to make new friends.

Other places to borrow or buy a book include the *British Council Library* in the British Institute in Lisbon (Bairro Alto) on Rua Fernandez, 3. Nearby is the *Livraria Britanico* (the English bookshop), which offers a wide range of titles. It is a comprehensive bookstore for the English-speaking community. It is located on Rua S. Marcal, down from Principe Real.

A new children's lending library has opened in Estoril with a good variety of books. It is on Av. de Biarritz, 14 B.

Without doubt, the most interesting experience in Portugal, to many, is the bullfight *(tourada)*. For pageantry, drama, bravery, machismo, beauty, and good fun, the Portuguese *tourada* is a must.

Anyone in Lisbon on *tourada* night should see it. The bullfights at *Campo Pequeno* are scheduled between Easter and October. Campo Pequeno, the nineteenth-century bullring in Lisbon, should be visited even if a tourist is not attending a *tourada*. It is a unique red-brick Moorish style building with many cupolas. The tiny and dusty museum (that few seem to visit) offers a good sense of the game. One should also visit the little chapel where the *cavaleiros* and the truly brave men of the *forcado* pray for their lives before the fights.

Bullfighting is a sport that evokes mixed emotions. If one has witnessed a Spanish *"corrida,"* one knows of those emotions. The principal difference between the Portuguese and Spanish bullfight is that the bull is not killed in the Portuguese ring. No matter what one feels about Spanish bullfighting, the kill, the moment of truth, is high drama and tends to drain one's emotions. The Portuguese bullfight does not provide that kind of drama, but it does provide an evening of elegant horsemanship, bravery, and excitement. Bulls have not been killed in the Portuguese bullrings since the eighteenth century when the infamous *Marquis de Pombal* outlawed the practice after the death of a friend in the ring. More of a game than a drama, the bulls' horns are now dulled and covered with leather sheaths for safety (such as it is!).

There are no bad seats in Campo Pequeno. The arena is small, and even those in the cheap seats have a good view of the action. Once one is past the delightful but persistent souvenir sellers, the museum, and the chapel and finally seated, the pageantry begins. The bullfights in recent years have suffered in popularity in deference to soccer matches but aficionados of the *tourada* still exist in Lisbon. True aficionados seat themselves in section 1, below the president's box. These people, and others of similar persuasion, are pressing for the reintroduction of the kill in the Portuguese bull-ring. This group is serious! It is interesting to watch them watch the bull.

At 10:00 P.M. (2200 hr.), the fun begins with a signal from the box of the president of the Campo Pequeno. A trumpet announces the ceremonial entrance of the *corrida* in their colorful costumes. Next come the band of young men who make up the *forcado*. They are dressed in snappy green and red capes and look very distinguished—no sign of fear yet. The *bandarilheiros* enter followed by the *cavaleiros,* decked out in their ornate eighteenth-century costumes with the feather-trimmed tricornered hats. The horses, beautiful beasts with rippling muscles and shiny coats, seem to parade in time to the music of pageantry. The first-time visitor is generally enthralled with the ceremony. During second and subsequent visits to the bullring, one will see more details of this ancient spectacle and will be equally thrilled.

After the entourage's elaborate salute to the president, each other, and the gathered public, the ring is cleared. A hush falls over the crowd, a pause, and then a trumpet blare signals the first bull's entry. At this time one should watch the bull carefully. If he hesitates as he charges out of the pen or acts timid, he is not a good bull. If he is spirited and brave and looks alert and mean, it promises to be a good fight and may even please the aficionados. A glance back to section 1 will show the reaction of the aficionados to the animal.

Enter the *cavaleiro*, adorned in his gold-embroidered coat of silk or velvet, silver spurs, and highly polished boots, riding on his fancy steed. The action begins. The bull, now aware of the horse and rider's presence, takes stock of the situation and assumes his territorial stance. With that, the horse and rider prance and taunt the bull into a spectacular charge, which will surely catch the fleet-footed horse. But, no, the bull stops, and again the two adversaries assume their territory. This time the bull charges head-on into the horse, which careens at the last split second while the *cavaleiro* plants the short colorful spear, or *bandarilha*, in the bull's shoulder. Success! The horse resumes its original position. More *bandarilha* are taken, and the *cavaleiro* taunts the bull with *"Ah touro!"* The bull responds violently now because he recognizes the source of his irritation and frustration. After three such hair-raising charges, the horse is changed. Three more *bandarilhas* are strategically placed in the bull's shoulders during the next segment of the exciting spectacle.

When the bull shows signs of tiring and appears unable to respond to continued taunts from the *cavaleiros*, the president signals the beginning of the something the Spanish only dream of: the *forcados!* The bull is tired, but he is not seriously wounded and weakened by the picador as in the Spanish fight. In fact, by the time the *cavaleiros* leave the ring, the bull has regained his liveliness and becomes even more furious and irritated—ready for the fight to continue.

Enter the eight *forcardos*. The leader of the group, wearing a green stocking cap, stands about ten yards ahead of the seven remaining men lined up for the onslaught. The leader, brave one that he is, carefully moves toward the bull in a defiant, hands-on-hips, head-thrown-back posture, yelling, *"Touro, touro!!"* The bull checks him over, wondering what this new menace means. The first *forcado* moves in closer, stamping his right foot. The bull is still puzzled, but some primal instinct tells him this thing must be destroyed. The bull charges with renewed fury. The leader dances lightly backward, measuring the bull's charge carefully as the animal gathers incredible speed, fury, and powerful energy.

Then, at the exact moment that the angry horns rise to attempt to gore the young man, he jumps on the bull's head, grasps the bull around the neck, and hangs on. If all goes well, the remaining men throw themselves on the beast and wrestle it to a standstill. One of them, in charge of the tail, controls the swing of the bull's hind quarters. This fight is known as the *pega*. Often the *pega* is not successful and another attempt is made to subdue the beast. This is very dangerous business. The leader is often carried by the bull, thrown about, and stomped while his brothers in mayhem unsuccessfully try to deal with the fury of the bull's torment. When the bull is finally subdued after one, two, three, or more attempts (the *forcados* never give up), the crowd is ecstatic. More times than not, the *forcados* were wildly cheered, while the *cavaleiros* were applauded.

The danger and thrill of the *pega* are obvious and appreciated wholeheartedly. Only the aficionados understand the real risks taken by the horseman, the split-second timing and the skill of the *cavaleiro*. If you can appreciate this, the show is heart-stopping.

After the first three bulls, there is a much-needed and calming intermission. Now is the time to have some refreshment: beer, wine, or coffee. The *forcados* usually are there too. By now blood-spattered and bruised, they have the smell of the bulls on them. Spectators mingle with them, give them a greeting or shake their hands, buy them a beer. They have earned it. But there is more to come. The second half is about to begin. Now the tourists know what it is all about and can sit back and watch the details—the horses' moves, the *cavaleiros'* costumes, the *forcados'* bravery bolstered with beer. The men in section 1 under the president's box will show signs of approval or disdain. These are the aficionados!

Usually the Thursday-evening Lisbon tradition boasts of six bulls. The spectacle will end at about 1:00 A.M. (0100 hr.).

Other than those in Lisbon's Campo Pequeno, there are bullfights in Cascais during the summer. These are good, to be sure, but the atmosphere of Campo Pequeno is missing. Those who have the chance to visit the towns of *Santarém* and *Vila Franca de Xira* will witness bullfighting at its best. This is the area where the bulls are raised, and the people—all those in the arena—know the best when they see it. Both of these towns are a short train ride or drive from Lisbon.

Bullfighting is not without its critics. For example, the Parliament of the European Economic Community has proposed a ban on bullfights in all member countries, and the Portuguese Animal Rights League has denounced the *corrida* as barbarous, bloody, and cruel entertainment. Visitors to Portugal should witness the spectacle before it is gone forever.

As the reader can see, there are many things to occupy one's time in addition to museums and monasteries. Even the avid museum freak needs a break once in a while. Of course, one can always put oneself quickly to sleep by just watching a little Portuguese television.

CHAPTER 11

Fairs and Festivals: If Only We Were Saints

*F*airs are a way of life in rural Portugal. Every town has its fair, where the tradition prevails for bartering and selling livestock, produce from garden plots, bounty of farms, and handicrafts. Many of these fairs are held regularly. A good example is the market or fair at *S. Pedro de Sintra*. Every second and fourth Sunday of the month the fair takes place. In *Lagos* there is a weekly market or fair each Sunday. These fairs, like so many others in Portugal, are remnants of times past when Sunday, a day consecrated to God, was a day in which everyone would gather in the village or town to attend church service. After church, tradition had it that goods, livestock, and services were exchanged. It was convenient, fun, and practical. In many towns and villages across the land the tradition survives. The goods and produce one can purchase seems limitless. But today there is no significant religious meaning attached to such gatherings. The markets have evolved into commercial ventures only. That is not to say, however, that religion plays no role in the fairs and festivals of the country.

173

In Portugal one can enjoy many country trading fairs associated with religious holidays, feast days, or *romarias* (pilgrimages). Few, if any, pilgrimages exist without a fair. Portugal has many *romarias* and religious celebrations and, therefore, many alluring and enjoyable fairs. In the past the church played a meaningful and powerful role in everyday life. Today the influence of the church has certainly declined, but the traditions associated with the ancient feast days remain alive. The visitor will soon realize that Mary, the Virgin Mother of Christ, is represented in nearly every religious building and throughout secular Portugal. Ask any girl or woman in Portugal and the odds are great that "Maria" is one of her names. Most churches are named in honor of the Virgin, for example, Nossa Senhora da Nazaré and Nossa Senhora da Fatima. Our Lady of Sorrows, Our Lady of Pity, and Our Lady of Wounds are other illustrations. Feelings run deep. The feasts, festivals, and fairs in honor of the Mother of Jesus are not held for the tourists. Most have been celebrated for centuries; tourists have only recently discovered the delights of these country fairs.

In addition to the myriad feasts to honor the Virgin Mary, the saints too have their days. Each city, town, and village has its patron saint. The feast days of those individual saints become times for both prayer and merriment. Over the years the imagination of the Portuguese people has turned these celebrations into true holidays. In Lisbon, for example, the *Popular Saints Day* is an official holiday on which all commercial activity comes to a halt, so that processions, religious services, dancing, eating, and fun can commence. Other towns and cities have similar holidays. Often adjacent towns will celebrate alternate holidays; one town will close its businesses and schools while the other remains operating. Particularly during the month of June, when many of the popular saints' festivities take place, travelers must consult official calendars to predict with accuracy their ability to conduct business or carry out normal activities in the Lisbon-Cascais line of suburban communities. In some towns it may be business as usual. The neighboring town, however, may be celebrating its patron saint. There is never a dull moment.

Fairs are part of Portugal's way of life. The names given by the Portuguese to the days of the week indicate the importance of fairs. Language is always an excellent measure of the meaning of an idea or a thing. If an item or concept does not exist in a culture, it has no corresponding word in the language. The more important it is, the more often it appears in words and variations of words. The Portuguese word for fair is *feira*. The names of the days following Saturday and Sunday (*sabado* and *domingo*) are merely indicators of fair days. Monday is *segunda-feira* or second fair day. Tuesday is *terça-feira*, or third fair day. Friday, *sexta-feira* is the sixth fair day. Sunday (*domingo*) is, of course, the first fair day.

The idea and reality of the fair runs deep in Portugal. Prior to Christmas few fairs take place because all attention is devoted to that major holiday. During the period between Christmas and *Carnivale* few significant fairs are scheduled. *Carnivale* is the last major party before Lent. Since Ash Wednesday is a religious holiday, the day before—Fat Tuesday, Shrove Tuesday, Mardi Gras, or *Carnivale*—is celebrated with gusto. Tradition has it that parties, feasts, and general merrymaking be part of the celebration. This is also the beginning of the spring season. The Portuguese who can afford it often take the days prior to *Carnivale* as time to travel to nearby Spain for the more boistrous Spanish festivities or to relax in Portuguese luxury. In fact, *Carnivale* is the time for local tourism. The foreign tourists have yet to arrive in any great number, and so the week prior to *Carnivale* has become the time to prepare for Lenten sacrifices. Youths who can afford it head south to Algarve for fun in the sun. This is equivalent to the American "spring break." Families fill the *Pousadas*, and singles migrate to the beach resorts. This is the Portuguese vacation time.

The serious fair-goer can find several festivals to attend just prior to *Carnivale*. Some festivals in celebration of *São Bras* are worth a visit. In *Almofrela*, near Porto, the festivals are also called *"Festo dos Salpicões."* *Salipicões* are a type of sausage that is the main feature of a traditional dinner served at the beginning of the festival.

In the town of *Sta. Cruz do Bispo*, near *Motosinhos*, there are processions in honor of São Bras that are reminicent of ancient fertility rites, akin to the rites still performed in remote mountain areas of the country. In these mountain towns, groups of young girls of marrying age climb a small hill covered with blooming mimosas. The chapel of São Bras is on the hilltop. After much prayer, the girls begin to dance around a granite statue called the "apple man." The plea is for his help in finding a husband. The statue is ultimately doused in wine and covered with flowers during the dancing. Viewing this, the tourist cannot fail to be impressed with the interesting mix of Christian and pagan ritual.

In *Nazaré*, São Bras' day is celebrated with copious amounts of grilled sausage, raisins, and pine nuts. The idea of the festival is to pay the saint for all wishes and favors granted throughout the previous year. The payments usually consist of tiles symbolically stolen along a processional route.

In the small town of *Salia* in Algarve, there is the *Festival of St. Louis*. It too is called the "Sausage Festival." After the religious processions, there is an auction sale of fresh local sausages. Grilled ones are sold in abundance during the fun.

Throughout Lent no festivities take place. Good Friday is a national holiday in Portugal. Easter, the major religious holiday, marks the beginning of fair and festival season, which extends well into November. Within that long season of celebrating life, there are a number of nonreligious festivals and fairs. Most have been created in response to a growing demand for organized cultural activities as well as tourism promotion. A superb example is the *Algarve Music Festival*. Others, such as the *Fiartil* (summer fair) of Estoril, are purely for the sale of regional arts and crafts. Many of the festivities are movable feasts so it is important to check the exact dates with a nearby *Tourismo* office. Dates indicated here are approximate.

Toward the end of May and stretching through June, the activities of the Algarve Music Festival usually take place. This fine collection of music and dance performances are staged in the three Algarve cities of *Lagos*, *Portimão*, and *Faro*. Visiting groups include the Gulbenkian Chorus and Ballet and the Lisbon Philharmonic Orchestra, as well as international performers. Mostly classical in style, the concerts often take place in the spectacular and solemn settings of churches, chapels, and cathedrals.

In the province of Algarve during the first week in June, there is also a relatively new but very popular festival. The *National Beer Festival* was first organized by the Silves Football Club and now sponsored by the town of *Silves* and the Algarve Tourist Board. It is five days of fun and merriment on the castle grounds of Silves near Portimão.

Nearby, during the same week depending on scheduling, is the *Algarve Cinema Festival*. About seventy films are shown at various locations in Algarve. Some films are well worth seeing.

June is the month when fairs and festivals take place in earnest. In *Santarém*, for example, another secular fair created in recent years draws thousands of people. It is called the *National Agri-*

cultural Fair and offers exhibits and activities related to the country's farming activity.

Religious festivals and related fairs abound in June. In *Vila Real* the festival is in honor of *São Antonio*. Parades, fireworks, and solemn religious processions honor the town's patron saint.

A series of seminars, parades, folk dancing, and sporting events are included in the week-long festivities taking place at *Fiqueria da Foz* during the *Festival of the Sea*. It is held during the last week in June. In this coastal town, one can watch the traditions of the fisherman, learn the facts of Portugal's fishing industry, partake in a wind-surfing contest, or just watch a parade.

Braga, in the north, celebrates *São João* day with processions, fireworks, and dancing. The whole town joins in the celebration. In fact, Braga, a gray granite-toned town, takes on a new air as it is decorated from one end to the other with brilliant color.

Always on the night of June 23, *Porto* comes alive with dancing, singing, and feasting in the streets and public squares. This is the climax to the *Popular Saint's Festival*, which lasts through the last half of the month. It is a joyous time to visit Porto.

The small town of *Povoa de Varzim* celebrates its *St. Peter's Festival* on June 28 and 29 with candlelight processions, dancing, and copious amounts of grilled sardines and wine.

Sintra's great music festival, which has been held for about twenty-five years, begins the first of July each year. In years past the festival featured the Zurich Symphony Orchestra, resident Portuguese musicians, the National Ballet Company and the Gulbenkian Orchestra. What is wonderful about this festival is that the concerts are performed in places like the Queluz Palace, the Swan Room, the National Palace in Sintra, and the gardens at the Seteais Palace. What settings for great music!

During the middle of July one can enjoy traditional foods and shop for handicrafts at the very popular *Fiartil* (summer fair) in *Estoril*. Its location is a cool pine wooded area opposite the Estoril Tennis Club. The fair, because of the large number of tourists in the area, attracts artisans from all over Portugal and Madeira. A stroll through the fair will take one past at least one hundred different booths, including small cafés serving typical Portuguese food. One can watch bread being prepared and baked in traditional coal ovens and even watch lace being made by hand. If one has not tried grilled sardines, this would be a good place to give them a try. The craft booths, however, are the center of attention. Many of the artisans are in the process of producing fine work. Stone masons, weavers, potters, candy makers, tile makers, and wood carvers all gather to demonstrate their talents. In addition, a stage performance of folk dances takes place at regular intervals throughout the fair. The fair remains open through August and into the first week of September.

At *Ermelo*, on the bank of the Lima River, sits a lovely little chapel that once belonged to the Benedictine monastery. On July 11, an age-old tradition lives on as a procession carrying offerings to *São Bento* (Saint Benedict) winds its way to the chapel. The offerings include salt, eggs, hens (all white), and white carnations. São Bento is also honored elsewhere in *Varzia* and *Caldas de Vizela* near Braga on July 14. In Varzia the procession is fairly elaborate. It includes floats covered in carnations and folk dancers who dance their way along the procession route. In Caldas de Vizela the stones and boulders surrounding the church are ceremoniously whitewashed in preparation for the celebration.

Near Porto lies the town of *Santo Tirso*. Between July 11 and 14, the townspeople hold a fair on the grounds of the ancient Benedictine monastery (A.D. 978). Good pottery and locally made *vinho verde* is sold. As expected, the fair ends with dancing and fireworks.

The tourist particularly interested in ceramics must visit the *National Ceramics Fair* held at *Caldas da Rainha* in the middle of July each year. Manufacturers and craftsmen offer a fantastic selection of ceramics. The selection represents all types produced throughout the country.

A very colorful festival begins on July 13 in *Matosinhos*, a small fishing town near Porto. Saint Sebastian is the patron saint of fishermen. On his feast day, the fishermen of Matosinhos carry the saint's statute down to the water for an elaborate blessing-of-the-boats ceremony. During the following days, people are invited to the fair, folk dancing, band concerts, and fireworks.

On July 14 the medieval castle town of *Arraiolos* holds its fair to honor its patron, *St. Bonaventure*. The neat little town, which has a commanding view of the Alentejo plains, is famous for its rugs and tapestries. The fair is a good time to view the wide array of patterns and colors of the world-renowned Arraiolos carpets.

One of the oldest celebrations in Portugal takes place each July

14, in *Forijes* near Braga. It is the *Festas de Santa Marinha*. The festivities begin with a surprisingly grand parade. Later, there is a solemn religious procession. Each day of the festival there are band concerts, dancing, and fairs.

In the far south of Portugal in the city of *Faro*, a century-old tradition honors *Our Lady of Carmo* from July 14 to 21. Parades, dancing, and general partying follows the religious ceremonies on a daily basis.

In the little town of *Paredes* near Porto, one can watch a very majestic procession that lasts for hours. Filled with paintings depicting the life of Christ, it is the longest religious procession in Portugal and highlights the *Feast of Our Divine Savior*. Of course, the week is filled with other festivities.

The little town of *São Pedro do Sul* lies near Viseu. Set in a natural amphitheater surrounded by woods, this charming place celebrates its patron saints feast from July 20 to 22. Here one can witness horse racing, Portuguese style. Very informal, it is one of the few horse racing events in the entire country.

On July 21 the *Clamor da Roda* (Circle of Waiting) takes place in *Vale de Bouro* near Braga. The ancient tradition earns its unusual name from the religious ceremonies. During the *Feast of Santa Maria Madalena*, a procession circles the entire town. In this procession of penance the worshipers chant archaic canticles for the forgiveness of their sins. The procession can last for many hours, depending on how sinful the townspeople have been.

A change of pace would take one to *Mafra* on July 21 for the annual *Garlic Festival*. Garlic is obviously the featured attraction, but other items can be enjoyed as well. Regional wines, agricultural produce, cheeses, and fresh bread make this festival worthwhile. One of the regional food specialities includes an interesting broad bean *(fava)* dish that uses copious amounts of the aromatic garlic in honor of the festival theme. This is genuine country food.

The month of August is both fun-filled and solemn. In fact, there are more festivals in August than any other month of the year. A unique example takes place at *Santa Maria de Sintra* and is held only at twenty-five-year intervals. The last one was in 1986, so the next will be in the year 2010. Tourists who plan ahead should mark their calendars! This festival has been held faithfully since the thirteenth century and will probably continue for many more centuries. The festival revolves around the statue of *Our Lady of the Cape*. The story begins in the year 1215 when a storm wrecked the English merchant ship "Haldebrand" off the Barbarie Point. In the turmoil a small statue of the Virgin was lost. The statue was a gift to the Benedictine monk Augustine from St. Gregorio Magno. After the storm was over and the loss of the ship and statue was known, the story becomes complicated. Witnesses told of seeing a shining light on the cliff near the wreck. An old man in *Alcabideche* and an old woman in *Caparica* both dreamed of images of the Virgin. The two communicated these dreams to the authorities, who were then led to the *Espichel Cape*, where a dark wooden statue was found.

Later the people of Caparica built the first chapel to honor the Virgin. Then pilgrimages began. A convent was built in 1428, and in 1606 a Confraternity of Our Lady of the Cape was formed that embraces twenty-six parishes. It is through those parishes that the image travels over a period of twenty-five years. Each year the Virgin is carried to another parish church in candle-lit splendor. Participants in the procession traditionally dress in seventeenth-century costumes to commemorate the founding of the Confraternity. August 25 is the date to mark on the calendar. The festivities also include a fair, dancing, and fireworks through the following week.

Earlier in August the visitor can enjoy one of the larger and more colorful fairs. It is dedicated to *Our Lady of Agony* and takes place at *Viana do Castelo*. For three days beginning on the Saturday before the third Sunday in August, about thirty thousand people gather to watch the brilliant procession honoring the Virgin. The focal point is the Virgin's image, carried on a platform balanced on the shoulders of a cadre of men. Hundreds of little children dressed as angels walk before the statue. Older girls are dressed as saints. The procession winds through the flower-decorated streets late into the night. The next morning everyone is awakened by the drums and bagpipes of the official band. On the second day tourists can witness a four-hour ethnic parade. Hundreds of floats dominate the parade, which represent the surrounding villages of the Minho region. There is a certain amount of good-natured rivalry among those villages as they present their elaborate floats. Also on parade are the magnificently costumed people of the Minho. Women are dressed in richly embroidered costumes with black girdles and gold necklaces, earrings, and bracelets. Some younger women wear heavily embroidered red dresses. The women who are traditionally known as *sargaceiras*, or seaweed gatherers, have less fancy costumes and wear no shoes. The men in the parade are usually in the costume of fishermen. After the parade the streets are filled with dancing that usually lasts all night.

Sunday, the last day of the festival, is dedicated to the fishermen. Highlighting the day is the "Procession of the Sea." For this the streets are redecorated with incredible numbers of flowers. The procession, in full gear, winds toward the sea with the statue of Our Lady of Agony carried on the shoulders of the fishermen to their boats. Thousands of people gather to witness the Bishop of Braga blessing the boats and the fishermen praying their thanks to the Virgin. That night, the highlight is a fantastic fireworks display over the river. Accommodations are scarce during that long weekend, so tourists planning to enjoy the festival should make reservations well in advance.

The festival at Viana do Castelo has the ambiance of major religious feasts and celebrations and equals any in the world. This is a world-class festival. Visitors should be prepared for crowds, noise, and copious amounts of food and wine. The feast also has deep religious overtones that are not lost in the wine. The people of the town and region are proud of the celebration and will be overjoyed at the visitors' pleasure as they witness this example of an elaborate traditional celebration.

A much smaller affair, but very agreeable nevertheless, takes place during the second week of August in the village of *Malveira da Serra* between Cascais and Sintra. The roads leading into the village are trimmed and decorated with colorful paper arches. The celebration is in honor of *Our Lady of the Assumption*. The procession takes place toward the end of the week and includes floats and dancers with the usual array of civic and religious organizations represented.

The last weekend in August in the small village of *Macas de Dona Maria* near Alvaiazere, one can witness the celebration of the festival of *Senhora dos Aflitos* (Our Lady of Affiliation). Here, too, is a procession with gifts for the Virgin. The difference is that the gifts are later auctioned off to support the small church.

In *Foz do Ouro* near Porto (in late August), the *Festival of Saint Bartholomew* is celebrated with what is known as the "paper procession." The participants are dressed in paper costumes. Mostly of a satirical nature, the costumes lend a unique ambiance to this pro-

cession. Not as solemn as others, the parade begins at the Foz
Castle and winds down to Ourico Beach, where a symbolic battle is
fought between the pirates and the land people. After that dramatic
display, everyone spontaneously jumps into the water and
splashes about. The costumes, of course, don't survive the melee.
The *Festas de Santa Maria* takes place during the last week in
August in the town of *Arca de São João* near Caminha. Following an
ancient tradition, the people of the area walk to the town's church,
bringing offerings of salt or "stealing" carnations and tiles for São
João. The "stealing," of course, is merely symbolic since flowers
and tiles are conspicuously placed along fences and walls. What is
symbolic about the "stealing" is a mystery!

The month of September sees considerably fewer festivals and
fairs than previous months, but tourists need not despair. Fair-
goers will find the *Festa da Senhora das Vitorias* (Our Lady of Victories) at *Vila da Lixa* near Felguerias to be refreshingly different. Here
the women of the town exhibit their delicate and intricate embroid-
eries in front of their houses. This is the place to buy fine linens
and needlework. The religious procession is usually on the first
Sunday of September.

The very popular festival of *Our Lady of Nazaré* is celebrated also
on the first Sunday in September. At the beach of Cortegaça in *Ovar*
the fishermen carry a statue of Our Lady to the shore to bless the
boats, the sea, and themselves.

The second week in September witnesses fairs in several Algarve
locations. The folk-dancing festival in *Praia da Rocha* is the largest
and best of the lot.

The so-called "New Festivals" in *Ponte de Lima* near Viana do
Castelo are held in honor of our *Our Lady of Agony* around September 15. The name "New Festivals" is curious since the fair has been
taking place regularly since the 1600s.

In the Beira region lies the town of *Casteljo*. Celebrated here in
mid-September is the festival of *Santa Luzia,* patron saint of sight.
Also around September 15, there is a procession of fishermen in
honor of *Our Lady of Succor* at *Espinho* near Aveiro. The fair focuses
on onions. It is a wonderful fair where one can buy most local craft
items and also many onion products.

On September 16 in the small village of *Milagris* near Leiria, one
can witness the pilgrimage to celebrate the *Festival of Our Lord of
Miracles*. The faithful are seen winding their way to a tiny church

built in the eighteenth century. Later in the evening worshipers participate in a torch-light procession through the streets while singing religious hymns.

Much activity occurs in *Elvas* during the third week of September. During that time Elvas becomes the site of an elaborate agricultural fair. Additionally, there are two religious processions in honor of *Our Lord of Mercy*. The visitor can remain in town for the horse shows, bullfights, and dancing in the streets.

The grape harvest is celebrated with gusto in the grape-producing region near Braga. In the last week of September, the town of *Cabeceiras de Basto* holds a series of fascinating festivals, including a huge livestock fair and a religious procession. This fair is unique because it retains the medieval traditions of cattle trading. Another event to look for is the demonstration of an ancient form of self-defense that has been practiced for centuries. It is called *jogo do pau*. The fair is also an excellent place to buy the heavy woolen goods of the region.

For an excellent display of Portuguese-style bullfighting, visit *Viana do Alentejo* near Évora during the last week of September. This festival, in honor of *Our Lady of Aires*, dates from the thirteenth century. Six centuries of time have bestowed upon this festival a refined ambiance of well-worn tradition.

As summer ends and the days become cooler, the fairs change with the weather. Agricultural products become more of a focus. The great harvest of fruit and nuts seems to dominate the fair themes.

Certainly the most important, best-known, and largest of the pilgrimages or *romarias* is the October procession to *Fatima*. The great pilgrimages actually begin on May 13, the day of the first apparition of *Our Lady of Fatima* in 1917. Worshipers negotiate their way to the shrine in any way they can: walking, riding—in cars, trucks, or buses—and hitch-hiking. Timing is important to the pilgrims. Many walk for weeks just to arrive on the thirteenth day of the month. Between May 13 and October 13 (the date of the last apparition), the pilgrims pour into Fatima by the thousands. The October 13 great pilgrimage includes torch-light processions, celebration of solemn masses in the Basilica, and prayers for the sick and infirm.

Food and good eating is the focus for the *Fair of St. Francis* in *Moimenta da Beira* near Viseu. The attractions here include the famous grilled pork steaks, served in vast quantities during the first week in October.

Also in the first week of the month of October, tourists visit *Redondo* near Evora to buy some beautiful ceramics or the famous Alentejo capes and coats.

For something unique, also during the first week in October, the town of *Requengo do Fetal* near Batalha celebrates its ancient and traditional *Snail Festival*. The festival derives its name from the fact that the route of the religious procession is lit by thousands of lamps made from snail shells. Snails are harvested in the early spring, and so they are not part of the festival's cuisine.

Near Beja lies the town of *Moura*. In this first week of October, the town organizes a dignified procession to honor *Our Lady of Carmo*. In this instance the statue of the Virgin is completely covered in white flowers. Bullfight enthusiasts will enjoy the informality of the small town's bullfights.

In the north the town of *Godomar*, famed for its filigree, holds the procession of *Rosario*. This distinguished procession dates from the sixteenth century. Visitors can enjoy folk dancing, fireworks, and a fair. Held in the second week in October is the *Nut Fair*, a place to purchase the autumn harvest of nuts and dried fruit.

Around the twentieth of the month is an old fair held in *Castro Verde* near Beja. The first time this fair was held was 1636, but the products sold have changed very litle over the years. One can still buy fruit and nuts, handicrafts, and wine.

There is an ancient fair also held around October 20 in *Tomar*. Called the *Saint Iria Fair*, this festival tradition began in the seventh century. Bouquets of flowers are thrown into the river with great ceremony, but the true meaning of this lively tradition is lost in time.

The town of *Merces* is near Lisbon. Usually during the last week in October a tasty little fair is held in this town. The visitor is obliged to try some *pão saloio*, or peasant bread. One must also try the sweet herb bread with roast suckling pig or grilled pork steaks. Local wine is of top quality. The celebration is in honor of *Our Lady of Merces*.

Long ago in the fifteenth century, the first explorers sailed from the bay at *Lagos*. During that time, *St. Gonçalo* was an inhabitant of the city. His name is honored every October 17 with a fishermen's festival.

The last of the fairs in October is the *All Saints Fair* in *Montalegre*. Here one enjoys not only the usual processions, dancing, and feasting but also a very unusual form of bullfighting. Literally a bullfight, this one takes place between two bulls. It is called the *chegas de bois*.

November winds down the festival and fair season. November 1, of course, is *All Saints' Day*, and towns throughout Portugal use the occasion to celebrate. An interesting festival called the *Glutton's Fair* is held in *Alcains* near Castelo Branco and focuses on the sale of the autumn harvest.

In *Tentugal*, near Coimbra, one can also stock up on fruits and nuts. But in the old town of *Alvito* near Beja, the holiday is celebrated with a fair that highlights the famous Alvito bean dish that includes *favas* (broad beans), Portuguese *choriço* sausages, and smoked ham.

In the town of *Mangeralde* near Viseu, visitors are obliged to consume huge quantities of grilled pork steaks famous in the region. The pork steaks are marinated for a few hours before they are grilled. While being grilled, the steaks are basted with the marinade. The aroma alone on fair day draws visitors from miles around.

St. Martin's Fair in *Golega* near Santarém is also known as the "Horse Fair." Usually held in the second week of November, this fair is a horse-lovers delight. Along with the spectacle of numerous riding competitions, horse trading, and selling, one can enjoy the locally grown roasted chestnuts and sip plenty of wine.

For cattle shows, the tourist should visit the *St. Martin's Fair* in *Penafiel* near Porto. Here, too, one can feast on grilled pork steaks of the region and also enjoy a rare taste of beef steaks. Of course, all is washed down with the fresh *vinho verde* of the region. The fair usually lasts from the second to the third week in November.

Further to the northeast near Bragança is the town of *Mansores*. *St. Martin's Day*, November 11, is celebrated with an old tradition of dancing in the streets. Here, however, there is a unique wine-cauldron tradition. The young men of the town carry a large cauldron of wine through the streets during the celebrations. Those wishing to partake of the beverage must do so by drinking face down. The messy practice evokes much laughter and fun. Others pass around huge baskets of roasted chestnuts for snacking.

The second and third weeks in November mark the fair in *Gon-*

çalo and the *Raisin Fair* in *Estremoz*. The Gonçalo fair is most interesting for the horse-blessing ceremonies. Also called the *Festival of St. Andrew*, the fair at Estremoz is a good excuse to visit these interesting medieval towns.

There is a wonderful fair toward the end of the month in *Albufeira* in Algarve. The weather remains quite warm in Algarve so the visitor can enjoy that bonus while feasting on the fruits and pastries indigenous to the area.

The last fairs of the month, and essentially the last of the season, take place in *Mafra* and *Mesão Frio* near Vila Real. The fair at Mafra is held in front of the huge monastery. Good food and good fun are easily found here.

At Mesão Frio one can buy nearly all of one's needs for the winter months ahead. The cuisine at this fair consists mainly of grilled pork. The aroma is mouth watering and the local wines are refreshing.

The listing of fairs presented here is certainly not all inclusive. Nearly every town has its fair or festival at some time during the year. Those listed are considered to be the best known and the most interesting, fascinating, colorful, or convenient in location.

There are other celebrations in Portugal that do not include a religious theme. For example, on January 1 the people celebrate *Universal Brotherhood Day*. April 25 is the *Day of Liberty*. This commemorates April 25, 1974, the day of the revolution. Many streets and squares are named April 25 *(25 de Abril)*. The first of May is *Labor Day*. June 10 is also a national holiday now called *Portugal Day*. That day corresponds to the anniversary of the death of Camões. The fifth of October formerly was *the* major national holiday. The day commemorates the establishment of the republic after the monarchy was overthrown in the early part of this century. October 5 has taken a back seat to April 25 as a day of national pride.

December 1 is called the *Restoration of Independence Day*. This day commemorates Portugal's independence from Spain in 1640.

The celebration of these national holidays is rather subdued compared to the hoopla associated with the religious fairs, festivals, and *romarias*. The tourist, for example, who visits Portugal on the anniversary of the revolution would expect wild and crazy celebrations similar to the United States bicentennial, the one hundredth anniversary of the Statue of Liberty, or a British Royal wedding. There is, of course, patriotic music on the radio and television, but not the outburst of national pride that one might expect. All tends to be subdued and dignified. The parade in Lisbon is short, and the day ends with a small fireworks display over the Tagus. Most small-town fairs have more elaborate celebrations. The country festivals are more fun, more lively, and more entertaining than the national holidays.

CHAPTER 12

Cities and Towns

This chapter presents short sketches of the principal cities and towns of Portugal. Because of its importance, Lisbon will be dealt with in a separate chapter. Described here are the main features, attractions, and ambiances of Portugal's other cities and towns. For this discussion, Portugal will be divided into areas; all cities and towns will be categorized as north of Lisbon, east of Lisbon, south of Lisbon, or the Lisbon area. The chapter begins in the north with Portugal's "second" city, Porto.

North of Lisbon

Porto (OPorto) is considered to be the city in Portugal second only to Lisbon. When you think of the city of Porto, you think, naturally, of the incredible port wines. It is true; Porto is the center of the port wine industry, which thrives in the Douro River Valley. But Porto is more.

You can approach Porto by train from the south, by air, or by road. The fast train commute from Lisbon takes only four hours on the *Rapido*. By rail you are afforded the best first view of the city. As the train crosses the high bridge at the river, the city spreads before you. Frankly, this is Porto's best face. The train station is attractive and inviting, and the taxis are cheap. The neighborhood of the station is "downtown" and you can find many suitable hotels, sociable cafes, pastelerias, and restaurants within a few blocks.

Porto is a big city. Although not on the scale of Lisbon, it is crowded and noisy just like any big city. With only about one-third of a million people, Porto feels smaller than Lisbon. Many visitors feel that Porto lacks the prepossessing ambiance that Lisbon has. Few cities do, however. Being only about a third the size of Lisbon, the city suffers in relative prosperity. Porto is slightly dingy, is not as lively as Lisbon, and offers food that is a bit lacking (except at a fancy hotel). Northern Portugal has a distinctive cuisine, and visitors should sample a few regional dishes while in the area. Although hearty and savory, the regional cuisine is more austere than further south.

One regional dish dates from the fourteenth and fifteenth centuries and has become a Porto tradition—tripe. Usually this delicacy contains beans, onions, tomatoes, and garlic. Fancy versions include pine nuts or almonds.

Another regional dish worth consideration is the *sardinhas frescas de caldeirada*, or fresh sardine stew. It contains fresh sardines, potatoes, onions, and the usual spices layered together.

After a good meal there are certain things you must see while in Porto. You may wish to visit the *sé* (cathedral). Take advantage of the interesting views of the market and old neighborhood from the belvedere near the cathedral entrance. The cathedral itself dates from the twelfth century. The interior is surprisingly baroque in style. The altarpiece of the Chapel of the Holy Sacrament should be studied. Wander into the Gothic cloister and study the eighteenth century *azulejos* (tiles).

Probably the best of all things to see in Porto is a medium-sized church at the intersection of *Rua de Cedofeita* and *Rua do Carmo*. On the Cedofeita side is a most impressive outside street wall of the Portugese *azulejos* anywhere to be found. This wall is one of the better ones in all of the country. If you do not have a city map, write the street intersection on a slip of paper and give it to a taxi driver. Seeing this church wall is a must. Photograph it, study it, and remember it for years to come.

Tourists should also visit one of the wineries along the river for a glimpse of the port-wine-making process. After a taste and maybe a purchase of wine, you may want to take a photograph or two of the river, the winery, the city, and the *barcos* (traditional boats transporting wines on the Douro River). The port-wine industry is dominated by the British. Notice the English names on nearly all of the major products.

In this district, known as the *Vila Nova de Gaia*, shop for the wines of the Douro Valley. Here, on the bank opposite the city, are nearly a hundred wine shops. This is the center of the Portuguese wine industry. Its importance is indicated by the fact that prior to 1986, all port wine, by law, had to pass through the warehouses of the district. The monopoly, however, was abolished as Portugal entered the European Economic Community (EEC), or Common Market. That change of rule did not diminish the district's premier position in the port wine trade.

For a choice view of the city, visit the convent of *Nossa Senhora da Serra do Pilar* on the same side of the river. Enjoy the grand vista of the bridge and Porto. Ask any taxi driver to take you there. The view is worth the cost.

Porto dates from the middle ages and as its name implies has acted as a significant port, since here the Douro River enters the Atlantic. It is also surmised that in this region surrounding the city the nation of Portugal emerged. Obviously, Porto has its "old" section of town. Visit the old quarter and wander down alleys and narrow streets. The picturesqueness is enhanced by the orientation of the narrow streets toward the river and the quay along the river bank. This is where medieval Porto began.

There are museums, of course, but one seems especially worthwhile. It is the *Ethnographic Museum* on the Largo de São João Novo. Tasteful displays of life, crafts, and the art of the region can hold your interest. Of the other museums, the *Soares dos Reis Museum* offers little for the casual tourist, and the *Guerra Junqueiro Museum* is merely a display of the poet Junqueiro's collected "objects d'art." Neither of these is outstanding.

Another "must" is the *St. Benedict Station (Estação de São Bento)*—the main train station in downtown Porto. Why visit a train station? Well, in this one there are some genuinely beautiful *azulejos* covering the walls of the entire waiting area. These are not old (1930s), but they are worth seeing. Most depict everyday life in the Douro valley and city. Some of an historic nature depict early monarchs and their deeds of heroism.

A day or two may be enough to see the city's highlights. Time is better spent exploring nearby towns and wandering the Douro valley. A short train or bus ride will get you to the quaint towns of *Braga, Vila Real, or Viana do Castelo*. Remember, this is the most densely populated area of the country. You are never far from a town or village. The landscape is densely cultivated with grapes (on trellises) and food crops. Do not expect wide open spaces in this region of the country.

Of the three cities listed above, if you have time to visit only one, choose Braga. Vila Real is pretty, lively, and animated and is a good place to buy local pottery, but it offers little else. Viana do Castelo is an old middle-ages harbor town that today acts as a weekend resort community for the Porto wealthy. So, of the three, Braga is the best.

Between Porto and Braga the terrain slopes steeply. Nearly every space is cultivated in grape arbors with an understory of vegetables for home consumption.

Historically, Braga was a rather important Roman outpost. It had experienced the invasions of the Visigoths and Moors and survived to prosper again under Christian domination. The town, like so many others dating from the same era, is dominated by the cathedral. A visit to it is marked by its pathetic treasury and dismal chapels. The treasury is a dusty collection of locally important artifacts and ecclesiastical treasures. It should be seen, if only for its pathos. Each tour is "guided." That is, you are led in silence throughout the church's attic. The guide's function is merely to turn lights on and off as you wander through the dusty and dingy rooms.

Nearby are many old *pastelerias* crowded with old people, old tables, and old waiters. In the same vicinity, discover the *Garden of St. Barbara (Jardim de Sta. Barbara)*. This is a good example of a sumptuous Portuguese garden. The varieties and colors represented by the pansies alone are worth some time in Braga. Admire the *Casa do Raio*. It is an eighteenth-century palace known locally as the House of the Mexican. Its best feature is the fact that its entire facade is of brilliant blue *azulejos*.

If you have time, attend Mass at the cathedral or one of the smaller parish churches in the city. Your perspective of Portuguese churches can change dramatically as the interiors are illuminated to enliven normally dimly lit carvings and ecclesiastical artworks. The atmosphere glows with candles and lights while the mood is mellowed by the throaty blasts of an old pipe organ. Any Portuguese church is best seen on Sunday morning. Braga is in a poor region of the country, but the Sunday glow of a church's interior belies that fact. Tourists should leave generous donations to help support the maintenance of those special buildings.

Braga is a walking city, small enough to see entirely on foot. It is a cheery little town to ramble through for a day and evening.

After you visit Braga, travel into the middle-ages by the ever-so-slow train from Porto. Or drive the scenic route from Porto, through *Vila Real* and *Vidago*, to *Bragança*. You are now in the northeastern extremity of the country in the province of *Trás-os-Montes*. This region is one of the least known tourist areas in all of Europe.

Bragança is a mountain town, not big in size but fascinating to view. The medieval city on the heights above the modern town can be a walk back in time. The old town is within the fortified walls on the hilltop. Walk up from St. Vincent Square and visit the castle built in 1187. The view from the castle makes the climb worth the effort. Absorb the ancient landscape and envision the knights of old. The hilly terrain possesses a medieval quality that must be seen to be appreciated. In the town, check out the oldest town hall in Portugal. This is a five-sided building of unique architecture dating from the twelfth century. See the pillory and at least one of the churches of São Bento or Santa Clara. Accommodations are scarce in Trás-os-montes, but the Portuguese government has propitiously provided one of their excellent *Pousadas*. Reservations are necessary at the beautiful *Pousada de São Bartolemeu*.

Heading back toward the south you may choose an interior route via the rugged mountains and hills of the *Serra da Estrela* and the cities of *Guarda* and *Viseu*.

Viseu is the home to one of the better wines in Portugal, *Dão*. Stop for a few hours to visit the cathedral square and the main *praça* at the center of the city. You may wish to spend the night at the *Pousada de São Lourenço* in *Mantegas*, not far away, or you can proceed to *Guarda*.

Guarda is in the province of Beira Alta. The town of Guarda is the highest in all of the country, and its site has been occupied for millenia. The Romans (maybe Julius Caesar himself) had a military outpost here. The Visigoths, the Moors, and the Spanish all found the site to be strategic as well as climatically pleasing. The name Guarda gives away the function of the town: it is one of a series of fortified towns near the Spanish border. Most of the medieval fortresses were built in the seventeenth century. There are at least fifteen such fortresses in the immediate area. You can easily visit those nearby: *Belmonte, Sabugal,* and *Celorico da Beira.* The latter has the superior view from the heights of the ancient castle.

If you take the coastal route to the south, there are other beguiling stops along the way. You must visit *Coimbra.* Try to make it an overnight visit because Coimbra is a pleasure at night.

Coimbra would have made a respectable political capital for Portugal. It is old, distinguished, more or less centrally located, and yet detached from the economic mainstream of Lisbon and Porto. It is also the center of Portuguese academia. Indeed, it was Portugal's first capital but soon lost prominence to the mighty economics and politics of Lisbon. Even with its reduced status it is easily reached by train, bus, or car. Hotels are surprisingly scarce in this university city, but there are dozens of *pensãos* that seem to be clean, cheap, and centrally located. Coimbra has many outstanding restaurants. Lunch of grilled pork steak, potatoes, and wine can be enjoyed for little money.

Coimbra is another city for the walking tourist. The city has an ambiance that most visitors appreciate. Walk through the town up a wide and beautifully landscaped boulevard to the *Jardim Botanica.* You should spend significant time here. Meander through the narrow lanes and cobbled streets of old Coimbra. Stroll to the river's edge and cross the bridge where you can witness a scene centuries old: women laundering clothes in the river water. Wander through old Coimbra and up the steep streets to the famed university.

Coimbra University is the oldest in Europe but, as discussed elsewhere, never has commanded the academic respect given other European universities. This complex is well worth a visit, however. Most of the buildings date from the seventeenth century even though the university is over four hundred years old. The ceremonial hall is magnificent with its painted ceiling. As you walk out on the catwalk balcony, you are rewarded with a grand and dazzling view of old Coimbra and the countryside beyond the Mondego River. Also see the Manueline-style chapel and its ceiling and spectacular *azulejos.* The university is a good place to spend a few hours conversing with the students or just inconspicuously observing the daily routine. Note the colored ribbons adorning briefcases. These are indicative of the individual student's field of study. Coimbra and the university have a long tradition-filled history in the arts and letters. The students, only about seventy-five hundred in residence, maintain the romantic ambiance as they band together in communal living arrangements, gather at cafés to sing the dulcet tones of the *Fado,* and generally groom themselves for positions of national leadership.

Downtown Coimbra has few tourists. As you walk the streets and sip coffee in the cafés and *pastelerias,* you will mingle, not with other tourists, but with the Portuguese people. There is one rather large *pasteleria* on the main shopping street near the cathedral that seems to be *the* gathering place for Coimbra's solid citizens, but tourists are accepted without notice. Nearby is the cathedral, which dates back to the 1100s. The Gothic altarpiece, flamboyant in its gilded opulence, dominates the dimly lit interior. The remainder of the church, frankly, seems somewhat morbid and out-of-place in happy Coimbra. Walk in, say a prayer, light a candle, make a donation, and then hurry to that extraordinary *pasteleria* down the block toward the river.

The region of the Beira Littoral, where Coimbra is located, has a distinctive cuisine. One menu item you may find is the *Pe De Porco Com Feijao Branco.* This is a traditional dish of pig's feet and white beans. Coimbra, steeped in academics and history, maintains a strongly traditional cuisine.

Between Coimbra and Lisbon there are several towns worth visiting and some that should not be missed. These towns include *Leiria, Tomar, Almoural, Alcobaça,* and *Batalha.*

Leiria is a good one-day trip (combined with other stops) from Lisbon. A cheerful town with rivers, parks, and *pastelerias,* it lies about midway to Coimbra, near the coast. Its main attraction is a captivating castle situated on a peak towering above the town. In this moist coastal location more often than not the town will be shrouded with morning fog. The clouds of fog give the castle a mysterious "Dungeons and Dragons" aura. In fact, it is, even without Hollywood special effects, one of the most picturesque castles in Portugal. The original was built in the twelfth century, rebuilt and expanded in the fourteenth century and again in the sixteenth century. Originally a Roman fortified site, the first Portuguese castle was constructed in 1135 and formed an integral part of the front line of Portuguese defense. At that time the Moors still occupied the southern half of the territory. The existing restored buildings date from the sixteenth century when King Dinis chose the site as one of his homes. Today it is a perfect place to wander and wonder, appreciating the marvels of castle architecture and imagining the people who occupied the huge structure. Leiria is not on the tour-bus itineraries, so few tourists make their way to the castle.

Leiria is the setting for the famous Eça de Queiroz novel *The Sin of Father Amaro*. The book presents a realistic view of nineteenth Century Leiria as well as a wry and candid appraisal of the clergy at that time. Queiroz describes the sight of Leiria thusly:

> Around the bridge the view is wide and tranquil. . . . Below, among the great trees, are the houses, giving the melancholy scene a character more alive and human, with their joyful whitewashed walls shining brightly in the sun. . . . An angle of the Jesuit-style masonry of the cathedral, a corner of the cemetery wall [is] covered with wallwort and the dark green needles of the cypresses; the rest is hidden by the solid mass of the bristling wild vegetation, among which the castle ruins stand out with a grand historic air, silhouetted against the sky and enveloped in the evening by the circling flight of owls.

Tomar, a small town, is noted mainly for the *Convent of Christ* built in the twelfth century. Follow the signs through the town and up the hill to an enchanted, quiet site, parklike in appearance. Roam through this spacious cluster of buildings, cloisters, and church. Some of the features are remarkable. It is said that the window in the St. Barbara Cloister is the best example of Manueline-style ornamentation to be found in all of Portugal. Study its detail. Note the nautical motifs, the cork-tree images, and the royal crest of Manuel I.

The Templar's Rotunda, a twelfth-century replica of the Holy Sepulchre in Jerusalem, requires some study. Imagine the medieval gatherings of the Order of the Knights Templar in this setting. Here too, at a later time, the wealthy Knights of Christ gathered to discuss, ponder, and eventually finance the great discoveries of the fifteenth and sixteenth centuries.

On the drive toward Lisbon, follow the signs to *Almoural Castle*. The little castle is perched upon a small island in the Tagus (Tejo) River. The site, obviously a strategic one, was originally occupied by the Romans. The present castle, built by the Knights Templar, dates from the twelfth century. The site is reached by a gravel road and is surprisingly undeveloped. You can hire a small boat for the short ride to the island or, better yet, take a circle boat tour of the castle. This is, truly, one of the more photogenic sites in the country.

Alcobaça's claim to fame is the fact that it is the site of the Cistercian Monastery of Santa Barbara. This dates back to the twelfth century when much was happening in Iberia. It is an imposing structure in terms of its size and architecture. The church is particularly pleasing with its light, airy, and spacious interior. The facade today is the result of reconstruction in the eighteenth century. Some of the original features, such as the magnificent rose window, remain in good repair.

Certainly the reasons to visit this lovely structure are enhanced by elaborately carved tombs of Dom Pedro and Ines. Located in the south and north transepts respectively, both should be studied carefully. The exquisitely rendered tombs depict various scenes from their lives, including Dom Pedro's last moments of life, and biblical scenes.

The monastery at *Batalha* is a masterpiece of Portuguese architecture. This building is relatively new. Dating only to the fifteenth century, it was the result of King João I's vow to honor the Virgin Mary if victory over the Spaniards secured Portuguese independence. The Portuguese won the battle of Aljubarrota in 1385, and the monastery was duly built to be admired even today. In Founder's Chapel lies João I, Henry the Navigator, and other kings. The structure is the Portuguese equivalent to Westminister Abbey in London since it serves as the final resting place for many Portuguese monarchs. The church is remarkably light and is entrancing because of the few embellishments, the fine limestone, and the gorgeous stained-glass windows, which illuminate the whole of the interior space. Batalha Monastery is worth a few hours to admire the work of Portuguese masters of Manueline style. The detail is stunning. Even the unfinished chapels possess an endearing charm that encourages visitors to linger.

The town of *Fatima* stands alone. It is often regarded as one of the most famous holy places in the world. For millions, it offers inspiration and hope. For a few, it is a disappointment.

The story of Fatima began on May 13, 1917, when the Virgin Mary appeared on the hillside before three shepherd children—Francisco, Jacinta, and Lucia. Her message, a call for peace, was repeated with each appearance on the thirteenth day of the following months. Word spread of this apparition and miracle. Finally, it is said that on October 13 no less than seventy-thousand people saw the sun revolve in the sky. That spectre was taken as a sign from the Virgin.

In 1930, after long deliberation and inquiry, the church in Rome determined that a shrine should be constructed to celebrate the Roman Catholic belief in *Our Lady of Fatima*.

The town is crowded between May 13 and October 13 each year. During that period, the number of people making their way to the shrine is truly remarkable. Along every road, pilgrims, some on foot, some even on their knees, travel to the shrine. The town, as a result, has become a massive collection of inexpensive but very clean lodgings to accommodate the throngs. All is distinguished and well ordered. The buildings are neat and tidy and the shrine is strikingly grand with its basilica, the Chapel of the Apparitions, and a massive paved area stretching before the basilica for the faithful to gather in prayer. The incredible devotion of the thousands of worshipers boggles the mind. Many pilgrims can be seen making their way to the basilica and up the main stairs on their knees. This is no mean feat since there are hundreds of steps.

Adjacent to the shrine are numerous shops devoted to the sale of sacred artifacts. Much for sale is pure junk, but there are some interesting remembrances to be purchased in Fatima. Despite the commercialization, the shrine and the people who come in prayer and devotion deserve respect.

Fatima is only seventeen kilometers from Batahla over somewhat difficult roadways. The basilica crowns the vast site with its high, steepled bell tower covered in bronze. Inside, near the altar, are the tombs of two of the three shepherd children. The interior of the basilica is rather ordinary. Outside, a short distance from the basilica, stands an oak tree (not the original) like the one from which the Virgin is said to have appeared. Nearby are candle-vending areas where the faithful purchase their candles (some in the shape of body limbs and children) to be lit and placed on vast candle-burning platforms. Thousands of candles burn, their wax collected for reuse in huge vats beneath. The glass chapel (Chapel of the Apparitions) houses the statue of Our Lady of Fatima. The statue itself is stunningly radiant. A normal sight in the chapel is of many elderly women, dressed in black as if in mourning, "walking" on swollen knees as they pray the rosary.

Santarém and *Vila Franca de Xira* share a common heritage. Both towns are known for their roles in Portuguese bullfighting. Some aficionados claim that the bullfights in these towns are unequaled.

Nevertheless, this is the area where the bulls are bred and raised. Breeding farms can be located on local maps found in the Tourismo offices in either town. In Vila Franca there is a small museum devoted primarily to the bullfight.

Closer to the coast but still north of Lisbon are the towns of *Mafra, Ericeira, Óbidos, Nazaré,* and *Peniche.*

If you like monasteries, you will love *Mafra.* The town is small and exists because of the great monastery there. This monastery is a new one (eighteenth century) and like many others was the result of a promise to God if the Almighty would answer a certain prayer. In this case, it was a king's (João V) wish for an heir—a simple enough wish for such a great monastery! This building covers ten acres. Other incredible statistics include forty-five hundred doors and a perimeter wall twelve miles long. It is said that more than fifty thousand workers were needed to build the entire structure in just thirteen years. Inside the walls are the basilica, the monastery itself, and a palace. The basilica's elegance is due to the generous use of marble, which is rarely used in Portuguese churches. If you are lucky, you will hear the two famous carillons of the Mafra Palace. They were recently restored (1986) and each of the one hundred ten bells was cleaned, balanced, and positioned for clarity. After thirteen years of restoration, the bells, some of the finest in the world, are once more being heard for miles around.

While this huge monastery was under construction, King João V, the builder and financer of the project, took advantage of the many architects, sculptors, and artisans working at the site and founded the Mafra School of Sculpture. Many foreign sculptors were not only commissioned to create the magnificent statues gracing the basilica, but also asked to pass on some of their artistic knowledge and skill to local artists. The result was a true success: great art for the basilica and a legacy for the future. Portugal's most famous sculptor, Joaquim Machado de Castro, arose from the school, later to enhance Lisbon's urban scene with his great monuments.

A few kilometers beyond Mafra is the town of *Ericeira.* It is a small town but very picturesque. The harbor area is the focal point of this little community. Many tourists relax here over coffee and pastry and watch fishing boats on the beach. Many plan to have lunch because the town is full of delightful seafood restaurants. During the summer months Ericeira is a bustling resort town packed with visitors from Lisbon. Some home owners will even rent their homes and camp in their own gardens.

Óbidos, where you need reservations to stay at the elegant *Pous-ada* in the sixteenth-century royal palace, is a village on every visitor's itinerary. As you approach the town from the south, note the view. Here is a fortified town of resplendent medieval character. Óbidos, when built, was actually a fort on the coast. Now it is about six miles from the ocean. Over the centuries, a lagoon was created by natural beach action. Eventually the lagoon filled in and left Óbidos high and dry. The town's origins date from the twelfth century.

In the thirteenth century, King Dinis gave the town to his queen (Isabella) simply because she liked it so much. The tradition pre-vailed until the nineteenth century, when the town passed from royal ownership.

As you enter the town by car, you pass through the zig-zag gateway and proceed down the main street toward the *Pousada* at the far end of town (only a few hundred yards). Cars, which are not necessary in Óbidos, can be parked here. In fact, there is much concern by preservationists about tourists being able to enter the village by car. Some feel that eventually all vehicles will be banned from the streets since they are not needed and are not appropriate to the town's medieval character.

Óbidos is a strolling place. Walk through the tiny village. It is a friendly and most picturesque setting. Walk along the city ram-parts where the view of the town and surrounding countryside takes you back to the middle ages. Shopping is available on the main street. The favored items for local purchase are exquisite hand-woven cotton rugs. Evenings in the small town offer little entertainment except a stroll along the darkened lanes to enjoy the smells of home cooking, Portuguese style. The visitor can occasion-ally catch a glimpse of people in their tiny houses watching televi-sion, talking, or praying. The evening is short; by 10:00 P.M. the cafés are empty. It is a time for most activity to cease.

Mornings begin naturally in the village with the call of the roosters. Many visitors prefer the early morning to walk along the ramparts or linger at the church square to view the morning's activity. By 9:00 A.M. the shops open, the mailmen are beginning their rounds, and the song of *"Bom Dia"* is heard everywhere.

Accommodations at the pousada in Óbidos are difficult to get during the high tourist season. Visitors must plan well in advance. Originally the lodging place was a twelfth century castle. It was converted into a royal palace in the sixteenth century and now serves as a five-star hotel of impeccable quality. Rooms with views are available. The most popular rooms overlook the courtyard. The restaurant offers traditional Portuguese dishes of the best local cuisine.

Not far from Óbidos, along the coast, is the town of *Peniche*, situated on a peninsula. The port of Peniche is a notable and significant fishing port. You can easily tell when the town is nearby; the sardine canneries become obvious. Drive around town a bit. Park the car and walk to the Citadel, a sixteenth-century fortress used as a prison before the revolution in 1974. Peniche is a clean and pleasant little town where many visitors plan to have lunch. There are many tolerable restaurants and *pastelerias* to satisfy hungry tourists.

From Peniche a one-hour boat trip wll take you to *Berlinga Island*. This small granitic island, with its many marine caves, offers interest to the naturalists.

Along the precipitous and spectacular coastline to the north lies *Nazaré*. The town nestles at a natural indentation in the otherwise rugged coastline. The tour buses from Lisbon stop in Nazaré to allow the tourist to have lunch and a bit of shopping time in the beachfront shops. But the town offers much more to the visitor. For many, the main attractions are the grilled sardines, salad, and cold beer served at any beach café by the ocean. Visitors also enjoy the fish auction, the funicular, the fishermen's quarters, the rugged beach at *Praia do Norte*, the view at *O Sitio*, and watching, as well as helping, fishermen haul their nets on the beach. Nazaré is a lively break from museums, churches, and monasteries. This little town is worth a visit because it is what it is *now*, not what used to be.

Ride the funicular up to the area known as O Sitio. It is more than three hundred fifty feet above the beach and town and offers a spectacular view of both, as well as the coastline north and south. A short walk to the west takes you to the lighthouse. There is a path and an iron staircase, which hangs on the precipice, leading to a small point that allows a magnificent view of the seascape. You can climb down from the road to Praia do Norte (north beach). This is a spectacular beach of stones, polished granite, and sand. Few tourists venture to this otherwise unspoiled beach. One reason is perhaps the difficulty of access and the strenuous climb.

The beach at Nazaré itself includes two notable areas. At the extreme north end, tourists, sunbathers, and swimmers can gather. The remainder of the beach is reserved for the town's principal activity—fishing. A typical Nazaré beach scene shows people working hard. Usually groups of people—men, women, and children—are seen pulling in nets from the surf. Tourists are sometimes asked to lend a hand ("*Ajuda!*"). Catches are usually meagre; the nets are surprisingly empty. Only a few fish and crabs constitute a catch, after much work. Visitors can spend time at the beach observing the traditional fishing methods. Other than using the seine nets, fishermen launch boats from the beach. Nazaré has no harbor (one is under construction), so the boats must be hauled to the surf and wrestled out to sea. Handmade models of these brightly painted boats are available at most shops.

At day's end, the boats return. The boats are hauled back through the surf and onto the sand by a long cable attached to a tractor. Not too long ago, a team of oxen did the work of the modern tractors.

The fish, if any, are cleaned immediately by the women. Always dressed in black, the women pile the cleaned fish on pans and balance them on their heads as they walk swiftly to the market and auction nearby. Fish destined for the families of the fishermen for home consumption are dried on wooden platforms and rails near the boats.

Nazaré is a gastromic delight. Grilled sardines are served by the ton along the beach. Additionally, a plethora of outstanding seafood restaurants line the beachfront. A few blocks inland, simpler restaurants frequented by the local people offer cheaper and less fancy dishes. Fresh fish purchased at the market can be enjoyed at home as well. Most visitors prefer to find a small seaside café with only a few tables and a charcoal brazier. Here they can enjoy fresh swordfish, hake, sardines, prawns, and lobster grilled in the open sea air. You cannot afford to miss an evening in Nazaré!

East of Lisbon

Strike out from Lisbon in an easterly direction and you enter a different world. To the east lies the province of *Alentejo*. In this region, observe the triumvirate of Iberian staple foods: grain, olives and grapes. Many times all three crops are grown in close proximity. Additionally, the landscape is dotted with the ever-present cork oak—the source of Portuguese cork products. The terrain takes on a rolling to flat appearance, and so the vistas are much wider here than in the north. In fact, in some areas there are few features of local relief. Punctuating this flat landscape are substantial farmhouses, formerly the "big houses" of the large *quintas* or plantations. The villages and towns seem whiter and less crowded than in the north. Some of these towns are worth experiencing, but there are not many of them. Alentejo is an area of low population density. In fact there are only three relatively large towns: *Portalegre*, *Évora*, and *Beja*. The smaller towns include *Marvão*, *Elvas*, *Arraiolos*. There are, of course, many more villages, but the cities and towns listed are of most importance from both the tourist viewpoint and the economic viewpoint. Alentejo is a province that was made for the wanderer. The visitor can take advantage of this.

East-northeast of Lisbon, near the Spanish border, is the town of *Marvão*. It is an excellent example of the fortified medieval towns that flank the Spanish frontier. Marvão is particularly well known for its striking beauty. As you approach the town, it seems to be in a perfect place for a fortification. The castle and ramparts (constructed in the thirteenth century) are in rather good condition, considering the passage of seven hundred years, and give the town a decidedly medieval character. The vistas afforded from the castle affirm the strategic value of this site. The modern landscape below is a rich agricultural plain, which sweeps all the way to the mountains of Spain in the east.

Portalegre is nearby. In fact, driving from Marvão to the south, you would pass through it. At one time the town boasted of a castle, but little remains of it that may be of interest to the casual tourist. Portalegre has a rich history of tapestry production, and at one time the industry created great wealth. The evidence remains at the old Jesuit monastery, where the visitor can tour the tapestry workshops.

Directly out of Lisbon, toward the Spanish frontier town of *Badajoz*, runs the principal eastbound highway. To enter Spain by surface transport, one must pass through Badajoz, so this is the main thoroughfare. About midway between Lisbon and the Spanish border is a small town called *Arraiolos*. Despite its size, this little, isolated town has two claims to fame. Its major claim is the production of handmade, brightly-colored Arraiolos carpets. The other claim to fame involves food. The town is the source of savory *paios* sausages. Many tourists stop for lunch to try the sausage and then shop for wool carpets in the two major outlets or smaller shops. These famous carpets are discussed in some detail elsewhere in this volume.

Beyond Arraiolos, near the Spanish frontier, lies *Elvas*. This is a town of significance within the region. In terms of its market function, Elvas acts as the region's principal agricultural trade center. As a tourist center, it offers visitors the opportunity to see "new" fortifications, built in the eighteenth century. Note that the aquaduct built in the fifteenth century still functions to provide water for the city. Elvas, too, has a castle. This one, however, was built by Moors in the fourteenth century. The castle, therefore, possesses a different style than the others in the region. The view from the castle ramparts offers a magnificent picture of the agricultural base of the region: grapes, plum orchards, and olives.

Évora is considered as an individual destination. It lies almost directly east of Lisbon and can be reached by train, bus, or car. The drive from Lisbon is short and bus service is reasonable. The train trip requires a change, but the slow ride offers the best views of the Alentejo countryside.

Évora is a delight to behold. The town site has been occupied since Roman times and a Roman temple to Diana still exists near the cathedral. The square has been beautifully landscaped and enhanced with modern works of sculpture. This intriguing juxtaposition of the ancient Roman, Christian Gothic, and modern may take you by surprise. Surprises like this are typical of Évora.

Évora is larger than you might expect. Nearly thirty-five thousand people live within the walled town. The whole of Évora is bounded by fortifications built or rebuilt at various times between the first and seventeenth centuries. Many visitors try to find the various portions of the wall by date. The town was also the capital city for Portuguese kings from about the twelfth century to the sixteenth century. This is one reason why the city shines with such elegance and is filled with rich palaces and fine religious structures and treasures. The cathedral, for example, with its octagonal dome, rich treasury, and beautiful cloisters, could not have been built in such opulent style without royal support.

From opulence to the macabre, Évora will surprise you. Visit the *Casa dos Ossos* (Chapel of Bones). From a separate entrance of the cathedral, you will walk into one of the most incredibly bizzare works of religious art anywhere in the world. This, indeed, is a macabre chapel built in the sixteenth century. The walls and pillars of the entire chapel are faced with the bones of five thousand Franciscan monks arranged in intricate detail. You must pay an extra fee to take pictures to prove to the folks back home that such a sight exists and was built in the name of religion. Seeing the Chapel of Bones is a humbling experience, and this is probably the reason for its construction. It was a sixteenth-century monk's idea to humble his fellows as they worshiped in this unusual setting. The streets of Évora were built primarily for pedestrians. Visitors should take advantage of that medieval characteristic and stroll the streets. One delightful destination is the public gardens south of the main square. Well maintained, manicured, and absolutely beautiful, these gardens are truly a people place. Light music is piped in, and benches and kiosks are vividly decorated. The centerpiece of this lovely setting is a nineteenth-century gazebo. Do not miss the ambiance. Few public attractions are this affable, this much fun, and free. Originally, the space belonged to a sixteenth-century palace of the famous King Manuel.

Évora, because of its Alentejo location and the long-time influence of the Moors, displays a pleasing mix of Moorish and Christian cultural and architectural styles. The houses are whitewashed in North African style. Massive chimneys and hanging gardens are other influences from further south. Wander down narrow streets with characteristic Moorish arches. Note the small churches, crosses, and other Christian symbols blended into the clean and refreshing townscape. Évora, too, has its *pastelerias*. The interiors of some are surprisingly Moorish, with vaulted ceilings and low arches. Two items worth tasting while you are looking in pastry shops include the locally prized *bolo de mel* (honey cakes) and locally produced marzipan.

Generally, the climate in this region of Alentejo is warm and dry. Even in winter the weather will be mild. In summer the days may be quite warm. Plan a few days, no matter the season, to see all of Évora's offerings. In addition to the cathedral, for example, you should visit the Museum of Ancient Art, housed in a sixteenth-century bishop's palace. The museum possesses a good collection of Roman artifacts, Manueline sculptures, and primitive paintings of the Flemish school. Several sixteenth-century paintings of the Portuguese school also command some attention.

The *Palace of the Dukes of Cadaval* is open to the public. The gallery collection of historic documents and ancient paintings indicates that this palace was once the home of Portuguese kings. There is much to see. The Convent dos Lóios, founded in the fifteenth-century has been converted into a twentieth-century *Pousada*. This five-star lodging requires reservations well in advance. Rooms surrounding the Gothic-style cloister have been converted into tourist accommodations. The restaurant of the *Pousada* is in the old convent's refectory.

There are several smaller churches of note. The visitor should see the Church of St. Francis, the Church of Our Lady of Grace, and the fortified fifteenth-century, St. Blaise Chapel. Évora seems to be studded with royal palaces. Most are not open to the public and can be viewed from the exterior only. But perhaps the most interesting aspect of Évora, the single most important feature that gives it its particular charm, is the fortified wall, a considerable amount of which still remains. You can even view portions of the original Roman wall. The best section of the wall forms the border of the public gardens at the southern extremity of the city.

Since Évora is the economic as well as the cultural capital of the Alentejo province, it is a culinary center. Visitors will likely be introduced to at least two classic Alentejo dishes while in Évora. The first is the typical soup of the region, *Sopa de Alentejana*, which consists of an olive oil and garlic broth served over stale bread. The soup is considered to be the Portuguese cure-all, equivalent to Yiddish chicken soup. It is said that infants are fed this soup to improve their disposition. The other, a pork dish with clams, is discussed elsewhere in this volume and has become a Portuguese classic.

South of Lisbon

To the south of Lisbon lies a distinctive countryside. This area is quite different from the other regions of Portugal. The change is discernible in the scenery, climate, house types, people, and food.

There is only one principal road southbound from Lisbon. The road crosses the bridge over the Tagus and directs the tourist to *Algarve*. Algarve is the southern province of Portugal with a decidedly more Mediterranean climate. The road wanders through the western portion of lower Alentejo, which also has much to offer in terms of attractive landscapes. This is the region of cork oak trees, vineyards, and olive groves. At some of the larger farm homes, note the piles of curved cork bark waiting for shipment. The further south the road winds, the more noticeable the changes in the agricultural landscape become. The obvious change in cultivation is from olives and cork to citrus and other fruit.

As an alternative to driving, some people recommend the bus ride from Lisbon to Lagos. They claim it is comfortable, fast, and scenic. It is probably fast and scenic. But for the same price, the visitor can travel leisurely by train, pass through the classic Iberian landscape, and have an unspoiled view of the countryside as the train makes its way along the one-track southern route to Lagos.

From the vantage point of the train, which disturbs the routine of the countryside only momentarily, you can view scenes from centuries past: oxcarts, families working in the fields, and homesteads as ancient as the olive groves. Each of the nineteenth-century train stations is a delight. The train pauses at such places as *Alcaçer do Sal*, after passing through the flooded rice fields to the north of the city. The station at *Grandola* with its *azulejos* decor is particularly pleasing as it hugs the tracks. From Grandola the train begins a slow ascent on the edge of the *Serra de Grandola*. This is a hilly area in contrast to the heavily cultivated plains below and further east. Along many miles of track, you will notice a distinctive lack of roads crossing the track. In this part of Portugal there are few roads, and those that do exist are merely trails or dusty ruts.

Further along the route the train must wait until the northbound train passes since this is a one-track line.

As the train proceeds in a southerly direction, there is a noticeable change in climate. During winter, when Lisbon temperatures are hovering around 50° F., in Algarve the almond trees are in bloom, the oranges are ripe, the beans are blossoming, and the fruit trees are budding. Everywhere you smell the fragrance of blossoming fruit. The sky is generally a brilliant blue. The houses glare white in the sun, while their stylized chimneys catch the eye of a first-time visitor.

The chimneys, in fact, are a unique feature of Algarve's landscape. Some are so elaborate in stone filigree that they become showpieces only—too fancy to be efficient as chimneys.

Algarve was the land of the Moors. The art and architecture indicate that cultural heritage. The small towns and villages of Algarve have whitewashed, thick-walled homes and domed not steepled, churches. Orange-tile roofs seem to be growing from the cultivated countryside of almond groves and painfully gnarled and windswept fig trees. Long after the Crusaders had won back the remainder of Iberia, the Moslems of North Africa continued to trade in the towns of the coastal south. In Algarve the people are proud of their heritage and have an affinity for the culture of North

Africa. A true Algarvian claims to be very comfortable with the people, customs, and landscapes of Morocco, feeling a blood kinship.

It is true that Algarve is in a different cultural milieu. Although it has Moorish touches, it is still Portugal. The people are friendly and charming with tourists even though this area has many of them.

Some tourists prefer *Lagos* as the starting point to visit Algarve. Lagos does not require the tourist to walk through dismal cathedrals or musty museums. Its singular pleasure is its attitude. The town is clean, fresh, and friendly. The restaurants are numerous and varied. Obviously catering to the British tourists, the many English pubs serve "bangers" and "real English breakfasts," as all the signs tout. Seafood is plentiful and fresh and is available in so many tempting restaurants that deciding which to patronize is an arduous task.

The main street, facing the canal and harbor, offers an appropriate beginning for a restaurant tour. The principal shopping streets are one or two blocks to the west. Within this area there are many mouth-watering dining places. Wine-marinated and grilled tuna steaks are an integral part of local cuisine.

Lagos has become an international resort community favored by Germans, Britons, and Scots. Because of this, it transcends the local fishing-village image and has a seductive international mood. The yacht harbor, for example, is the mooring place of some very elegant vessels carrying some very elegant people. To attract wealthy people from around the world, Lagos holds an annual international yacht race.

In addition, Lagos has its historical imprint. From its harbor the great Portuguese explorers set out to navigate around the continent of Africa. In fact, the port of Lagos was Prince Henry the Navigator's main departure point.

Many travelers today use Lagos as a land base to explore the western end of Algarve. Car rentals are numerous, and when traveling off-season, you can expect significant discounts. Lagos is the consummate base for seeing western Algarve even without renting a car. Bus service from the main terminal will deliver you anywhere in the region cheaply but, of course, with less flexibility.

Leaving Lagos you venture to one of the grander sights in the world—*Cape St. Vincent* near *Sagres*. Sagres is only a short (36 km) drive from Lagos. A slight diversion at lovely little *Vila do Bispo* is worth the trip. Follow the road in a westerly direction toward *Praia do Castelejo*. The road meanders over ridges with ocean views and over windblown plateaus of stark barrenness until it reaches a boulder-strewn beach of the Atlantic. The scene is unsoiled—ice-blue water, multicolored cliffs, and brilliant azure sky.

After you return to Vila do Bispo, the remainder of the journey to Sagres is short. Sagres, at first glance, is a desolate, bleak, sand-strewn small town of little note except for one very important fact. Here Henry the Navigator learned to navigate. Here the great voyages of discovery were planned. Here at Cape St. Vincent Henry established his "school." From here Europeans ventured out to change the course of economic and political history.

Sagres is both fascinating and foreboding, nestled on the cliffs facing the Atlantic. The wondrous and spectacular cliffs are accessible by foot or car. Several hundred feet of sheer sandstone do not deter the local fishermen from their daily acrobatic fishing feats. Visitors watch in awe as these men lean at terrifying angles to check their catch dangling far below.

The best place for lodging is within walking distance of the town center, perched on high cliffs above a golden beach. It is another *Pousada*, called the *Pousada do Infante*. Each room has a view of the seascape that Henry admired. As usual, the food is excellent. There are not many other choices for accommodations in this little town. An excellent hotel, an *estalegem*, *pensãos*, and campgrounds make up the limited selection. The more adventurous may prefer to sleep in the hostel in what is left of Henry's navigation school. It is inexpensive and cozy.

Cape St. Vincent marks the most southwesterly point of Europe. Walk out the few kilometers from Sagres or drive the short distance. Visit the remains of Henry's residence and school. Walk beyond to the cliffs and contemplate what Henry and his men must have felt—wonder, speculation, excitement, and courage—as they gazed at that treacherous horizon and the unknown. The world looks huge from that vantage point. Linger at the fort and contemplate the fate of the tuna boats rounding the Cape. Stay awhile and count the ships as they pass ghostlike on the hazy horizon. Contemplate your own fate on this immense expanse of sea. This is a place for wondering.

As you return to Lagos, you will approach it from its best side. The western approach offers a fine view of the city. Leaving Lagos in an easterly direction, you will find that the next town of significance is *Praia da Rocha*, or rock beach. Although there are some rocks, this area has become one of the most popular resort areas in Algarve because it has beautiful white sand beaches with no rocks. The town of Praia da Rocha stands on a picturesque promontory facing the blue waters of the Atlantic. To see the whole of the coastline and resort area, drive just a bit to the west to an overlook near Dos Castelos Creek.

Further eastward lies the town of *Portimão*. There is little to interest the casual visitor in Portimão except tuna canneries and fishing-boat construction. Both are interesting industries in their own right, however, and persons wishing to visit a cannery or boatyard should ask at the Tourismo office in town.

Further east on the road toward *Faro* lie the popular resort towns of *Albufeira* and *Vilamoura*. Albufeira generates the classic image of a captivating resort town. The golden hills, green gardens, umber cliffs, whitewashed houses, orange-tile roofs, incredibly blue sky, white beaches, and sparkling water make it one of the best known seaside resorts in Algarve. Like many old fishing towns, Albufeira too, has its picturesque quarter. Walk up the steep streets from the *Largo Duarte Pacheco* in the center of town and lose yourself in cobbled lanes where Moorish arches span the narrow spaces. Here you can find a small café and relax as you prepare for resort-type entertainment in the evening.

Vilamoura was an ancient Roman outpost that apparently had a sizable population. Excavation into the ruins at *Cerro da Vial* continues to reveal buildings and beautiful artifacts. Now centuries after the Visigoths and Moors abandoned the site, the tourists— mostly British—have taken over. If you are worried about where to berth a yacht, you may want to consider Vilamoura. The marina, adjacent to the Roman ruins, can berth several hundred vessels, so you can rest easy.

Because all of these towns are now oriented to tourist trade, they offer a wide variety of restaurants from which to choose. There is an abundance of those specializing in freshly caught seafood. In addition, Algarve offers some interesting regional dishes and preparation techniques that you should try.

Probably the most unique dish is called *cataplana*. The whole dish—including clams or mussels, chicken, sausage, fish, pork, garlic, and assorted herbs—is cooked in a circular copper utensil that has a tight-fitting lid. The device allows the entire mixture to be turned and cooked on the opposite side to ensure even cooking and a delicious blending of juices and tastes. These utensils make interesting and functional souvenirs, which can be purchased anywhere in Algarve.

East of *Faro* is the little town of *Olhão*. Only about five miles from the larger Faro, Olhão is famous for its sardines, its Moorish-style houses, and narrow streets, and its barrier islands. The best way to pass the hours in this town is to consume quantities of fresh-grilled sardines, hard-crusted bread, and cold beer at any café near the port area.

Faro is a town worth visiting because it is so unresortlike. A non-tourist town is unusual in Algarve. The reason Faro seems to have fewer tourists is that it has no beach in town. Because of Faro's position relative to the protective barrier islands and salt marshes, the beach is a short bus ride away. Faro Beach will disappoint those looking for high-rise condominiums and flashy nightclubs. If, however, they want a wide expanse of white sand as far as the eye can see in both directions, they won't be disappointed. Sun-drenched and relaxed, Faro Beach is a place for seasonal residences, some rentals, *pensãos* and a few campgrounds. The city of Faro itself does enjoy some tourism since many people stay at the large Hotel Eva or Hotel Faro. A good view of the city can be gained from the rooftop pool and bar area of the Hotel Eva.

A major feature of seaward Faro is the so-called "yacht basin." It is pretty, but don't believe for a minute that you can moor your yacht there. Its shallowness is a real handicap. What really occupy the yacht basin are fishermen's dinghies, dories, and punts—no yachts.

Astride the basin rests Faro's most pleasant venue, the *Manuel Bivar Gardens*. This splendid city park offers lush tropical vegetation, benches, a bandstand, a newstand, vendors, many people, and a good sea breeze. Parks seem to be a Portuguese speciality, and this park is superior.

In the evening, you can enjoy the view of both the park and the yacht basin from the second-story bar of the Hotel Faro. In the distance, you can see the surprising amount of air traffic landing and departing at Faro's relatively new international airport. In recent years, it has become the transport hub for Algarve resort towns.

Faro has an old town that offers a welcome change of pace from the modern Faro. Check out the great *azulejos* decorations in the cathedral and spend a few minutes strolling the narrow streets of the ancient city.

Museums are not Faro's strong suit. See the Maritime Museum, the Municipal Museum, and the Ethnographic Museum, but don't linger. There is much activity on the streets. In the main shopping area, located just east of the park, are innumerable cafés, shops, and restaurants to delight visitors. Faro's year-round mild climate mitigates for many sidewalk cafés and al fresco dining experiences.

A classic *pasteleria* stands adjacent to the Hotel Faro. It extends between two streets and can be entered from either side. Try it for dessert. Note the vaulted ceilings, the nineteenth-century decor, and the nonstop activity.

Because Faro is the provincial capital, it also is the economic capital. There are many cork factories, marble-finishing factories, and canneries, which process the fruit and vegetables of the bountiful Algarve. Faro, like most coastal towns in Portugal, has a population engaged in fishing. It has also become a processing center for the tons of sardines and tuna taken each year. Fresh tuna should be on your list of gastronomic experiences while in Algarve. You should also try almonds in their myriad forms: in pudding, in candy, or plain. Figs are also an integral part of the dessert cuisine of Algarve. Most are served dried or preserved as jam.

Lisbon Area

Lisbon lies within an area dotted with smaller surrounding towns. There are a few that visitors must see, such as *Cascais* and *Sintra*. Others make interesting day trips because they have a special attraction or feature that beckons.

Most of the bus tours of Lisbon take their groups along the Estoril Coast west of Lisbon to the smaller town of *Cascais*. Cascais is now a sizeable suburb and condominium center for many Britons and Americans. It maintains its small-town charm in the sense that you can visit its principal sights on foot. The tour buses all seem to leave their passengers at Fishermen's Beach in front of the Hotel Baia. This is a perfect place to begin to feel the ambiance of Cascais.

Originally, the town was a small fishing village. Legend has it that a Cascais fisherman actually discovered the new world and passed the information to Christopher Columbus as he was passing through. It is possible that Columbus visited Cascais. His in-laws had a pretty *quinta* (farm) not far away where he was known to have visited with his wife. Whatever the truth of that story, the village portion of Cascais and the fishermen's beach are quite picturesque. The small, crescent-shaped beach is nearly totally occupied by the boats and gear of the local fishermen. An interested tourist can spend many happy days studying the techniques of these hardy men as they go about their daily activities. Every evening they moor their boats off-shore and unload their catches. Hefty crates and boxes full of fish are then rowed to the beach in small dorries. The fish are carted a short distance to the auction house opposite the hotel, where the fun of the sale begins. It is impossible to follow the fast pace of Portuguese auctioneers, but the auction is a so-called "Dutch auction." That is, the auctioneer starts high, and the price descends until there is a willing buyer at the specified price. The buyers at this auction are mostly restauranteurs and shopkeepers.

Nearby—in fact, one block to the right as you face the auction buildling—is Cascais' "Restaurant Row" *(Rua das Flores).* No cars are allowed on the narrow street. Here you can find a collection of some of the best (and most expensive) seafood restaurants in Portugal. Many display the evening purchases in the windows in decorative arrangements of shellfish, fish, and assorted edibles of the sea. The aromas are mouthwatering.

On the beach a charming and picturesque scene awaits the sunset. The brilliantly painted fishing boats seem to glow in the twilight. Few harbors in Portugal are so pretty. All of this loveliness is framed by the uphill slope of the road and the huge homes of the Portuguese wealthy or deposed European royalty. The Hotel Baia bar happens to be a good place to sip one's after-dinner port and watch the sunset. There are several other restaurants nearby that also offer a splendid view of the harbor. The Hotel Albatroz offers the most elegant place to enjoy the seascape. Seek it out; it is a few blocks west of the harbor and sits on its own spectacular rock promotory. The lounge and restaurant are beautiful, the service is superb, and the view pays for the extra cost.

The main shopping street in Cascais meanders only a few blocks. Note the mosaic design in the pavement; no cars are allowed here. Count the many restaurants. In all of Cascais, as you lose your way in the cobbled byways and alleys, you will find a wide variety of cuisine: Indian, Chinese, Italian, Korean, and so on. The best restaurants specialize in fresh-caught seafoods.

Cascais is the western terminus of the Estoril Line electric train from Lisbon, so it is very easy to find. It has many excellent hotels and is a short walk or train ride from the Casino at *Estoril*. The Casino, as discussed elsewhere, is the principal attraction in this very attractive and expensive suburb of Lisbon. Just east of Cascais, Estoril offers the first of the better beaches west from Lisbon.

Between Estoril and Cascais lies *Monte Estoril*. This is mostly a residential area, although more and better restaurants and pubs are springing up in old Monte to serve the huge number of British tourists. Monte is considered very elegant and sophisticated by Portuguese standards. It, like Estoril and Cascais, would be considered a prestige address in Portugal.

The Estoril Coast combines past glories and present chic so that it is also known as the Portuguese "Riviera." Throughout Estoril, Monte Estoril, and Cascais are the magnificent villas of the wealthy. Built many years ago, these were the second homes of the Portuguese elite and European aristocracy. Times change and lifestyles change even faster. The result was that many of these fine old mansions were abandoned. In recent years, however, restoration has become more evident. Saving the unique architectural styles, their warmth and stateliness, is a task that only the well-to-do can afford. Fortunately, many unique villas are being rejuvenated. Stroll the *Rua do Lido*, *Avenida Saboia*, and *Rua de Nice*. Note how the new pride in ownership restores this special area of Europe. Visitors interested in historic preservation will find these restorations of special concern. Tourists seeking unusual architectural styles, elegance, and hints of eras past will enjoy strolling the residential streets that wind through the hills of Estoril and Monte Estoril. Street maps are available at the *Tourismo* office in Estoril at the Arcade (west corner). Without a map, it is easy to lose your direction as the streets and lanes twist and turn past splendid villas and blooming gardens.

Setúbal is a rather large town near Lisbon that you can visit for several reasons. First, it is Portugal's third largest port and industrial center. That fact alone makes it an interesting place to see. Second, it has two intriguing museums and an interesting church (*Jesus*) with fascinating, twisted, Manueline-style columns. Third, it is a fun place during the month of June because June tenders many feast days and patron saints' celebrations in elaborate street parties and parades. Fourth, it is close to the *Serra da Arrábida* and the natural park therein. These limestone hills rise directly from the sea and give the illusion of great height. The road westward from Setúbal toward *Portinho* presents unparalled views. The panoramas are stunningly beautiful. The road curves, winds, and meanders around the hilltops high above the water and the *Troia Peninsula* in the distance. As the highway twists and turns over precipitous terrain, notice the *Convent of Arrábida* founded by St. Peter of Alcantara. Above the road, in still virgin forest, are many small chapels and hermitages built for the ancient monks. This, in fact, is the only remaining original forest cover in the region.

The return trip to Lisbon via *Palmela* provides much to see. The great castle on the hill at Palmela is one of Portugal's great *Pousadas*. The old town of Palmela draping down the hill from the castle still charms visitors with its clustered houses on narrow lanes. The view from the castle exhibits the richly fruited plain from Setúbal in the south to Lisbon in the north.

Near the town of *Azeitão*, take the road leading to the village of *Vila Fresca de Azeitão*. Opposite the village bus station, there is an inconspicuous entry leading to the *Quinta da Bacalhão*. Ring the bell and ask to see the gardens. The gardens contain the best sculpted boxwoods in Portugal. The intricately designed hedges lead to the fountain and the pavilion with its three towers. These towers contain the oldest dated tile panel in the country (1565). The sixteenth-century house remains in superb condition.

Your return trip to Lisbon could be punctuated by a stop at the winery in *Azeitão* for a brief tour of the storehouses and aging rooms. This famous winery, *J. M. da Fonseca*, produces the popular Lançers and some twenty other wines. The aging rooms have exhibits encased in cobwebs that look centuries old.

While in the vicinity of Setúbal, check out the new tourist complex on the *Troia* Peninsula. This pure sand strip at the Sado River estuary can be reached by ferry, motorboat, hovercraft, or road (the long way). It is interesting to see planned development in a very spontaneous country. You can also enjoy the view of the *Arrabida* range and visit the archaeological digs at the Roman ruins of *Cetobriga*.

If you have had enough of fishing ports, beaches, monasteries, and noise by this time, you should be ready to seek relief at *Queluz*. To the northwest of Lisbon stands the royal palace at *Queluz* and the palace and castles at *Sintra*.

The royal palace in Queluz is now completely surrounded by urban development. At one time the location, only eight miles west of Lisbon, was a secluded country estate. Urban development in the second half of the twentieth century completely surrounded the grounds and palace. The approach, therefore, is not grand. In fact, your first sight of the palace may be disappointing. The street-side entry displays a rather shabby and uninspiring facade. The rose-colored stucco needs a touch-up and landscaping is desperately needed. Near the main entry is one of the better and more interesting places to dine in the Lisbon area. The government manages a very elegant restaurant within the palace. You may wish to plan your visit around the midday meal, but expect to pay, by Portuguese measure, very high prices.

The small but elegant palace, you may be surprised to learn, still functions in official state visits. For example, in recent years Queen Elizabeth of England, Ronald and Nancy Reagan, and many other heads of state have graced the halls of Queluz Palace. One can only wonder what the queen's and Nancy Reagan's first impressions were as they emerged from their vehicles to see the rather shabby entry.

Inside the palace is a different story. The palace was built after the design of Versailles and reminds one of that distinctive edifice. Begun in 1758 and completed in 1794, the palace was originally the residence of Queen Maria until her death in 1816. Over the years, it has been furnished and embellished in a royal fashion.

All tours are guided, and English-speaking guides are available. The tour is conducted through much of the palace, including the Ambassadors' Hall, the Queen's Bedroom, the Don Quixote Room decorated with scenes from the story, the Music Room, and the Throne Room. The latter's stunning beauty and impressive elegance looks like everyone's dream of a throne room.

The guided portion of the tour ends at the entry to the main garden where you step into a sculptured green world. The shaped boxwoods, flowers, pools, statues, and fountains will hold your attention for hours. Stroll to the far edge and photograph the main facade of the palace. Compare it later to photos of Versailles. The gardens were designed by a Frenchman named *Robillon* who also had much influence in the architecture of the palace itself.

The *Canal Basin* remains one of the more fascinating features of the garden. Built in the eighteenth century and lined with gorgeous *azulejos*, the canal was designed for the sailing pleasures of royalty. Its original splendor can only be imagined, but it certainly represents royal excesses of the past. When you see it, you can understand the commoners' impatience with such works. The tiled Canal Basin remains a wonder to modern Portuguese and other visitors.

Sintra, the small town on the edge of the *Serra de Sintra,* is only a short drive beyond Queluz or a thirty-minute electric train ride from Lisbon. If you take only one tour outside of Lisbon, it should be to Sintra.

Nestled against the granite block known as the Sintra Range, the town has a climate that is milder, moister, and more pleasant than towns even a few miles distant. For nearly six hundred years Sintra was the favored summer residence for Portuguese kings. Royalty liked the climate and the way the landscape framed the pretty little town and their palaces. The English poet Byron spent much time in Sintra and called it his equivalent to Utopia. The famous Portuguese epic poets Camões and Gil Vincente praised the little town in stanza and song. Kings, poets, and modern tourists have all appreciated Sintra.

The loveliest section of Sintra, as well as the liveliest area, surrounds the royal palace. You can linger for hours at a café watching the tour buses come and go, sipping great coffee, and nibbling pastries. *Queijadas,* small cheese- or fruit-filled tarts, are one of the many Sintra pastry specialties you should try.

You can also wander the hilly streets and passages of the town, popping into shops or admiring the old and elegant houses nestled in rich vegetation.

From afar, you can see the Serra da Sintra. More likely than not the morning finds the hills shrouded in clouds. The weather can be sunny and bright everywhere surrounding Sintra, but the massif and the town will be receiving its usual gentle morning shower to refresh the flowers and clean the air. By midmorning, Sintra is sunny yet pleasantly cool. It is no wonder that ancient kings, poets, and wealthy people of today have chosen the gentle climate of Sintra for their summer residences.

You may wish to visit *S. Pedro de Sintra.* Not long ago it was a separate village, but it now connects to old Sintra. The attractions for tourists include antique shops and shops where you can purchase Portuguese artifacts and leather goods. S. Pedro also has a lively fair every second and fourth Sunday of the month.

The modern city of Sintra is the area known as *Estafania.* There is

not much here to attract the tourist, so stick to old Sintra and visit
the royal palace. More than likely you will approach old Sintra from
the east on the S. Pedro side. As you negotiate the sweeping turn
into the town, watch for the spectacular view of the palace's unique
conical chimneys. The palace sits serenely in the valley. Note its
irregular shape. This is due to the many additions built over the
centuries. The main structure dates back to the famous João I and
the fourteenth century. Other additions took place in succeeding
centuries, thus giving the palace a trans-historic character and
feeling. The palace was built on the site of a Moorish fortress after
its capture by Portugal's first king, Dom Afonso Henriques, in
1147. But not until the fourteenth century did the palace take its
present shape. You can, however, still note the Moorish elements
in the complexity of rooms (many at varying levels). The windows,
doors, and arches possess much Moorish influence. The interior
gardens and fountains also retain the atmosphere of a Moorish
alcazar.

Inside, visitors will be enthralled. The guided tour takes you
through each of the noteworthy rooms. The kitchens are of particular interest since they are the places from which emanate those
strange conical chimneys. Look up through the chimney for an
unusual sight. The kitchens remain as the oldest part of the palace.
Note the walls decorated with pale green tiles. Under the vast
chimneys, in the circular hearths, at least two oxen could have been
roasted for ancient royal banquets.

Adjacent to the kitchen is another Moorish-style room, decorated
in Mudejar tiles from the seventeenth century. These are some of
the oldest tiles in the palace. Note the small fountain set in the
center of the room.

The chapel is a serene combination of reds, browns, and gold.
The chapel's upper walls are lined with fifteenth-century frescoes
while on the lower portion of the walls are examples of the finest
early Portuguese *azulejos* anywhere to be found. The chapel ceiling
is the palace's oldest decoration. The carved Gothic rosettes date
from the time of João I.

The tour leads to (but not into) a small room next to the chapel,
which is said to be haunted by the ghost of Afonso VI. The story is
that in the seventeenth century, Afonso was imprisoned in this
very room by his not-so-loving brother Pedro II. Locked in this one
room for nine years, his only exercise was to pace the floor. (Note

where the tiles have been worn away by incessant pacing in front of the heavy door.) He died, obviously insane, in 1683.

The Chinese Room is so named because it is replete with oriental furniture acquired from the Far East colonies centuries ago. Look for the incredible ivory pagoda given to Portuguese royalty by the emperor of China in 1806.

Passing through the huge bedroom, look carefully at the oversized seventeenth-century bed. The room is decorated with unbelievable sixteenth-century tiles. Look closely and note that each tile has a raised green vine leaf.

In the following room, called the Mermaids' Room, the visitor can see some very rare fifteenth-century black tiles. The ceiling gives the room its name. Notice the ship and the mermaids rising from the sea.

The tour next leads to the Coats-of-Arms room. The reason for its name, too, is the ceiling. The domed and coffered ceiling presents the coats of arms of no less than seventy-two noble families. The walls are of eighteenth-century *azulejos* depicting hunting adventures. Look out the windows to the south. The view will be of the old town. Then look up into the hills for a superb view of the Moorish castle and its seventh- and eighth-century ramparts. The castle lies in ruins, but it is worth a taxi ride or brisk hike to catch a view of the ocean, the plains, and the unusual *Pena Palace* nearby.

Back inside the palace, the tour continues with the magnificent Magpie Room. An interesting story accompanies the name. The ceiling and frieze of the room are decorated with paintings of magpies with the words *"por bem"* (for the best) sealing their beaks. Legend has it that João I's wife caught him kissing one of her ladies in waiting. Palace gossip proliferated and became unbearable for old João. His infuriated statement against the gossip was to have the room painted with as many magpies as there were gossips in the court—their chattering beaks sealed "for the best."

The Swan Room is the last on the tour. This room is spacious. Note the green and white diamond-shaped *azulejos* in the recesses and doorways. The carved ceiling, however, is the real prize. The octagonal panels are adorned with twenty-seven gold-collared swans. Note the rectangular pond outside the windows the full length of the room. It is told that live swans once gracefully glided in the water for the delight of João I's daughter, Isabela, and her husband, the Duke of Burgundy. The patio offers a closeup of the famous chimneys. These chimneys are the distinguishing marks of the palace and are the symbol of the city of Sintra. On the opposite side of the patio there is a good view of the Moorish castle in the heights of the hills. Below, behold the courtyard in front of the palace.

A horse-drawn carriage can be hired for a trip through the streets of Sintra and up the massif to the incredible *Pena Palace*. The carriage is a bit expensive, but the ride offers a leisurely, entrancing, and scenic experience. Taxis are also available, but the ride to Pena is at the usual breakneck, hair-raising speeds through the cobbled streets.

The unique Pena Palace is not very old (built in the nineteenth century), but it looks like something out of a royal bad dream. Study its architecture and note the combination of Gothic, Moorish, baroque, Manueline, and Renaissance styles. It has been criticized roundly as a mishmash of architectural blunders, an eyesore. Critics notwithstanding, Pena Palace exudes its own beauty. The combination of a Moorish dome over a Gothic window may sound absurd, but such mixes do exist at Pena. The result is visually better than it sounds. Don't be too critical of those unusual touches. Look at the whole and relish the net result. You can argue that the best of Pena is the site. What a place to build a palace! The vista surpasses that of even the Moorish castle. Observe the scene clear to Lisbon, the Caparica coast far across the Tejo estuary. Look west to the ocean and the vast plain, green with vegetation and orange with tiled roofs. You can also gain an excellent grasp of the Serra da Sintra, the granite block stretching to the ocean that traps cool ocean air and makes Sintra so climatically pleasing. You are standing at its summit.

Spend some time in the center of Sintra. Have lunch or dinner at any of the many restaurants near the royal palace. The range of price is broad. If you plan to spend the night, there are also some superb hotels quite near the palace. To wake up in this poetic setting can be a treat. A unique experience would be sipping morning coffee near the royal palace with the Moorish castle and Pena above.

The *Seteais Palace* lies only a fifteen-minute walk from the town center along the Colares Road. Completed in 1787 for the Dutch consul in Lisbon, its architectural lines are neoclassical. Over the years of changing ownership, the palace has had many additions, including a duplicate of the original building linked to the original structure by a magnificent arch. Eventually, royalty grew tired of the palace, and it was abandoned and allowed to decay. In 1955 the palace was acquired by the national government. Under state ownership it was renovated and opened to the public as a five-star hotel. This is a great place to spend a few nights. The royal bedrooms occupy the lower floor. If you are fortunate, you can sleep in these beautiful chambers with their frescoed walls and grand views of the far coastline and the palace gardens. All of the rooms, even those on the upper floors, are impeccably decorated and furnished with period pieces. Visit the dining room and bar. Both are hand painted with old country scenes. Walk through the garden and note the rock outcrop where Byron found solace and the atmosphere to write so enthusiastically about Sintra. Here you will totally understand his sense of ease and pleasure.

All visitors should see *Cabo da Rocha*, the westernmost point of Europe. This is the spot on the continent closest to North America. The vistas of the rugged coast are impressive. On this isolated cape a few hundred feet above the Atlantic, the wind is usually strong and chilly. But here there is also a nice little restaurant, a respectable place for warming your bones or having a good lunch. On the drive back to the main road, look for farm fields sheltered from the constant ocean wind by woven cane windbreaks. Such structures are unique and present an intriguing study in agricultural adjustment.

CHAPTER 13

Lisbon:
Lisboa, Lissabonne

The story of Lisbon is a long one. There is some evidence to suggest that the Greeks, in their trading, visited the Tejo River estuary. Historians tell us that the site of Lisbon might have been a Phoenician settlement, and certainly the Romans laid claim to the site. The story continues with the Visigoths, the Moors, the great Portuguese Empire, and modern Lisbon. What one sees today in this city on the Tagus (Tejo) River is the consequence of the decisions and events of thousands of years of occupation by varying cultural groups.

During the age of the great discoveries, Lisbon was indeed, the center of the world. Its importance was never greater. It has lost that prominence to be sure. By modern European standards Lisbon is a small capital city, even a poor capital city. Because of various economic strains over the decades of the twentieth century, Lisbon has lost the glow and glitter of "Princess of the World," as Camões called the city. But *"Iacta alea est"* (the die is cast), and Lisbon has taken on a unique facade.

Despite peeling paint and a little deferred maintenance here and there, Lisbon is a happier, friendlier, more energetic capital city than most. Lisboetans, the people of the city, are happy. It is an edifying and safe place to experience the relaxed Iberian way of life. Juxtaposed to Madrid, its Iberian sister, Lisbon suffers by comparison. Madrid is bright, fast, flashy, dynamic, and a bit stuffy and officious. There are too many police with guns in Madrid, and too much organization. The contrast between the Iberian capitals is startling. Travelers who visit Madrid first will love it. If they visit Lisbon immediately thereafter, they will be amazed at the difference in attitudes of the people. Lisbon is scruffier, true. Lisbon is less flashy, true. But Lisbon is more fun. It is a city where the visitor can walk nearly the entire central area. Old Lisbon (Lisboa Antiga) has a charm that cannot be matched by other cities. Lisbon by the Tagus, with its hills and valleys, its trams and narrow cobbled streets, is like no other European capital city.

Modern Lisbon possesses the mundane as well. Unfortunately, midtwentieth-century urban architecture, the so-called "international style," abounds in modern Lisbon. The population, except in old Lisbon, is homogeneous in income, education, and social standing. It is, therefore, very difficult to identify neighborhoods based upon income or other social or economic indicators. As a result, much of modern Lisbon looks alike. Each block, however, has it own identity with the ever-present *pasteleria*, restaurant, and tiny grocery shop. Perhaps there will be a shoe store, hardware store, jeweler, or tailor located in the block. Some of the restaurants in the newer neighborhoods are even quite good. All are inexpensive and most offer similar simple fare. Ah, but in old Lisbon— Alfama, Rossio, Graça, Bairro Alto, Chiado, Praça do Comércio— the ambiance grabs hold of you and beckons you to walk, linger, explore, and enjoy.

By far the best known part of old Lisbon is *Alfama*, which predates the devastating 1755 earthquake. So terrible was the quake that most of the buildings in the lower town (Baixa) were destroyed. An estimated forty thousand people lost their lives. Alfama escaped major damage because the buildings were built, by accident, very well. Each of the thick walls of brick and stones abutted other walls of similar composition. The result was that the neighborhood shook and rolled in the quake, but virtually none of the buildings collapsed. As evidence of the integrity of the old buildings, there is a very narrow street in Alfama that is nearly closed at the roof line because the eaves of the houses are actually leaning together in support of one another. Could they survive another major earthquake?

To discover the oldest part of Lisbon, you need to walk. The tour can be strenuous as the walk ascends to the castle and through the narrow streets. Begin your walk at *Praça do Comércio* (also known as *Terreiro do Paço*). The square, said to be the most exquisite in Lisbon, is in reality nothing but a parking lot. The great equestrian statue in the center is surrounded by Renaults and Fiats. Too bad. At one time in the not too distant past, the square was the showplace of the gilded city, the entryway from the sea. It has lost that function, but the surrounding buildings are in the classical arcaded style and worth a look. Most are governmental offices. Look carefully at the magnificent nineteenth-century baroque-style arch leading into the *Baixa* (low area). The Baixa area was completely destroyed by the earthquake and was the original site of the royal palace—hence the name Terreiro do Paço, or Palace Terrace.

From here, walk eastward toward *Rua de Alfandega*, passing the ruins of a sixteenth-century church known as the *Conceição Velha*. As the street begins to climb the hill toward Alfama, you pass the *sé* (cathedral). Tour the *sé* if you have time. It is an old one, built in the twelfth century after the Crusaders recaptured Lisbon from the Moors. Some of the details are fascinating in this Romanesque structure. Once a fortress like its contemporaries in Porto and Coimbra, it has parapeted towers at the front. The sacristy now serves as the museum. An excellent representative work of Portugal's premier sculptor, Machado de Castro, rests in a chapel on the north side. You must pay a few *escudos* to enter, but the exquisite baroque-style Nativity is worth the cost. A visit to the Gothic cloisters will remind you of the Cistercian style so prominent at Alcobaça. The cathedral has undergone much restoration since the quake of 1755. Today there is constant restoration and renovation, so visitors should expect some confusion and disarray. The cathedral remains an interesting mixture of styles, periods, and techniques of architectural restoration.

As you leave, passing the north wall of the huge structure, look for the low relief carvings at the base of one of the pillars. These are Visigothic carvings that date from the sixth century. Unless these ancient works are preserved soon, pollution, wear, and many hands will continue to waste them away.

Continue up the hill and stop at the belvedere of *Santa Luzia*. This lovely overlook is usually crowded with old women knitting in the sun, old men playing dominoes or checkers, and youngsters just playing. Before you are lost in the view of Alfama's maze and the harbor, look at the wonderful *azulejos* covering the walls of the Church of Santa Luzia. These panels are excellent examples of the decorative depiction of historic events so common throughout the city.

Further, beyond the belvedere, is the *Largo das Portas do Sol*. There is a pretty view of the Alfama here, but before turning down into Alfama, you must first visit the *Castelo São Jorge*. This monument, from the eleventh century, dominates the cityscape. The castle, built on the promontory above the city, is nestled in a setting of luxurious splendor. The grounds are the home of peacocks, the famous black swans, and other fowl. The fortress is, in a real sense, the true beginning of Lisbon. The city grew up from and around the castle. In medieval times, for example, the city encompassed most of the area on the heights surrounding the citadel. As population grew, the built-up area cascaded down the south slope of the hill toward the river. The castle walls were extended both north and south in the fourteenth century to protect the residents from barbarian threats.

Enter the castle grounds through the main arched portal. Look for the painted statue of St. George on the left. Once inside, you will be struck by the peacefulness of the surroundings. In contrast to its stormy and violent history, the castle is now quiet, an almost demure place. Spend some time climbing the castle ramparts to catch breathtaking panoramas of the city. You can see nearly the entire urban area of Lisbon from the castle. The vista of the river, hills, orange-tile roofs, and green parks gives an excellent picture of the city. From these heights the city looks like a sea of orange and green wavelets. Visitors often spend hours entranced by the sights from the castle heights.

After leaving the castle grounds, locate the *Tourismo* office near the entry and acquire a map of Alfama. You will need it now because after a good lunch at one of the many restaurants near the castle, you are ready to venture into the heart of Alfama. There are some superior night spots near the castle. Some of the famous *Fado* houses of old Lisbon are in Alfama. In June, which is the best time to come, the streets are alive with song and food during the festivals associated with the popular saints.

Walk a little further to the Church of *Santa Engraçia*. The church itself is a masterpiece of baroque styling and is built in the form of a Greek cross. Visitors can climb the cupola for an unusual view of the city. But the fun is nearby on Tuesdays and Saturdays at *Campo de Santa Clara,* near the church of *São Vincente de Fora,* which has beautiful *azulejos* panels. On those days the *"Fiera da Ladra"* is celebrated. This flea market is unequalled in Lisbon. You can find anything you can imagine. Some vendors have a wide selection of fascinating antique maps. Others sell memorabilia of bullfights, including the old photos. Still others specialize in the interesting antique door knockers seen so often in old Lisbon—a lion's head molded of solid brass.

Walk back to the *Largo das Portas do Sol.* Continue down the stair-street into the Alfama. First-time visitors will no doubt notice the number of areas referred to *largo* in this part of Lisbon. This is a Portuguese word meaning simply "a wide area." There are many in Alfama. But "wide" in Alfama is not the same as "wide" elsewhere. Because the area has narrow streets and lanes, a *largo* may be an area only twenty feet wide. Nevertheless, *largos* act as convenient landmarks for visitors and open spaces and gathering places for residents.

You can easily become confused in the labyrinth of streets, stairs, and *largos.* Alfama is, in the words of a Portuguese author ". . . confused, heaped-up, multi-colored, twisted and re-twisted, lots of embracing narrow streets and overhanging eaves." Alfama is an intriguing collection of archways, stairways, tiny houses with lace curtains, back yards, roof gardens, blind alleys, and terraces. Al fama is the aroma of grilled sardines, the squawk of the chicke॒ soon to be dispatched for the evening meal, and the chatter of ol women leaning out of windows to gossip or scold noisy childre॒ Alfama is also the sound of ubiquitous canaries singing happily in their cages hung carefully in the sun and the mournful melody of the *fado* sung by the young woman scrubbing the stone threshold of her family's small home. The sights common to Alfama are window shutters, women dressed in black, flower-covered walls, coats of arms, *azulejos* panels, window boxes, and dripping laundry overhead. Some of the houses are so old that they have no running water. All water must be carried from a public water tap. There are common bath houses, common laundry rooms, and noisy gathering places. There are a million photo opportunities. Alfama is also myriad balconies, railings, forgotten doorways, columns, Moorish walls, ancient foundations, loose stones, elaborate gas lanterns, gables, and overhanging stories. It is a place of many corners and jumbled roof lines. The views of Alfama from high belvederes or from the castle show clearly how building upon building was added or changed, creating a crazy-quilt patchwork of orange-tile roof lines that defy the modern sense of organization. Alfama is a place that accumulated, growing as its residents' needs dictated. Alfama is lazy dogs, an army of cats, a thousand tiny taverns, a chorus of street cries, perpetual motion, and the aroma of fish, beans, and cabbage. Visit early in the day and listen to the vendors bargaining in the streets. In the spring you can buy snails by the kilogram, fresh sardines, a live turkey, fresh-baked bread, and fragrant cheeses at the small shops everywhere. You will delight in the cheerful greetings of "Bom dia" as Alfama residents pass. Alfama is a salutary place to linger and absorb a lifestyle that has evolved for centuries in the Portuguese sunshine.

The Rio Tejo, or Tagus River, is the reason for much daily activity in old Lisbon. Beyond the commuter train station at Cais do Sodré is an area to the west known as Madrogão. Between Cais do Sodré and Santos, the atmosphere is filled with the hustle and bustle of port activities, the smell of the river, and seedy characters. The busiest time is sun-up, when the fishermen auction their catch to the varinas, the fish women. Usually stocky and big-boned, these women all dress in wide black skirts and wear gold earrings and gold crosses on their necklaces. With ruddy cheeks and throaty voices, they are the fish hawkers you see and hear in Alfama, singing their sales pitch in the streets as they carry dripping wet baskets of fish on their heads. Yes, on their heads! These are some of the genuine characters remaining from a way of life centuries old. The smell of the fish market is powerful, so be prepared.

If you continue westward along the Estrada da Marginal (the main road along the river), you will arrive at Belém. You can also ride the electric train or the tram from Cais do Sodré. A taxi is also inexpensive and easy. Belém is the seat of Portuguese political power and the site of many historic events associated with the great discoveries.

When you arrive, stroll through the Praça Afonso de Albuquerque. The huge rectangular space of sculpted hedges and trees lies between the main sights of Belém. On the north side of the Praça, note first the National Palace of Belém, the official residence of the President of the Republic. It is a lovely rose-colored stucco building that some residents and visitors affectionately refer to as the "Pink House." You can view the ceremonial changing of the guard, but it is advisable to check first with your hotel concierge for exact times.

The *Coach Museum* is attached to the building. This museum will be discussed with all other museums later in this chapter.

To the west of the palace lies the *Praça do Imperio* and the *Jeronimos Monastery*. The monastery dates from the beginning of the six-teenth century and is a prime example of the Manueline style of Portuguese architecture. Built by King Manuel, the church and monastery are today the principal visitor attractions in Belém. The best Manueline decorative embellishments are on the two portals, the west one being the better. Inside you will marvel at the very thin columns that support the pure Renaissance-style network vaulted interior. Note the tomb of *Vasco da Gama*, a famous explorer during the period of the great discoveries. It was from this area, the so-called *Restelo Harbor* that the Age of Exploration, the great dis-coveries, and Portugal's vast empire commenced. The harbor no longer exists. The monastery itself was built on the water's edge but years of filling and natural change left the building some distance from the river.

Near the river, facing Jeronimos, is a magnificent stone monu-ment evoking memories of the great explorers. The shape is unique. The *Monument to the Explorers* was designed to resemble the shape of the bow of the old sailing ships, the Portuguese *caravels*. At the prow of the ship is a powerful statue of *Henry the Navigator,* pointing the way of discovery to the persons represented by the sculptures. Included in the parade are *King Manuel* and the author *Camões*. Other figures are of the great explorers, such as *Da Gama* and *Magellan*. Note the surrounding mosaic pavement (wave-like) and the beautiful inlaid compass rose given to Portugal as a gift from South Africa upon the dedication of the monument in 1960.

The most photogenic monument at Belém is the *Torre de Belém* (Tower of Belém) built in the fifteenth century by King Manuel. It is an unparalleled example of the Manueline style. Built originally in midstream of the river, it is now on the north bank of the river opposite and a bit west of Jeronimos. The tower has become a symbol of the discoveries and is often used as the symbol of Portugal's golden age. Built by Manuel as a lighthouse, fortress, and royal residence combination, it was also intended as the orig-inal monument to the explorers—a tower that would see them safely back to port. The tower is five stories high and embellished in the Manueline tradition with battlements decorated with the shield of Manuel's Order of the Cross of Christ. On one of the terraces stands an elegant statue of Our Lady of Safe Homecoming. The tower is balanced nicely by the rounded sentry boxes at each corner. Unfortunately, the interior of the tower has been closed to visitors for the past few years because of jurisdictional disputes concerning its management. These problems should be resolved soon so that visitors can enjoy the interior royal chambers.

Looking toward the river and to your left (eastward), notice the great suspension bridge (Bridge of April 25th) that links the north and south of Portugal over the wide Tagus. The view of Lisbon from the bridge is particularly good. Unfortunately, there is no stopping for pictures. On the south side of the river you will see a huge statue of *Christ in Majesty*, or *Cristo Rei*. Ninety-two feet (28 m.) high, it is a scaled-down copy of the famous statue in Rio de Janeiro. You can drive to it easily by following signs on the south side of the bridge. The observation deck at the foot of the statue is 371 feet (114 m.) above the river and offers a panoramic view of the city and the Tagus estuary.

The *Baixa*, or "low town," north of Terreiro do Paço (Praça do Comerçio) lies between the St. George Castle and the Bairro Alto. You will immediately notice that, unlike any other part of Lisbon, Baixa is an area of regular, straight streets crossing at right angles to one another. This rectangular grid system was the direct result of the rebuilding of Lisbon following the great earthquake of 1755. The *Marquis de Pombal* initiated the plan that gives Baixa its orderly character. Baixa is Lisbon's financial district, its principal shopping area, and the bustling commercial center of the city. Note the names of the streets: *Rua do Ouro* (Gold Street), *Rua da Prata* (Silver Street), *Rua Dos Fanqueiros* (Draper Street). Located on Rua do Ouro for centuries has been the gold-trading area of Lisbon. Likewise, Rua da Prata was the historical center for the silver trade. Today nearly all of Baixa is crammed with banks, jewelers, goldsmiths, silversmiths, and financial institutions.

The main street, *Rua Angusta*, leading to Rossio from Praça do Comerçio is lined with banks, jewelry stores, and bookshops. This area has more bookstores than any other part of Lisbon.

The *Santa Justa Street Elevator (Elevador)* on Rua do Ouro is one of Lisbon's unique sights and experiences. It was designed by the Frenchman Eiffel of tower fame. Take it to the top for a splendid view of the Baixa and Rossio area. Visitors are usually surprised by the elevator's size: fifty persons. It has no windows, so there is no view on the rise. Once out of the upper platform, follow the catwalk to the high neighborhood, or *Bairro Alto,* past the ruins of the *Carmelite Church.* The church, another victim of the earthquake, now serves as an archaeological museum. From the street level at Rossio you can easily locate this landmark structure in Bairro Alto.

Stroll to the left along *Rua do Carmo* to *Rua Garrett.* This is the district known as *Chiado.* The name is derived from the *Largo do Chiado,* which creates its heart. The *largo* itself is named in memory of the nineteenth-century Portuguese writer, Chiado. He and the famous novelist Eça de Queiroz sipped coffee, observed life, and argued politics and world affairs at the *Brasileira* on Rua Garrett. That café is still the scene for the city's freethinkers. Note the elaborate wood carvings embellishing the walls, the brass bar trim, the mirrors, the small tables, and the people (some of who are probably aspiring poets!). This place has atmosphere and a sense of history. Best of all, it has yet to be discovered by tourists.

The Chiado district is the busiest in all Lisbon. This is *the* shopping area. This is where Lisbon's largest department stores are located and where the smart shops are found. Look around and do some shopping. You can purchase beautiful leather goods, shoes, and clothing along Rua Garrett. Even though this is Lisbon's fashionable shopping street, the first-time visitor should not expect Fifth Avenue or Rodeo Drive. No, in Portugal the shops, though impeccably arranged, are not full of the wide-ranging inventory Americans have come to expect. The department stores present their goods nicely but are unimpressive. There are, however, incredible bargains to be found. Enjoy the bustling, busy atmosphere, the *pastelerias* (some very fancy ones), the candy shops, the book shops, and the jewelry stores. This is the area of the huge fire in the summer of 1988. The 19th century buildings are being reconstructed in their original style.

Follow Rua do Carmo down the hill to what has been called the center of town, *Rossio.* The word *"rossio"* simply translates to English as "square." But the Rossio is more than that. Its official name is *Praça Dom Pedro IV,* whose statue adorns the central fountain.

Rossio has been serving as a trading and meeting place for five or six centuries. Since the 1755 earthquake, the Rossio has had a "new" look. It is surrounded on three sides by eighteenth-century structures that were suggested by the Marquis do Pombal in his reconstruction plan. The fourth side (north) is occupied by the *National Theater,* built in 1840. Look for the statue of *Gil Vincente* at the front near the entrance. Vincente was the originator of the Portuguese theater tradition.

Rossio today is not what Pombal envisioned. Twentieth-century transportation demands have destroyed what was once a quiet but busy urban square with fountains and flower stalls in the center. The fountains remain and the flower sellers are still there, but the square is choked with the fumes of buses and taxis. It would be awkward at best to purchase flowers from the sellers at the fountain. To get to them one must subject oneself to the crossfire of Lisbon traffic at its worst. The pedestrian, remember, in Rossio, is virtually nonexistent in the eyes of bus and taxi drivers.

Nevertheless, visitors should spend an adequate amount of time at Rossio in order to enjoy the interesting cafés at the square. The *Café Suiça* is the best and most popular place for people watching. The huge café has a delectable selection of pastries, ice creams, wines, and other drinks. Visitors *must* try it. Opposite the Suiça, on the far side of the square, remains one of the venerable old nineteenth-century cafés that offers an historic review of that era's lifestyles. It is the *Nicola*. You may be intimidated by its staid facade, but have a look at the rich interior.

The square, because it is a transport hub, is always busy. It also seems to be where Lisbon's "street people" gather. This is a hapless and harmless collection of off-beat young and middle-aged characters. Some are beggars, some just loafers and professional lottery players, but none are terribly unpleasant.

A better venue than Rossio, more lively in a people sense, is a lovely square just two blocks east. It is the *Praça da Figueira*. There are some good cafés here too. This square enjoys much less traffic noise and has a beautiful view of the St. George Castle on the hill above the city. The castle looks remarkably noble from this view, demanding a photograph.

Behind the National Theater exists a short pedestrian-only street, *Travessa Santo Antão*, running from the foot of the Av. da Liberdade eastward. Along it are some good restaurants. As the Travessa meets the narrow street connecting to Praça da Fegueira, you enter a seafood-lover's heaven. Turn left. This is the *Rua Portas de Santo Antão*. Along this little narrow way are many of Lisbon's finest restaurants. They are not necessarily expensive, but they do offer a wide range of seafood delicacies. Such a concentration of seafood establishments is not found anywhere else outside of Cascais. All restaurants display their menus conspicuously on the front window, and some menus have English translations to make it easy for tourists.

To the west of the theater is the *Rossio train station.* At this station, you can catch the electric train to Sintra. The interesting aspect of this station is its unusual facade. It has been described as neo-Manueline, ugly, and comical. Study the arch-shaped entries for a short time to form your own opinion. The area near the station is a busy part of Lisbon. During rush hours you can barely make your way through the throngs of people moving to and from the station.

One block to the north, the area known as *Praça dos Restauradores* is decidedly less hectic. Here there are fine restaurants, shops, and bookstores. The grand obelisk central to the square commemorates the 1640 revolution against Spanish rule.

The square is also the beginning point of the *Avenida da Liberdade.* Simply known locally as the Avenida, it is Lisbon's most formal and attractive avenue. This, too, was part of Pombal's postearthquake plan. The avenue is a tree-lined, European-style grand avenue suitable for any capital city. Along the way there are lovely fountains, palm-lined promenades, benches, and the best of Lisbon's mosaic sidewalks. The avenue is the location of Lisbon's principal movie theaters, some hotels, restaurants, embassies, and airline offices.

The further from Rossio that you walk, the more modern Lisbon becomes. At the upper end of the Avenida, surrounding the *Praça Marquês de Pombal* and its huge monument to this man, are located the glittering and expensive new hotels. Group or package tours make their reservations in these comfortable hotels. They are conveniently located next to the splendid *Parque Eduardo VII,* which is formally elegant. The main portion is landscaped in a strict formal plan. Seen from the upper end of the park, the spreading view of the city and the river presents an interesting optical illusion. Far distant vessels on the river appear to loom huge above the foreshortened cityscape below. Nevertheless, you can get a good overview of the city's layout from here. Note the position of the castle on the left, Baixa in the center, and Bairro Alto on the right. This point is a favored stop of the city tour buses.

Most visitors would agree that one of Lisbon's better features lies in this magnificent park. In the upper or northwest corner of the park spreads the *Estufa Fria* (Cold Greenhouse). Its charm, like many Portuguese gardens, is based upon its informality. Under several acres of lath or glass, the Estufa Fria's exotic plants number in the thousands. All are set amongst streams, pools, rocky grottoes, and natural hillsides. Many people come here for the peace and serenity. Its paths seem endless and the secluded benches are many. Mothers with young children bring them to Estufa Fria, where they can explore for hours in a safe learning environment. This place is a delight for the serious horticulturist, botanist, and tourist alike. Not only is the garden brimming with tropical and rain-forest species of plants, but it has a vast collection of arid-region and desert species as well. Bird lovers will delight in the hundreds of caged tropical birds. Spend some time in the park outside, too. Look for the black swans in the large pond near the entrance of the Estufa Fria. In the spring, the female swans will be keeping track of their broods of fluttering, light gray cygnets. Nearby is a *Tourismo* office. Stop in for maps and other information you may need for a continued walk through Lisbon.

Beyond Parque Eduardo VII, distances between points of interest become greater and the area is less amenable to those on foot. There are interesting places to visit, but it is best to use public transportation or taxi. Near *Praça de Espanha* is the great *Gulbenkian Foundation*, which will be discussed in detail later. The *Zoological Gardens* are located in the area known as *Sete Rios*. The zoo's garden setting is attractive but there are many more interesting things to see. For example, visit *Campo Pequeno*, the nineteenth-century Moorish-style bullring. Campo Pequeno and its charming attributes are thoroughly discussed elsewhere in this volume but are worth mentioning here as well. The building is one of the interesting sights north of Parque Eduardo VII on the *Avenida da Republica*. Beyond and further north on the Avenida is the *University of Lisbon*. Most of the campus's buildings were constructed during the Salazar years and have been described as wasteful and extravagant users of space. It is true that this is one of the few open areas in the city. The buildings do have spacious foyers and wide halls, which is very un-Portuguese indeed.

Back in old Lisbon, one of the more fascinating neighborhoods or areas is *Bairro Alto*. Some say the Bairro is not just a neighborhood but a frame of mind. It is not old and quaint in the style of Alfama; it has its own ambiance and atmosphere, which comes alive after dark. This is the center of Lisbon's night life.

If you want to experience quintessentially Portuguese entertainment—the *Fado*—Bairro Alto is probably where you will find the more popular *Fado* houses. The *Fado* is *the* entertainment at drinking and eating establishments generally called *Adega Tipica.* But *Fado* is more than mere entertainment. The Lisbon tradition is for the reveler to arrive about 11:00 P.M. (2300.), eat a hearty meal of a Portuguese speciality, drink large amounts of good Portuguese wine, and become enthralled with the wails of the *fadista* and accompanying guitar. That is easy to do. The typical *Fado* (translated "fate") is a song of tear-jerking emotion. It has a pleading, wailing quality that tears at the heartstrings. Most *Fado* singers are women (*fadistas*). A typical *fadista*'s throaty and sometimes piercing message comes from deep down. The best known *fadista* is *Amalia Rodrigues.* If you can, listen to her recordings before visiting a *Fado* house and compare the live performances you hear with the greatest *fadista* of them all.

In the *adega,* the mood of the *Fado* is further enhanced by flowing black dresses and shawls, dramatic facial expressions, and body language. The lights are always dim. The tables are candle-lit and the atmosphere is close. Meals are not obligatory, but there is usually a two-drink minimum and a small cover charge at most *Fado* houses in Bairro Alto. Cover charges vary considerably, depending upon the relative affluence of the *Fado* house. Some are mere dives. Others are rather stylish and have a correspondingly high cover charge. Choose to visit one or more *Fado* houses depending upon your mood and budget. It is absolutely necessary, however, to visit at least one *Fado* house. Visitors to Portugal must experience *Fado* to begin to understand it; they must hear the *fadistas* at least once.

Fado is a national folk tradition, yet some Portuguese actually dislike it. To be Portuguese is not to love *Fado* unconditionally. Apparently it is an acquired taste, like the taste for country music in the United States; not everyone is a devotee of Hank Williams. Likewise, there are many Portuguese who do not like *Fado.* On the other hand, there are *Fado* addicts who feel a week without *Fado* is a week without sunshine. Actually, this analogy goes awry when you realize that nearly all classic *Fado* songs have a sad, depressing theme: the sadder and more fateful, the better. Many observers see and perceive the *Fado* attitude applied to everyday life in Portugal. "It's our fate; it's the Portuguese way" are recurring phrases repeated in many everyday situations. "Fate" is used as a catch-all explanation for daily mishaps. If there is a power outage, no water, or some other upsetting occurrence, the attitude is always: "Don't worry, don't fret. It's fate. It's the Portuguese way; nothing can be done."

The origins of *Fado* undoubtedly stretch back to the fifteenth and sixteenth centuries. This was a time of great expeditions of conquest, discovery, and expansion of the empire. It was also a time of great sorrow for thousands of families who lost sons and fathers on ships that never returned. Colonization took its toll in family separation as well. The songs of the time reflected that grief, misery, and *saudade* (longing).

Today, in addition to the classic, mournful *Fado*, there are at least three other forms. The style of singing remains the same, but the themes of the songs vary.

There is a formal *Fado* song that is sung at special occasions. It is generally more sophisticated and much less fateful. The themes of these popular *Fado* songs would be, for example, "Springtime in Portugal," "April in Lisbon," and the like. Such songs are intended for a Portuguese audience.

A third type of *Fado* is closely related to the former, but its intended audience is quite different. Performed for tourists, these songs are happier and more upbeat. These are the songs heard in the tourist-oriented hotel lounges and nightclubs.

The fourth is a traditional form sung by the students at the University in Coimbra. This type of *Fado*, too, is more complicated and sophisticated but its themes are more likely to be involved with nature, birds, flowers, stars, or the sky. A recurring theme is the opposite sex and its particular virtues and foibles. Popular themes also include young love, looks of love, or love in general. While in Coimbra, visit the student hangouts near the university. Late at night these taverns and cafés will be filled with the sounds of this lively form of *Fado*.

A Portuguese *Adega Típica* meal at an evening of *Fado* in Bairro Alto would probably consist of a hearty soup and one of the following: roast veal in wine sauce, salt-cod, grilled Portuguese sausages, beans, cabbage, fried fish, squid, or sliced octopus.

If you approach the Bairro Alto neighborhood from the north, walk down the *Avenida da Liberdade* to the Praça dos Restauradores area and then ride the funicular up the steep *Calcada da Gloria* to the pretty belvedere *São Pedro de Alcantara*. This is, in every respect, one of Lisbon's more pleasing gardens, with a rich view of Rossio,

Baixa, and the opposite hills, including the castle. It is always cool and shady near the *azulejos*-adorned fountain. You can easily spot the famous landmarks by using the unique tile viewing table. From the belvedere, walk in a northerly direction along *Rua Dom Pedro V.* On either side of the street are excellent antique shops. One of the shops specializes in fine quality antique *azulejos.* The shopper can buy single representative tiles or entire pictorial panels at rather reasonable prices. All tiles are classified according to color, style, and age. The place is a veritable museum for sale. Wander through the seemingly endless cellars and galleries. (You will be asked to turn lights on and off as you enter and leave the myriad rooms.) It is the first shop on the right just beyond the belvedere. Other antique shops will have religious art, furniture, and many pieces of historic interest.

Walk further to the *Praça do Principe Real.* Look at the incredible tree that is the centerpiece of this delightful park. This Portuguese cedar provides a canopy and a shady haven for the whole area. Note how the spreading branches are propped with supports. Unfortunately it is difficult to photograph because of its size and the spread of its branches.

Surrounding the park on three sides are old aristocratic structures once occupied by Portugal's wealthy and royal families. Now many are used as government offices, apartments, or commercial office spaces. The facades remain as they did for centuries. If you are interested, the commercial buildings are open for viewing. Merely inquire at the reception area.

Walk a little further beyond the park. The street name changes to *Rua da Escola Politecnica* because this is the location of the politechnical school. Near the school, walk down the hill to the right to enter Lisbon's *Jardim Botanico,* or *Botanical Gardens.* At this point, if you wish, you can stroll through this typically Portuguese garden, with its excellent palm tree collection, back down to Av. da Liberdade.

Travelers whose accommodations are along the Estoril Coast will approach Bairro Alto from the south, leaving the train at Cais de Sodré. From there the neighborhood is only a short walk or tram ride up the hill on *Rua do Alecrim* to the *Praça de Camões.* This entry to Bairro Alto is also where Rua Garrett begins its bustle through the Chiado shopping district.

The Praça de Camões honors *Luis de Camões,* Portugal's most famous and beloved author. In fact, Camões is probably the only Portuguese artistic figure widely known outside of the country. He lived in the sixteenth century, and is best known for his epic poem *Os Lusiadas*, which chronicles the voyage of Vasco da Gama. Camões is a national hero; modern critics have judged him to be the greatest Iberian poet of all time.

There is a unique statue of another author near the *praça*. It is not the centerpiece, but it certainly is the focal point. The statue is actually a scene with *Eça de Queiroz* in nineteenth-century garb lending a hand to a scantily clad woman. The symbolism escapes most observers, but it is an engaging piece of sculpture. The nude woman is a symbol of his work, which in his own words represents ". . . the strong naked face of Truth." His quizzical look is rather amusing beside the serious face of the woman. That statue is beautiful but badly placed. To admire it properly and give it the attention it deserves, an observer must stand on the opposite side of the busy street. At one time the statue was considered by some to be quite naughty. Apparently when it was first unveiled in 1903, it created somewhat of a scandal. One of the aristocrats living in a palace facing the new statue was enraged enough to have all streetside windows sealed for fear his family and guests would be corrupted by the monument.

From Camões (as the area is called), walk northward for a few blocks. The sidewalk is narrow, and you are now in the heart of Bairro Alto. Look down the streets to the left. That is where all the *Fado* houses are located.

Walk a short distance to the *Igreja São Roque*. Visitors fancy this church for several reasons. The interior is elegant. The wooden ceiling is beautifully painted in the Italian style. The side chapels are exquisite in detail with outstanding *azulejos* panels and paintings. But the most important aspect of this church is the fourth chapel on the left as one faces the main altar, the chapel of St. John the Baptist. Note that the style is Italian baroque. Originally built in Rome in 1742 and blessed by the Pope himself, the chapel was taken apart, packed, and shipped to Lisbon in three ships. Spend some time looking at the details. The angels are carved from white Carrara marble and ivory. The friezes, capitals, and ceiling are gilded with gold and silver. Note the amazing mosaics on the floor and walls. Now look at the columns; believe it or not, they are made of *lapis lazuli*. The front of the altar is *amethyst*, and the pilasters are made of a *alabaster*. This chapel is sumptuous and opulent. A small museum attached to the church has other small items from its chapels on display, but it is an anticlimax.

After all this walking and looking at the splendor of ecclesiastical art, you should be ready for a break. The *Solar de Vinho do Porta* is the perfect place to relax in Bairro Alto. In English it is known as the Port Wine Manor House. It is very close to the São Roque Church, at *Rua São Pedro de Alcantara, 45.* Beautifully decorated and with comfortable easy chairs, it is a pleasant, cool place to wind down with a glass of port. The list of ports from which to choose is immense. The manor house, or *solar,* is operated by the *Port Wine Institute,* and all the wines on the list can be purchased. Choose a vintage port, relax, and enjoy it before venturing back out into old Lisbon. From here you could just wander the back streets of Bairro Alto for a few more hours or days.

There are other districts of Lisbon that are not well known to the tourist. These areas have a charm of their own and always offer something a bit different. The places are *Graça, Largo do Rato, Jardim da Estrela* and *Basilica da Estrela* and *Campo Martires de Patria.* Each of these neighborhoods of Lisbon is best reached by tram (trolley) so that you can enjoy the ambiance from which they grew.

Lisbon is a town of views and vistas from lovely belvederes, many of which have been mentioned. For spectacular vistas of the city for photography or just enjoyment, take a tram to the *Graça* area. Seek out the *Largo da Graça* for a homey atmosphere and a view of the city from the heights of the east. Most of the houses in this neighborhood were built in the eighteenth century. This is a comfortable working-class neighborhood. Feel free to visit the *tabernas, pastelerias,* and cafés. Visitors are welcomed with a bit of surprise since few tourists find their way to this neighborhood. An extra bonus awaits those who seek out the three well-known tile factories in the area: *Viuvo Lamego, Sant'Ana,* and *Constança.* These factories are occasionally open to visitors, but you should check the schedules in advance.

Another wonderful view of the city can be enjoyed from the area known as *Campo Martires de Patria.* Seek out the *Hotel Senhora do Monte* for the incredible view from the hotel's terrace. Nearby is the *campo* with its wide open spaces and terrific vista as well.

The *Basilica da Estrela* is worth a visit just to see its life-size Nativity scene with exquisitely carved figures. Opposite the church is the *Jardim da Estrela.* On Sunday afternoons the space is totally animated with families strolling, children playing, and ice-cream vendors selling their wares. The park itself is refreshing, with well-maintained walkways and many benches. Few tourists visit here so you see a part of Lisbon used by the people—the *Lisboetas*.

Another comfortable venue is the district known as *Rato*. The area surrounding the *Largo do Rato* is part of modern Lisbon, but note how each block has its *pasteleria, cervejaria,* restaurant and shops. The charm is here. Visit the *pasteleria* on the southwest corner and notice the impressive carved wooden bar, mirror, and entry. They may have been moved here from an old Lisbon location. Nearby is the *Palace of the National Assembly,* the former *Monastery of São Bento*. The legislature has been using the palace since 1834. It can be visited at regular hours on weekdays only.

Other areas of interest to visitors who wish to sample all segments of Lisbon life include the *Praça de Londres,* an area of modern commercial structures and many government offices; *Praça do Chile,* an area of older structures; *Saldanha,* a fashionable district with luxury restaurants, private clubs, and shops, surrounding the Sheraton Hotel at the beginning of the Avenida da Republica. The neighborhood beyond Campo Pequeno to the north, northwest, and east offer little that is unique or interesting to visitors.

One of the principal landscape features of Lisbon is the vast green space on the city's west side. In area, *Monsanto Parque* is nearly half as large as the urban area of Lisbon. Dedicated more than fifty years ago, it provides the citizens of Lisbon with much-needed breathing space. The park occupies a wooded hill that has been handsomely carved by roads, some of which provide broad vistas of the city to the east. The main road *(Auto Estrada)* that bisects the park leads directly from Pombal circle to the Estoril coast.

The *aqueduct* is a fascinating feature that you will glimpse along the Estrada. Still serving Lisbon, this amazing, eleven-mile-long (18 km) structure was built in the middle 1700s and survived the great earthquake of 1755. If you study the massive construct of 109 arches, you will understand why it lasted through the quake without crumbling. Other views of the structure are available from the *Avenida de Ceuta* and the *Avenida Maria Pia*.

Museums of Lisbon

The *Gulbenkian Foundation* operates the premier museum complex and is the principal supporter of the arts in Portugal. The

Gulbenkian, as it is called, was the gift of *Calouste Gulbenkian* (1869–1955) to the Portuguese people. Gulbenkian was an Armenian emigrant who amassed great wealth while living in his adopted Portugal. His fondest wish was to provide support for the arts in the poor country. So, before his death in 1955, he established his foundation to facilitate that support. The principal and most visible result was the construction in 1969 of the complex of modern buildings and gardens near the *Praça d'Espanha* on the *Avenida da Berna* and *Avenida Augusto Aguilar.* The impressive museum is the keystone of the complex. Gulbenkian's personal collection is at the heart of the museum's superb collage of ancient and medieval religious art, Renaissance art, and works of European artists up to the eighteenth century. The collection is small but wide-ranging, and the displays are exceptional. Most impressive are the tapestries from the Renaissance period. The foundation is constantly adding quality pieces to the original three thousand items of Gulbenkian's private collection.

Gulbenkian was an extraordinary art enthusiast. He had a rare ability to discern beauty and quality. In order to be able to cultivate his excellent taste, Gulbenkian accumulated immense wealth in the Middle East as an astute negotiator and financier. At the end of the nineteenth century, when the oil industry was beginning to blossom in the Middle East, he organized the Royal Dutch–Shell group, which turned out to be the link between American and Russian industry and provided the first incentive for the development of the Persian Gulf oil fields. He amassed tremendous sums of money, which he distributed generously. Coming to Portugal in 1942 in search of a peaceful home, he fell in love with the country and the people, eventually bequeathing his entire fortune to Portugal through his foundation.

In addition to the visual arts, the Gulbenkian offers a lively year-round schedule of performing arts, lectures, and seminars. Each May the foundation sponsors a comtemporary music festival with performers from the world over. The Gulbenkian Orchestra performs regularly in the accoustically superb main auditorium. The Gulbenkian Choir offers musical programs throughout the year as well. The tickets most prized and, therefore, most difficult to acquire, are those for the performance of the Gulbenkian Ballet.

The foundation also supports research and writing and gives stipends to artists. Temporary exhibits are promoted throughout the country by the foundation.

In addition to all of this, the new (1984) *Gulbenkian Modern Art Center,* adjacent to the foundation complex, presents one of the better collections of twentieth-century art to be found anywhere. The centerpiece of this beautiful building is a collection of works by contemporary Portuguese painters. Visitors can take photographs but only without a flash.

Off-site, the Gulbenkian, supports another museum that visitors absolutely must see. It is the *Azulejos Museum* at the *Igreja da Madre de Deus* (Church of the Mother of God). It is a bit out of the way, but any taxi driver knows the location on the east side of town near the river beyond the train station at Sta.Appalonia. You can also ride tram #3 or #16 from Praça do Comerçio.

The church itself is gorgeous. It is one of the lightest and more captivating in all of Portugal. The lower walls are covered with stunning *azulejos* panels. The altarpiece is of gilded wood. This is an inspirationally radiant setting. Since the church was originally part of a convent, attached buildings surround the cloister. Some of the buildings function as the *Azulejos Museum.* The displays here are the finest examples of *azulejos* panels. All are arranged in chronological order from the fourteenth century.

In addition to the Gulbenkian museums, Lisbon offers a plethora of first-rate museums. At Belém there are no less than four museums to occupy your time. The *Museo Nacional dos Coches* (National Coach Museum) is the museum of preference for most visitors. The facility is attached to the Belém Palace, home of the President of the Republic. It is a former riding school, so it has a unique interior with galleries surrounding what used to be the practice or schooling rings. The collection of seventy-four carriages and coaches is dazzling. Some date back to the sixteenth century, and one dates as late as the twentieth century. All are magnificent. Some are gilded and encrusted with elaborate carvings and molding. Studying the interiors illustrates clearly how immoderate were royal comforts. Notice the details of each coach's suspension, how the body is suspended from the chassis to provide a smooth ride. It is also fascinating to note that coach technology changed very little in the four hundred years of coach building represented in the museum.

The *Museu Nacional de Arqueologia e Etnografia* (Archaeological Museum) is at Jeronimos Monastery. In an attached nineteenth-century wing, the museum possesses a good collection of antiquities gathered from both Spain and Portugal. It presents a fairly comprehensive view of the ethnography of Iberia, but it is not the most exciting museum in the city.

The *Museu de Marinha* (Maritime Museum) is also a component of the Jeronimos Monastery complex of buildings. Since additions have been made to house more displays, this is quite a good museum. It chronicles Portugal's rich maritime history with attractively arranged displays of ship models, memorabilia, uniforms, and so on. Logically arranged, according to the classifications of merchant marine vessels, navy warships, and ships of the great discoveries, this museum is worth a few hours. One particularly interesting exhibit is the reconstructed royal stateroom of the ninetenth-century royal yacht, "Amelia." The best part of this museum is in a new addition beyond the Gulbenkian Planetarium. It is called the *Galliot Pavilion* (Galley Pavilion). Containing about twelve ceremonial galleys for royal use, the pavilion has several raised walkways to provide better views of unbelievable royal maritime opulence.

Beyond the busy Estrada Marginal lies the *Museu de Arte Populare* (Museum of Popular Art). A pedestrian underpass helps visitors cross the heavily traveled road safely. From the outside, the museum looks rundown and uninviting. After this first impression some people assume it is closed for repair or renovation. It is not. Once visitors are inside, their impression changes. The host of exhibits are arranged according to Portugal's regions. This regional approach gives a good overview of the styles, ingenuity, artistry, and craftsmanship of the various parts of Portugal. To enhance the mood, this museum has probably the friendliest guards and attendants of any museum anywhere. They seem to be eager to answer questions or explain a tool or strange contraption. Maybe this is because the museum has so few visitors.

Unfortunately, there are no English labels or explanations on the displays, but most items are visually self-explanatory. The Douro-Minho display from the northern part of the country, for example, includes wooden pitchers, nets, sweaters, and wool-processing items. None require English placards to understand.

The hall devoted to the Trás-os-Montes region has some interesting pottery. A puzzling display of a curved board, measuring approximately four by six feet (1.2 m. by 1.8 m.), with razor-sharp, imbedded flint pieces catches visitors' attention. Deduction and a few hints from a friendly guard will explain its function—a primitive grain-threshing device.

The Algarve display is colorful but has fewer pieces than you might expect. The collection depicting the popular arts and crafts from the Alentejo and Estremadura focuses on cork and cork artifacts. One display uses carved cork figurines to demonstrate the processes involved in cork production and manufacture.

All in all, this museum provides the best and most comprehensive picture of regional artifact styles in this small but varied country.

The *Museu Nacional de Art Antiga* (Museum of Ancient Art) has a misleading title. The oldest pieces date only from the fifteenth and sixteenth centuries. By European standards this is not ancient. Nevertheless, the museum, housed in an old palace built by the counts of Alvor, has a certain charm and a worthy collection. The gloomy, nondescript old building is located on *Rua das Janelas Verdes* (Green Window Street). Inside, the galleries are less gloomy and very dignified. In fact, the collection provides one with a first-rate overview of Portuguese painting since the fifteenth century. The so-called "Portuguese School" is represented by some magnificent paintings on the second floor.

Two excellent reasons to visit the museum are the Bosch painting and the six-paneled painting by Gonçalves. The Hieronymus Bosch painting *Temptation of St. Anthony* defies description. Typical of the Bosch method of depicting terror, this trio of panels offers surprises by the hundreds. The gift shop sells a passable copy of the panels for further study.

The *Adoration of St. Vincent*, by Nuno Gonçalves, is probably the highlight of a visit to this museum. Its six exquisitely painted panels have amazing detail and took ten years to paint. The museum graciously provides padded benches so visitors can study these masterpieces of the Portuguese artist leisurely.

One annoying problem with this museum, as with other Lisbon museums, is that it closes for the lunch break between 12:30 and 2:30 P.M. (1230–1430 hr.), the perfect time for museum strolling. Another quirk that can be bothersome is the practice of museum guards and attendants scurrying around from gallery to gallery, switching lights on and off as patrons come and go. The point is to save electricity, but the practice is a bit disconcerting. It almost makes one feel guilty if one lingers too long.

The *Museu do Cidade* (City Museum) is located in the *Pimenta Palace* at *Campo Grande*. The collection consists of some fascinating pre-earthquake maps and drawings of Lisbon. Beyond that exhibit is a series of paintings of the Tower of Belém, a wooden model of the tower, and many examples of architectural detail collected from old ruined homes.

This is also a museum for the study of Portuguese *azulejos*. There are many displays of tiles dating back to the fifteenth century. Some of the huge panels give a reasonable glimpse of life in the seventeenth and eighteenth centuries. A highlight of the museum is a diorama of Lisbon as it appeared in 1755. This is a splendid model that requires some study. Other displays include some nineteenth-century paintings, household artifacts, and furniture. The self-explanatory displays are well designed and present a valuable look at the history of Lisbon.

When you look at the *Museu Militar* (Military Museum) near Sta. Apolonia Station, east of Alfama, you will notice that it is not housed in a former palace but in a building built specifically for the collection. This huge museum filled with a wide selection of military memorabilia requires a guide. The guides, all of who speak some English, take tours through rooms filled with eighteenth-century armaments and military headgear, sixteenth-century armor, and nineteenth-century weapons. One intriguing gallery is dedicated to Luis Camões. Other galleries are devoted to collections of equestrian items. The final portion of the tour takes visitors through a courtyard surrounded by *azulejos* panels depicting Portugal's great battles. Appreciation for the collection of cannons must be left to the experts. The cannons are, however, interesting to inspect.

The *Ethnological Museum* in *Restelo* is a relatively new museum, located behind the stadium in Restelo. Opened at the end of 1985, it focuses on the people and cultures of the world, their art, and their artifacts. Rich displays of African sculpture are housed here as well as artifacts gathered from Portuguese experiences around the world. The museum also shows films of related interest on a regular basis. This museum will grow in importance in years to come.

The *Archaeological Museum* is located in the ruins of the *Igreja do Carmo* (Carmelite Church) at the upper entry to the street elevator at *Largo do Carmo*. The church was devastated in the 1755 earthquake and now provides a unique setting for a somewhat disorganized collection of pottery, Gothic tombs, and other assorted items. It is a very casual place. Many pieces are not labeled, and some items in the collection are labeled only with handwritten slips of paper. Some Portuguese themselves are embarrassed by this museum and its organization. The exhibits fall into three categories: (1) the sarcophagi, inscribed stones, and religious relics; (2) items retrieved from the excavation of Vila Nova de S. Pedro, including an awful, preserved human head; (3) miscellany such as mummified Peruvian Indians, coins, tiles, books, and stone items of little significance. If this kind of museum interests you, be aware of its limitations.

The *Museu de Arte Contemporaneo* (Museum of Modern Art) is a small collection on the *Rua Serpa Pinto* near Lisbon's city hall. It is not nearly as comprehensive as the Gulbenkian Center but does have some sensitive twentieth-century Portuguese works by Columbano and Malhoa.

Another very small specialty museum is the *Museu Numismatico* (Numismatic Museum) housed in the *Casa da Moeda* on *Avenida R. Pais*. This special collection of nearly fifty-thousand coins dating as far back as the twelfth century will be a delight for any numismatist.

The *Palacio Nacional da Ajuda* (Ajuda Palace) houses a valuable collection of royal automobiles. Because it was a royal palace in the eighteenth and nineteenth centuries, it contains some fine furniture and tapestries from the period. In 1986 Portugal's crown jewels were placed on display at the palace. It was the first time they had been shown in public since the end of the monarchy in 1910. Ajuda Palace, like other public buildings, does not look like much from the exterior. In fact, it looks a little worn and in need of serious repair. Inside it is much better. Don't despair. This is often the case in Portugal; first impressions give way to inside surprises.

Nearly all of Lisbon's museums are the present occupants of former palaces. The *Museu Nacional do Troje* (National Costume Museum) is no exception. The former seventeenth-century palace that houses this museum was the home of the Duke of Palmela. It is a bit out of the way in a section of Lisbon called *Lumiar*. The palace, built in the seventeenth century, stands in *Monteiro Park* and can be reached by bus #1, a forty-five-minute crosstown ride from Cais do Sodré. This is a tasteful little museum. In 1979 it won special mention in the European Museum of the Year Awards.

The exhibition comprises several rooms of party dresses, focusing on eighteenth-century gowns. One display is an early twentieth-century wedding montage. There is a "flapper" room, a boot display, a collection of extravagant accessories, and a display of parasols. The palace stables have been converted into an exhibit of eighteenth and nineteenth century fabric-making machinery and apparatus.

There are no guides and no English explanations, but such is not necessary. The museum is so well organized and the displays so well done that everything is obvious. The museum is closed for lunch.

Nearby is the *National Theater Museum of Lisbon*, located at Estrada do Lumiar, 10. The exhibits here are ephemeral. That is, because of the fragile nature of the clothes, the exhibits are changed every six to eight months. The photographs, posters, musical scores, and so on, are permanent. The effect is like entering a theater through the stage door. You will see a dressing room, the manual light boards of the São Luis Theater, and floodlights, footlights, and photos dating as far back as 1899.

The "stage" is alive with famous characters like Hamlet and King Lear. Various rooms focus on the Portuguese theater and its history. Upstairs, for example, are elaborate dresses worn by the famous *fadista* Amalia Rodriques. Portuguese musicals are featured with costumed mannequins assuming various scenes. Other displays throughout the museum include posters, set designs, personal belongings of famous Portuguese state personalities, autographs, and theater programs. This museum closes for lunch.

The *Museum of Decorative Arts* is like stepping back into time and visiting the eighteenth-century home of a Lisbon aristocrat. The building, located at *Largo das Portas do Sol* at the upper entrance to Alfama, was a seventeenth century palace. It is very unmuseumlike. In fact, visitors may have the feeling of wandering through an old house looking for the owner. Since not many people visit this museum, the chances are good for touring the collection alone. The many perfect examples of Portuguese and Indo-Portuguese furnishings are difficult to find elsewhere. This museum is also closed for lunch.

The *Vasco da Gama Aquarium* is quite far out of the way, west along the Estrada Marginal at *Dafundo* near *Alges* (almost midway between the train stations at Alges and Cruz Quebrada). Ride the train to either station and then catch the #15 tram to reach the aquarium. The place is small by American standards, but it has a fine collection of fish, shellfish, and other sea life. There is even a space for live seals and a huge tank for turtles. A self-guided walk (*trajecto recomendado*) leads the visitor through the second-floor galleries of stuffed or preserved sea life and birds. This is the least interesting aspect of the aquarium. Other rooms offer old nineteenth-century photographs, coin collections, stamps, and medals. The live displays are at ground level. Divided logically into six galleries, the live collection is quite comprehensive, well maintained, and clean. It is dimly lit and is very crowded on weekends. The aquarium opens at 12:00 noon and is open during lunch.

More Places of Interest

There are a few more palaces open to the public. Some post no hours so visitors must ring the bell, knock on the door, or otherwise make their presence and intentions known. Most of the former residences of the rich and royalty are now used as headquarters for government agencies or departments. For example, the *Palácio das Necessidades*, at the *Largo das Necessidades*, now houses the Ministry of Foreign Affairs. Constructed during the years 1745–50, it was the home of all Portugal's kings until the last monarch.

The *Palácio Foz*, in *Praça dos Restauradores*, was built in the eighteenth century and is one of the most sumptuous in Lisbon. Many of the rooms are decorated with the paintings of the Portuguese painter Columbano.

The *Palácio da Independência*, at the *Largo de S. Domingos*, was named and built by the Count of Almada in remembrance of the restoration of independence in 1640. Here there are some worthwhile *azulejos* panels depicting the events of the time.

At Campo Pequeno is the *Palácio Galviras*, which dates from the seventeenth century. It was built by the Marquis de Tavora and today is the municipal library.

Casa dos Bicos is a striking and unique building near the lower end of Alfama on the *Rua dos Bacalhoeiros*. The name literally translates as the "house of points." Built in the sixteenth century for the son of Afonso de Albuquerque, it is one of the more curious palaces in the city. The entire facade is made up of diamond-faceted stones. Notice the placement of the unique windows. To many observers they look awkward.

In addition, two small galleries may be of interest. The *Museu Rafael Bordalo Pinheiro*, at Campo Grande, 382, has numerous fine examples of Pinheiro's work. Knock on the door here for entry and viewing the collection.

The *Museu do Ultramar* (Overseas Territories Museum) at the Rua das Portas de Santo Antão, has an historic theme. It has many interesting pieces of art and artifacts collected from Portuguese overseas territories throughout the centuries of Portugal's colonial domination.

Libraries

There are always some visitors deliberately seeking in-depth study of the culture, history, or geography of the country. Portugal has many libraries open for such research. Most welcome visitors with helpful staff, but visitors must present identification (passport) to be admitted.

The *Arquivo Nacional* (National Archives) at the National Assembly building possesses ancient manuscripts and records dating from the ninth century. The *Arquivo Historico Militar* (Military Archives), on the Rua do Paraiso, 8, documents most military events of the country. For documentation of Lisbon's past, visit the *Arquivo Historico Municipal* (Municipal Archives) on the Largo de Pelourinho. There is even an *Arquivo Historic Ultramarino* (Archives of the Overseas Territories) on Calcada da Boa Hora, 30.

The *Biblioteca Nacional* (National Library) on Rua Ocidental do Campo Grande possesses more than one million volumes and eleven thousand manuscripts. The *Bibliotico da Academia das Ciências* (Library of the Academy of Sciences), Rua Academia das Ciências, 19, is the principal depository for scientific information. The *Bibliotico Da Fundacão Gulbenkian* (Gulbenkian Library) on the Avenida de Berna has for your use over fifty thousand volumes related to the arts. The *Bibliotico da Imprensa Nacional (National Press Library)* has a valuable collection of the classical Portuguese works including those of Camões. It is located on the *Rua Escola Politicnica.* Finally, the *Bibliotico Municipal* (Municipal Library), at the Largo de Afonso Pena, maintains a good collection of historic volumes.

Miradouros

The word *miradouros* translates to English as "terrace with a fine view." The root word is "mirage," but by no means are the views described here mirages. They are all genuine and some even spectacular. It has been mentioned that Lisbon is a city of belvederes (places with beautiful vistas). They seem to be everywhere. Most are views from the natural heights of Lisbon's seven hills, but some, like the restaurant at the Sheraton Hotel or the suspension bridge, are manmade. All are worth a few photographs.

At the *Statue of Cristo Rei* (Christ the King), see the entire city across the Tagus River. On the Rua de Catarina is the *Alto de Santa Catarina* (Heights of St. Catherine), where one can gain a fine view to the east toward the castle. Certainly the *Castelo de São Jorge* (St. George Castle) offers the best view since it is placed on the highest hill of the city.

There are some great views from the heights in Monsanto Park. One called *Luneta dos Quarteis* (Eyeglass of the Barracks), another *Moinho dos Mochos* (Loft of the Owls), another called *Alto da Serafina* (Angels' Height), and yet another *Montes Claros* (Clear Hills), are all in Monsanto. You will need a car to get to them, however.

Drive across the suspension bridge for a splendid view of the city. Stopping for pictures or any other reason is not permitted on the bridge. In the city some great photo opportunities are presented at *Santa Luzia* near the *Largo das Portas do Sol* at the upper entry to Alfama. To see the castle from another angle, walk to the *Largo do Monte*. For an opposite view, go to the pretty and pleasant *São Pedro de Alcantara* on the Rua de São Pedra de Alcantara in Bairro Alto. For a unique view, ask at the *Basilica da Estrala*, Largo da Estrala. Visitors are able to climb to the cupola of the basilica to look back at Lisbon from an angle that complements the view from the Sheraton. With photos, slides, or few inches of video tape from each (or at least several) of the belvederes, you will have a comprehensive collection of Lisbon vistas.

A water-level view is one final picture that every visitor to Lisbon should have. The sight of the city is beautiful from the *ferry* that crosses the Tagus from *Terreiro do Paço* to *Caçilhas*. For a small amount of money you can enjoy a memorable round-trip ride and add another superlative picture to your Lisbon collection.

Conclusion

Lisbon is a fascinating city and an easy one in which to get around. It is manageable from the pedestrian's point of view. It is a photogenic city with a million subjects to capture the photographer's eye. Some of this charm is the result of urban deterioration. Wandering the back streets and alleys of the old quarters, one is struck by the picturesque hodge-podge of houses and shops. A closer look reveals solid, handsome edifices showing severe signs of deterioration. The decay ranges from peeling paint, cracked stucco, and chipped tiles to crumbling walls, sagging roofs, and splintering woodwork.

What has happened? Why is Lisbon crumbling? The answers to those two questions are rooted in the nature of the Portuguese economic system and the deferred maintenance resulting from a depressed economy. There are, however, people who are concerned. Persons at the Ministry of Quality of Life, at City Hall, and at the National Laboratory of Civil Engineers indicated to me that there are groups of government leaders, politicians, architects, planners, economists, and civic organizations that are working toward a solution. Consultants from abroad have studied rehabilitation schemes. Preservation is on the minds of many people. The solutions, however, are economic. There is no lack of concern or enthusiasm to commence restoration, but there is a serious lack of financial resources to renovate crumbling neighborhoods. Money is the key. Subsidies from the national level, education at all levels, and the creation of a legal and fiscal network for the distribution of funds for Lisbon's recuperation are absolutely necessary in the near future. Lisbon's continued efficacy as a tourist center is at stake. To lose the old city's charm of the past is to lose its principal drawing power. No one seriously wants to visit modern Lisbon. People tend to gravitate toward the Tagus and the hills on its banks to enjoy the atmosphere, ambiance, animation, and enchantment that have evolved through the centuries.

Within the framework of economic hardship, there are other problems too. For example, a proliferation of illegal building (*clandestinos*) has frustrated efforts at logical growth and planning. These are not buildings or structures hidden away out of sight. These are sometimes huge hotels, apartment buildings, and housing subdivisions that are begun without permit or government license. To the American and British way of thinking, it is difficult to reconcile this situation. Picture this: there are strict laws regarding building permits, zoning, construction codes, and so forth. These laws, however, are totally disregarded by the clandestine builders. Why? Why not enforce the laws, one could ask government officials as high as ministerial level? The answer is always the same: "Enforcement is very difficult." But why? The answer to that question is steeped in the traditional southern European system of bribery and favors. Nothing can be done if officials who have been bribed to ignore those who break the building codes refuse to act or never seem to have time to initiate action against illegal structures.

The age-old system is self-defeating. The problems, however, are compounded as Portuguese society becomes more complex and more interdependent economically. There is, for example, a major plan to refurbish the Estoril Coast (west of Lisbon) to improve its already attractive blend of coastline, sun, sea, and quaintness. Can the plan be carried out? Consider this: funds for development will come from money generated by the Casino concession, which is paid directly to the government agency in charge of governance of the Estoril Coast, the Town Hall of Cascais. Will the funds be equitably distributed by a system steeped in the Iberian tradition of payoffs? The plan calls for promoting investment in a wide variety of projects. New development, with the exception of new hotels, has proceeded slowly over the past decade. Again, lack of investment capital and incentive is to blame. With government investment, it is hoped private investment will follow. Some of the government plans include a complete marina in Cascais that is badly needed, two international-standard golf courses, and the control of beach erosion. There are plans to promote Guincho Beach as an international wind-surfing center by organizing various championship events. There is a plan for a new *Museu do Mar* (Museum of the Sea) in Cascais and another for reopening for development the hot springs next to the Hotel Palacio in Estoril. The Cascais Town Hall considers sanitation a top priority. New sewer systems are planned to maintain and improve water quality along the coast. None of this will happen unless the basic system, the infrastructure of payoffs and favors, changes for the better. Portugal and the Estoril Coast cannot afford to let the opportunity slip by. Tourism is far too important to the economy. It has become a major industry. The country cannot afford to let its attractions deteriorate for lack of viable government organization. The old ways will change.

Index

Other travel guides of interest from Hippocrene Books . . .

The Tropical Traveler
John Hatt
This book provides all the information needed for traveling in a tropical climate. Equipment, preparation, health, animal and human hazards, special precautions and getting around are all discussed. *Stars and Stripes* called it "One of the most practical guidebooks to be published in quite some time."

Traveler's Challenge: Sophisticated Globetrotter's Record Book
George Blagowidow
This is a record book listing the 1,000 most important and fascinating places in the world. It gives the traveler a list to record travel achievements and to suggest new possibilities for travel experience. A must for the serious traveler.

America's Heartland: A Travel Guide to the Backroads of Illinois, Indiana, Iowa and Missouri
Tom Weil
This is a new kind of guidebook because it not only covers what to see, but it also puts places in perspective by relating their history in a lively and interesting way. Weil has uncovered dozens of delightful, off-the-beaten-track corners of the Middle West, a surprisingly fascinating part of the country.

Himalayan Kingdoms
B. Gibbons and B. Ashford
The scenery of the Himalayas is legendary, comprising the highest mountains in the world, mysterious forests and dry countryside. The authors cover three Himalayan kingdoms: Nepal, Sikkim and Bhutan, looking at the real country and its people, little touched by Western civilization.

Traveler's Trivia Test: Questions and Answers for the Sophisticated Traveler
George Blagowidow
". . . excellent . . . both well-known and obscure facts." *Travel Holiday* ". . . for those who have traveled the world from pole to pole, climbed high mountains, explored deep caves . . . a test of travel knowledge."
—*New York Times*

Long Island: A Guide to New York's Suffolk and Nassau Counties
Raymond, Judith and Kathryn Spinzia
This is the first comprehensive guidebook to this popular resort area. Directions, telephone numbers, hours, and a short history are given for over 450 entries, including parks, nature preserves, museums, archaeological sites, beaches, lighthouses, fish hatcheries, churches, manors and estates, and much more.

An American's Guide to the Soviet Union
Lydle Brinkle
"Travelers should welcome this guide. It covers Moscow, Leningrad and Kiev in depth, as well as other stops such as Odessa and Novgorod, providing . . . useful information."

Exploring the Berkshires
Herbert S. Whitman, Illustrated by Rosemary Fox
"This gem of a book, with delightful pen-and-ink drawings by Rosemary Fox, takes you on six detailed motor tours of the Berkshire Hills in western Massachusetts and their foothills in northwestern Connecticut."
—Conde Nast's Traveler

The Hawaiian Islands
Carole Chester
This guide covers the six islands of Hawaii, introducing far more than just leis, hula dancers and luaus. Hawaii's rich culture and beautiful countryside are described in detail, and much practical information is given.

Traveler's IQ Test: Rate Your Globetrotting Knowledge
George Blagowidow
Thousands of questions, ranging from elementary to downright tough, on foreign places, people, language, food and drinks, and other travel topics.

Hippocrene Insider's Guide to Poland
A.T. Jordan, Introduction by Jerzy Kosinski
This guide explains how to break out of the sightseeing/hotel/restaurant trap, and see the real Poland. Full of friendly people, beautiful scenery and thousands of activities, Poland is an increasingly popular tourist destination.

The Netherlands Antilles
This first comprehensive guide to the Netherlands Antilles takes you to six of the best Caribbean islands: Aruba, Bonaire, Curaçao, St. Maarten, St. Eustatius and Saba. Increasingly popular, but still unspoiled, the Netherlands Antilles offer a refreshing change for the Caribbean traveler.